Mahabharata

An imprint of Om Books International

 Om Books International

Reprinted in 2021

Corporate & Editorial Office
A-12, Sector 64, Noida 201 301
Uttar Pradesh, India
Phone: +91 120 477 4100
Email: editorial@ombooks.com
Website: www.ombooksinternational.com

Sales Office
107, Ansari Road, Darya Ganj
New Delhi 110 002, India
Phone: +91 11 4000 9000
Email: sales@ombooks.com

© Om Books International 2009

ALL RIGHTS RESERVED. No part of this book may be reproduced or transmitted in any form by any means, electronic or mechanical, including photocopying and recording, or by any information storage and retrieval system, except as may be expressly permitted in writing by the publisher.

ISBN: 978-81-87108-25-2

Printed in India

10 9 8 7 6 5 4

Contents

The Great Indian Dynasty	4
The Illustrious Progeny	25
Duryodhana's Evil Designs Fail	53
Arjuna Hits The Fish's Eye and Wins Draupadi	79
Bheema Kills Wicked Jarasandha	101
The Ill-fated Game of Dice	123
The Years in Exile	147
Jaidratha and Keechaka's Misdeeds	169
The Peace Mission Fails	191
The War Clouds Gather and Sermon of Gita	221
The War of Mahabharata	247
The Land of The Dead	283

The Great Indian Dynasty

During ancient times, India, the land of Aryans (Aryavarta) saw a number of great kings rise to dizzying heights of prominence and glory. These kings followed specific lines of succession. Such lines of succession were called dynasties, each of which traces its origin to a certain ancestor after whom it was named. Amongst different dynasties recorded in the annals of India's history, one of the most outstanding was the Kuru dynasty.

The Mahabharata, one of the two great epics in Sanskrit (the other is the Ramayana, composed by Sage Valmiki), describes the outstanding feats of the kings who belonged to this dynasty. The Mahabharata was composed by Shree Krishna Dwaipayana, popularly called Sage Vyasa. Son of Sage Parashara and Satyavati (who later became the wife of the Kuru king, Shantanu), Sage Vyasa was a literary genius par excellence who mastered ancient learning with rare perfection. He compiled and edited the four Vedas. He witnessed the tragic end of the Kurus. Thereafter, it occurred to him that the story of Kurus must be written down in the form of a grand narrative. But he didn't know of anyone skilled enough to put down in writing, the great epic (Mahakavya) as he had envisioned.

Finding himself puzzled and clueless, Sage Vyasa invoked Lord Brahma, the creator of the whole universe. When the Lord appeared, Sage Vyasa made him aware of the problem he was facing and asked for his guidance on how to give verbal form to the epic.

Considering Sage Vyasa's peculiar problem, Lord Brahma said, "I am fully convinced that you require the service of a master scribe, who can write down the words that come out of your mouth. It is impossible for any human being to perform this daunting task. In my opinion, it's only Lord Ganesha who can successfully do this job." After saying so, Lord Brahma returned to his divine abode of Brahmalok.

Sage Vyasa followed the words of Lord Brahma as a divine command, and accordingly invoked Lord Ganesha, who appeared before Sage Vyasa. The Sage disclosed to him his heartfelt desire, "O Lord, grant your consent to the humble request of your devotees and be the scribe of my epic, so that the grand mission I have undertaken by your grace can be brought to completion for the welfare of the entire mankind."

After contemplating for a while over the proposal of Sage Vyasa, Lord Ganesha, who is known for his ability and strength to liberate the devotees from all troubles, replied, "O, Sage, I am willing to fulfill your desire. I have no problem in accepting the proposed engagement for such a noble cause as you cherish. However, I can do so only on the condition that while dictating to me, you shall not let my pen pause even for a moment. If you want me to be the scribe of your epic, you must take care of that."

Vyasa was momentarily taken aback, but recovered quickly. "I wholeheartedly agree to your condition, my Lord. But then, I too have a condition to put forth, which I beseech you to accept on your part. As per that condition, you will not write down any verse without understanding its meaning completely."

The Lord and the Sage agreed to each other's conditions, and thus, began the composition of the Mahabharata, one of the great masterpieces in verse of all times in the history of mankind. Originally written in classical Sanskrit, the Mahabharata embodies a unique fusion of history and imagination, which merits comparison with very few works in any language composed since the dawn of human civilisation to this date. The great epic starts with the description of the early kings of the Kuru dynasty.

The Beginnings

The beginnings of the Kuru dynasty can be traced back to King Puru, the son of King Yayati and grandson of King Nahusha. King Puru was followed by an array of successors for many generations before King Dushyanta, the next noted king of the dynasty. He was succeeded by his son Bharata, who was one of the greatest and most illustrious kings of the Kuru dynasty. It was because of his most excellent qualities, virtues and all round achievements that King Bharata became famous. After him, the Kuru dynasty came to be known as Bharata Varsha or The Dynasty of Bharata. King Bharata was the father of King Hastin, who built the great city of Hastinapur. King Hastin fathered King Kuru.

King Bharata was King Dushyanta's son from Shakuntala, the foster daughter of Sage Kanva. Though Shakuntala was brought up in the hermitage of Sage Kanva, she was actually the daughter of Sage Vishwamitra and Menaka, one of the *apsaras* or heavenly nymphs in the court of Lord Indra, the king of Gods.

Once it so happened that Sage Vishwamitra, who was originally a kshatriya ruler, started planning to conquer the heaven and overthrow Indra. Getting scared of Vishwamitra's might, Indra quickly sent the exquisitely charming Menaka to divert the attention of Sage Vishwamitra with her beauty.

Menaka reached the place where Sage Vishwamitra was performing penance to receive blessings from *Parampita Parameshwar* for the success of his grand plan. Obeying the commands of Lord Indra, Menaka captivated Sage Vishwamitra with her beauty and distracted him in his meditation. Saint Vishwamitra stopped the penance and started living with Menaka. As a result of it, Menaka gave birth to a girl child. Since the purpose for which she had been sent down to the earth by Indra was successfully achieved, she was supposed to get back to heaven without further delay. She could neither take the child with her to heaven, nor could she wait for the child to grow up to maturity, when she could take care of her herself.

So, Menaka left the new-born girl to her own fate on the bank of the river Malini, and departed. Lying by the riverside, the baby was protected by a pair of birds called Shakuntas, which gave her shelter under their wings and guarded her against beasts and the other threats of nature. After some time, Sage Kanva, who was passing by that spot, saw the baby lying there under the protection of birds. He hesitated for a while, but finding nobody around to claim her, he brought the baby to his hermitage. The baby came to be called Shakuntala because she had been protected by Shakuntas.

Shakuntala's Story

Shakuntala was brought up in Sage Kanva's hermitage with affection and care. Years passed by and Shakuntala grew up into a beautiful young girl. One day King Dushyanta, who was on a hunting spree, was roaming about in the forest. Suddenly, he came across Shakuntala and the two fell in love with each other. Soon after, with the permission of Sage Kanva, they got married. King Dushyanta lived in the hermitage of Sage Kanva for some time and then left for his palace. Shakuntala felt sad at the thought of living away from her dear husband. King Dushyanta noticed tears in her eyes. So he said to her, "O my dear queen, I know that you love me very much and it's difficult for you to spend even an hour without me. I suffer the same agony. Even I cannot bear the thought of separation from you. However, I cannot ignore my royal duties and responsibilities. So, I must depart now. Very shortly, I shall come back and take you to my palace. It's only a matter of time when we shall begin to live happily together, enjoying the pleasures of life. You will grace my palace as my queen." Saying these sweet and soothing words, King Dushyanta departed.

After some time, Shakuntala gave birth to a male child who was named Bharata. He was a very bright child with a divine aura and angelic countenance. When he was only five years of age, he made play mates with fierce wild animals like lions, leopards and tigers. Besides being well versed in ancient classical learning, he had an excellent command over all the skills that a scion of royal lineage was supposed to master those days. When Shakuntala noticed the extraordinary talent of her young son, her joy knew no bounds. At times, this joy even made her forget the sorrow of separation from her husband.

When the boy came of age, Sage Kanva asked Shakuntala to take the boy to his father. Taking the sage's advice, Shakuntala went to meet King Dushyanta and said, "O King, this is your son. Accept him and anoint him your crown prince." But the King pretended to not know her. "I do not know you or your son. You are just a hermit-woman. Why should I believe you?" he said harshly. Shame and anger overtook Shakuntala.

"O king, love and promises are sacred. Do not forget your love when you met me and the promises that you made. If you cling to your lie, I must go away. But my son will be king even without you." She started to go away when a heavenly voice echoed in the hall that Shakuntala told the truth and deserved to be honoured. Hearing the voice, Dushyanta acknowledged them. When King Dushyanta grew old, Bharata, donned the royal mantle and soon distinguished himself as a *Chakravarti Samrata*, or the most powerful ruler of his times.

King Bharata was a rare synthesis of all great qualities and was incomparable on every count with any of the rulers of his dynasty before and after him. He was brave, generous, benevolent, just and righteous. He never hesitated to sacrifice his interests for the welfare of his subjects.

As a ruler he set a rare example in *Bharata Varsha* when he decided not to nominate any of his nine sons as his successor to the throne because, in his view all of them were unworthy and incompetent. Instead of his sons, he appointed Bhimanya, the son of Sage Bharadwaja, as the *Yuvaraja* (heir-apparent). So, he is aptly credited as the first ruler to introduce democracy of some sort. In doing so, he might have violated the dynastic tradition of those days, which favoured *Jyeshthadhikar* or the primogeniture. As such the eldest son of a king was considered his natural successor to the throne. However, this incident went on to prove how lion-hearted, fair-minded and unbiased he was as a ruler, who was concerned about the larger interests of his subjects rather than the narrow interests of his family.

A couple of generations after King Bharata, King Kuru ascended the throne after whom the dynasty of Bharata came to be known as the Kuru dynasty.

The Mystery of Ganga

Shantanu, one of the illustrious kings of the Bharata dynasty, son of King Kuru, loved hunting. One day, when he was on a hunting expedition along the banks of the Ganga, he saw a girl whose beauty left him awe-struck. Her waist was as slender as a wasp's and her eyes were like the petals of a lotus. Her hair was dark and long.

Shantanu couldn't resist the temptation to marry her. "Who are you?" he asked, but couldn't wait for her reply. "I am King Shantanu. Marry me and I will lay the world at your feet," the king proposed.

The girl smiled, "My name is Ganga. I will marry you, but I have two conditions." "I promise to fulfilll all conditions," the king said, lost in the beauty of the maiden.

The maiden spoke in a plain but grave tone, "My first condition is that you will never interfere with, nor question any act of mine. And the second condition is that you will never utter one harsh word to me irrespective of what I do. I will leave you immediately if you break any of the conditions."

Shantanu was so deeply in love with Ganga that he hardly considered the two conditions as harsh. He instantly agreed to her demands. They married and lived as husband and wife, and led a life of marital bliss for the next two years.

Shantanu felt very happy when his wife conceived, and even happier, when their son was born. But Ganga, his wife, took the newborn to the river and threw the infant in the flowing waters. Shantanu, who had slyly followed his wife, was aghast at what he saw with his own eyes. But he didn't retaliate for fear of Ganga leaving him forever. Six more sons were born to Ganga, one after the other. And she treated them all alike. She threw them in the river without the least trace of guilt. Each time Shantanu followed her, only to helplessly watch her kill their sons. He bore the pain and suffering of her murderous acts, for he loved her too much to question her. Seven sons were thus consigned to the flowing waters.

Then the eighth son was born to Ganga. She took him down to the river immediately. Shantanu followed her again but this time he was determined to put a check to her cruelty. As she was about to throw the baby in the flowing waters, he shouted, "Stop it. Who are you? How can you kill your own children? Have mercy at least on this baby. Are you a woman or a demoness who can kill her own children without remorse?"

Ganga turned around to face Shantanu, the baby still in her arms. "I must leave, because you have broken your promise," she said. "Before leaving, however, I must let you know who I am," she continued. "I am Ganga, Jahnu's daughter, worshipped by Bhahmarshis as I make my way through the matted locks of Lord Shiva. I chose you to be my husband and the father of my children on earth."

"I will also tell you why I killed my own children. The eight Vasus were cursed by Vasishtha to be born as men because they stole his cows. The Vasus requested me to be their mother on earth and to ensure they did not lead a miserable life as mortals. I agreed to their prayer and I have released seven of them from their mortal life. I will not kill our eighth son. His destiny is to live in the world. This extraordinary child shares his spark with the Vasus. Call him Gangeya, the son of Ganga, or call him Devavrata. He will remain with me till he is perfectly trained in every skill and art, and thereafter he will come back to you." The next moment Ganga and her baby son vanished, before Shantanu could find time to respond.

Shantanu came back to his palace utterly dejected and disappointed. He led a despondent life in the absence of his wife Ganga. He had lost the zest for life. However, he continued with his passion for hunting.

Years rolled by and King Shantanu adjusted himself to his loneliness. One day he came to the bank of river Ganga while chasing a stag. There he saw a handsome young boy who was shooting his arrows into the soft mud to build a dam. The boy was graceful. His bearing was noble and exuded wisdom and intelligence through his brilliantly shining countenance. Shantanu wanted to speak to the boy but before he could to so, the boy vanished out of his sight.

Shantanu thought, "If I could only meet that lad once again!" As he wished so, he found a woman appearing out of the gushing waves of the river leading the same boy by the hand. Shantanu's eyes beheld the woman in surprise as he recognised her. She was Ganga.

Shantanu was speechless with surprise and happiness. Ganga spoke in her lilting melodious voice, "O, King of Bharata, take a look at your son. I had promised that I'll bring him back to you. He will, from today, stay with you. He will be unrivalled in the world. Vasishtha, Parashurama, and Brihaspati have been his tutors. Treat him well. He will bring glory to the world." Saying these words Ganga vanished, while Shantanu held his son's hand gently, escorting him to the palace.

The Sacrifice of Devavrata

Shantanu appointed his son Devavrata as heir-apparent, satisfied that he had an able successor. A few years later, while he was hunting on the banks of the Yamuna, Shantanu found the atmosphere around redolent with sweet fragrance. He saw a beautiful lady and followed her. Shantanu was enchanted by her beauty and instantly decided to marry her.

He asked her to introduce herself. She said that she was Satyavati, daughter of the chief of the fishermen. Shantanu immediately proposed to her. Satyavati coyly replied that she would marry him but he must ask her father for her hand.

The chief of the fishermen was astounded to find the King of the Bharata dynasty right at his doorstep. Bowing his head low to the king, he asked what he could do to serve his king. Shantanu, without wasting his words, straightaway spoke out the desire of his heart.

The fisherman was cunning enough not to display emotions of happiness and surprise, which were only natural for any humble fisherman suddenly bestowed with such an honour. "You can marry my daughter O lord, but I have a condition," said the fisherman shrewdly.

Shantanu grew suspicious. "Yes, tell me what is the condition?" he asked cautiously.

"I want Satyavati's son to succeed you as king," the fisherman spoke distinctly and clearly.

Shantanu thought of Devavrata and turned speechless. Without saying a word, he came back. Once in the palace, the king's apathy and listlessness became obvious to all.

Devavrata too noticed his father's lack of interest in life. He decided to find out why his father had turned so sullen all of a sudden. "Father, I can see you have lost all interest in life. You neither sleep, nor eat properly. You don't even go outside the palace. May I know, what is it that is troubling you?"

Shantanu tried to hide his actual worry by saying that he was worried that Devavrata, his only son and successor, should remain safe and sound and should never be harmed. Should anything happen to Devavrata, he would be left heirless. But much as he would have not liked to see his line die out, Shantanu declared, he would nonetheless not marry again.

Devavrata could easily guess there was something more than what his father admitted. So he went to the king's personal attendant and asked what was the matter with him. "He wants to marry a fisherman's daughter," the attendant replied succinctly.

"Then, what is the problem in that?" asked Devavrata. "The fisherman has put a condition for the marriage," replied the minister without hiding any fact, "and the condition is that the son born out of that union should be the next king after him."

For a moment, Devavrata remained nonplussed. He thought deeply in silence, but soon enough an idea occurred to him and he smiled. The prince asked his father's ministers to accompany him to the bank of river Yamuna, where he was going to see the fisherman.

The fisherman was not surprised to see the ministers and attendants of the king, but was taken aback to see the prince himself arriving at his humble hut. Without wasting much time in formalities, Devavrata straightaway came to the point. "I have come here to ask your daughter's hand in marriage to my father," he said.

Bowing humbly with joined palms, the fisherman repeated his condition as he had done before, reminding the prince, "So long as you are there as the first born son of King Shantanu, I cannot expect my daughter's son to be the king ever."

"Take my word, your daughter's son will be the king after King Shantanu," said the prince with a determined look on his face.

The clever fisherman wanted no obstruction to the accession of his daughter's son to the throne. He said humbly, "I can see your will and determination and I believe you will keep your promise, but I cannot trust your children. They could, in all probability, oppose my daughter's son's accession to the throne."

Devavrata appeared even more serious and determined now. "Listen, I have already given you my word, but if that doesn't satisfy you, I swear, I will remain celibate all my life. Tell me, what more do you want me to do?"

There was stunned silence as soon as Devavrata swore. No man could have taken a harsher oath. The Gods from heaven rained flowers on the man who had taken such a stern oath only because he wanted his father to be happy. From then on Devavrata came to be known as Bhishma.

Bhishma escorted Satyavati to his father's palace in Hastinapur. When Shantanu learned what great a price his son had paid to buy him happiness, he was moved to tears. He embraced his son warmly saying, "My son, I cannot ever repay your debt, but I wish to bless you with a boon. No one will ever defeat you in a war. Death will never touch you, unless you choose it yourself."

Not much later, Shantanu died leaving behind his young wife, Satyavati, and two sons, Chitrangada and Vichitravirya. The sons were still minors. True to his word, Bhishma crowned Chitrangada as the king and himself acted as his regent. He looked after the two young boys well, just like his own children.

The Kingdom in Crisis

Chitrangada did not live very long. One day in the forest while hunting, he came across a *gandharva (heavenly being)* by the same name as his. The *gandharva* did not like a human being having the name Chitrangada. Therefore, he challenged the young king to a fight. Although he fought heroically, the *gandharva* being a superior warrior, killed him. Bhishma crowned Vichitravirya as the next king.

When Vichitravirya attained marriageable age, Bhishma began scouting for a suitable bride for him. About the same time he came to know that the king of Kashi was going to hold a Swayamvara for his three daughters Amba, Ambika and Ambalika. They were all beautiful, accomplished and skillfull.

Having been fully satisfied with his choice, he went to meet Satyavati to seek her permission. "What is the matter, my son?" asked Satyavati as he touched her feet. "I want your permission to seek the hands of the princesses of Kashi for Vichitravirya, as I have learned that they are beautiful and well accomplished. I will attend the Swayamvara and bring the princesses back."

After preliminary enquiry about the princesses, their lineage and reputation, Satyavati gave her consent. Bhishma arrived at Kashi with his large retinue.

As Bhishma strode in the Swayamvara hall, the great and mighty kings felt uncomfortable. They were surprised at his presence. He had no business to be there, having taken a vow of celibacy. Moreover, he was also in a somewhat advanced age for marriage. But no one had the courage to question his presence.

Bhishma stood up as the three princesses of Kashi entered the Swayamvara. "I am here to represent my younger brother Vichitravirya for whom the princesses of Kashi will be ideal brides," declared Bhishma to the stunned gathering of the princes. The protesting princes found their spirits daunted in the mighty presence of the son of Ganga. Bhishma continued after a brief pause, "A kshatriya king may take his bride in several ways, including force. It is said the bride carried by force after vanquishing the rival claims is the most honourable form. I am, therefore, taking these princesses. Free them if you can!"

There was a flurry of resistance as Bhishma carried away the princesses, but Bhishma's swift marksmanship ensured that no one posed a real threat. Those who did, lay wounded or dead. The brave ruler of the Shalva kingdom also had to lick dust.

Amba, the eldest princess, did not like being carried away by Bhishma. On reaching Hastinapur, Amba complained to Bhishma, "As you carried us away, you did not give me an opportunity to speak. But there is something I wish to convey to you. Even before the Swayamvara, I had decided to marry the prince of Shalva. Had the Swayamvara taken place, I would have garlanded him. Now I leave the rest on your wise decision."

Bhishma consulted Satyavati and arrived at the decision that Amba should be allowed to go wherever she liked. He sent her honourably to the Shalva capital along with escorts. But King Shalva refused to accept Amba, as she had been captured by Bhishma. Amba returned to Bhishma and asked him to marry her, to which he declined. Feeling humiliated and angry, Amba commited suicide, vowing to kill Bhishma in her next birth. (Later she was born as Shikhandi to King Drupada.)

King Vichitravirya wedded the other two princesses Ambika and Ambalika. The two sisters were happy to be married to a handsome and valiant prince. Not long after, however, Vichitravirya died of a wasting disease, leaving behind the childless widows. They became Bhishma's responsibilities along with the kingdom. The kingdom was once again heirless. Bhishma made no claim to the throne, bound as he was, by his vow.

Satyavati underwent a trauma at the loss of both her sons, but she maintained her calm, for she was the queen. She had to act courageously to save the Kuru line from extinction. At times, she also felt that these misfortunes resulted from the injustice she had done; and which her father had meted out to Bhishma. She called Bhishma and said, "The Kuru-line should not die out. You are Shantanu's son and you have a duty towards your father."

"Tell me, what do you want me to do?" asked Bhishma. "Perpetuate the Kuru line through the widows of your dead brother," Satyavati said boldly. "That is impossible. You, of all people, should know why that is impossible," Bhishma spoke in a determined tone. "But there is a way out, mother," said Bhishma, "society permits a widow to perpetuate progeny by someone who stands in an equal or a higher order."

Satyavati was reminded of Vyasa. "Yes, I have a son who is still alive. He was born to me when I was still unwed through the blessings of Sage Parashara," Satyavati said. "Mother, that would be the best solution. Don't waste any more time and call Vyasa immediately," Bhishma requested.

Satyavati wasted no more time. Vyasa came and touched Satyavati's feet. He found his mother in tears. "Don't weep, mother. I have arrived. Tell me what I can do for you."

"Vichitravirya, my youngest son, is no more. He has left two childless widows behind. You are my eldest son. Bhishma has taken a stern vow of celibacy. But you are under no such vow. It is your duty as Vichitravirya's half brother to perpetuate his lineage. You are also a brahmin, which makes you an ideal candidate to perform this task. Ambika and Ambalika should also have sons to hold in their arms."

Sage Vyasa wanted the princesses to undergo rites of purification for one year. But Satyavati requested the sage to arrive at some other option, as it was a question of heirs for the kingdom, which could not remain kingless for long. "In that case, the princesses should be prepared to withstand not just my ugliness, but also my unbearable odour," the sage stated clearly.

Arrangements were made for sage Vyasa's stay and union with the widows. The sage was dark in colour and had ugly features. His body reeked with an offensive odour too.

Ambika could not withstand his looks. She closed her eyes out of fear. The sage informed queen Satyavati that the son born to Ambika would be blind, though he would be a brave warrior.

Next, it was Ambalika's turn, when the sage would be visiting her. Ambalika too, found the sage so resentful in looks that she turned pale when she looked at his frightening face. Later, Sage Vyasa informed Satyavati, his mother, that Ambalika will be blessed with a child no doubt, but he would be pale in colour. "He would nonetheless be valiant," added the sage.

Queen Satyavati was not satisfied that the heir to Hastinapur would be blind. Therefore, she proposed that Ambika should once again contact the sage. She was sent once again to meet the sage, but Ambika did not gather enough courage to face him. Instead, she arranged for a maid to represent her.

The maid was intelligent, fearless and devoted to the sage. This time, the sage informed Satyavati that the son born to the maid would be highly talented and worldly wise. He would be a man of great political learning. His wise policies would take Hastinapur to glorious heights.

In due course of time, the two widows and the maid were blessed with a son each. Ambika gave birth to Dhritarashtra, Ambalika gave birth to Pandu and the maid gave birth to Vidura. Dhritarashtra was born blind. Pandu was congenitally pale but Vidura was quite normal and intelligent.

All the three children grew up together. Bhishma raised them as his own.

The Illustrious Progeny

The birth of the three children brought prosperity to the land of Kurus. The state coffers swelled and there was peace. The crops yielded bounteously and the citizens were happy.

Bhishma, who was at the helm of affairs, was running the state on behalf of his mother Satyavati. The three young princes were given the best training under eminent teachers. They were taught the ancient epics and lores, history and statecraft, archery, swordsmanship and riding.

Dhritarashtra proved his mettle in physical strength, Pandu was unrivalled in archery while Vidura mastered traditional wisdom, excelling in the Shastras and Vedas.

As soon as Pandu was of age, Bhishma enthroned him. Although Dhritarashtra was the eldest, his blindness came in his way to attainment of throne. Vidura, although qualified for the post, lost his chance as he was born of a maid. Since Pandu became the king, the Kuruvansha also came to be called Panduvansha.

The princes were now old enough to get married. Bhishma, as their guardian, made discreet enquiries about princesses from the neighbouring kingdoms. His choice fell upon the princess of Gandhar, the daughter of King Suvala of Gandhar. She was beautiful and virtuous. Moreover, she had been granted a boon by Shiva to be blessed with a hundred sons. That was indeed a decisive factor for the Kurus, a dynasty suffering from scarcity of sons.

A formal proposal was sent to King Suvala requesting Gandhari's hand in marriage with Dhritarashtra. Initially Suvala hesitated at the thought of Dhritarashtra's blindness, but after a little dithering he could not resist the offer from Kuru dynasty. Gandhari, the daughter of Gandhar, on learning of her proposed marriage to a blind prince, bound her eyes with a dark cloth, never to remove it again. "I too will share my husband's fate," she said with determination. Shakuni, her brother, escorted her to Hastinapur, where she married Dhritarashtra.

It was Pandu's turn to get married next. Bhishma sent the brahmins to all the kingdoms in the land to find a suitable bride. Of all the reports that came in, the most favourable was that of Kunti, the adopted daughter of Kuntibhoja. Kunti was the daughter of King Shoorsena, Lord Krishna's grandfather and Kuntibhoja's cousin. Shoorsena had promised to give him his first born, as Kuntibhoja was childless.

Durvasa's Blessing

Kunti was young, beautiful and charming. Once Sage Durvasa visited King Kuntibhoja. Being aware of his quick temper and the tendency to curse anyone at the slightest excuse, Kuntibhoja asked Kunti to take good care of the guest, so as not to invite his wrath. Kunti looked after Durvasa for one year, humbly fulfilling the slightest demand of the sage. At the end of one year, when it was time for the sage to depart, he expressed his deep satisfaction and happiness with young Kunti and told her to ask for a boon. She declined the offer saying the sage's satisfaction was reward enough. But the sage insisted that he must reward her and gave her a boon. According to this boon she could invoke any God any time, who would bless her with a son.

When Sage Durvasa left, Kunti decided to test the efficacy of the incantation taught to her by the sage. She invoked the Sun God and he instantly appeared. Kunti, who was trying the incantation for fun, got scared. She prayed to the Sun God to forgive her misadventure. But the Sun God stood adamant, refusing to go without blessing her with a son. Kunti urged that she would be disgraced as an unwed mother. When the Sun God threatened to curse her and her family for insulting the holy chant, she relented and made a request that the child should be born with a golden armour and earrings.

Kunti's request was fulfillled. When she gave birth to a baby, he was as glorious as the sun himself. Moreover, the baby was born with a golden armour and an earring attached to his ear. Kunti's heart missed a beat as she beheld the glorious child, resplendent like Surya himself. Fear of social disgrace was far more overpowering than the motherly love for the baby. Kunti decided to disown the baby. No one knew anything about the unwed mother and her baby, except Kunti's maid. She laid the

baby in a silk cushioned basket and consigned it gently over the waves of river Ganga, praying and beseeching the Gods in heaven for the well-being and safety of the baby.

The basket floated quietly over the waves till spotted by Adhiratha, a *suta* (charioteer) and Radha, his childless wife. Radha shrieked in delight when she saw a divine child in the basket, handed over to her by Adhiratha. The childless couple could not have been happier as they thought it was the most obvious divine blessing to them. The child came to be called Radheya, after his foster mother's name. He was also called Karna. Adhiratha fondly called him Vasusena because of his golden armour and earrings.

Kunti's Marriage

Kunti was already of marriageable age. She had grown into a fine young doe-eyed woman. King Kuntibhoja held a Swayamvara for her, to which all the kings of Bharatavarsha were invited. Kunti entered the Swayamvara hall and when she saw Pandu, she made up her mind about who her groom would be. She walked up to him and placed the lotus garland around his neck.

Bhishma was happy for Pandu. However, he thought one more wife for Pandu would be an added insurance against the abrupt end of the Kuru line any time. Bhishma decided to choose the bride himself this time and his choice fell upon Madri, sister of King Shalya of Madra. She was graceful and highly attractive in looks. When Bhishma spoke his wish to the king, he felt honoured to enter into an alliance with the Kurus. Pandu also married to Madri, who became his second wife.

Barely a month after his marriage, Pandu set out on an expedition of conquest with the blessings of Bhishma. Heading a large army, he easily trampled various kings and princes. The unpopular ruler of Magadh was vanquished and his treasury emptied. Mithila too met with the same fate as the brave Videhas surrendered to Pandu's might. He came back to Hastinapur, richer in men, and material resources.

Pandu received a rousing welcome from Bhishma and the other Kuru elders. Hastinapur was at the centre of the world and its treasury lay swollen. Pandu, however, dedicated everything he had, at the feet of Bhishma and Satyavati. A portion was of course offered to Vidura, whom he loved dearly.

Pandu's Misfortunes

Hard campaigning and wars had left Pandu with a desire to relax in the sylvan surroundings of a forest retreat. Bhishma consented to Pandu's wishes, who had a magnificent pavillion built in the charming forest retreat, where he retired with his wives amidst all comforts.

Everything was going well, when suddenly a mishap occurred which was later to prove to be the nemesis of Pandu. He noticed a large stag with his mate, while roaming in the forest one day. He shot arrows at them, fatally wounding the stag couple. The stag and his mate were, in fact, a sage king and his wife. As they fell, they transformed into their human forms and cried out, "O king, you have committed a grave sin. Even a hunter doesn't attack an animal at such a moment. Most heartless of men would not commit such a foul deed."

Pandu deeply regretted his act and had no words in his defence. The sage died with a curse on his lips. "There is a time for slaughter and a time for refrain. Your act was unbecoming of a Bharata King. I, Kindama, therefore curse you. You will die in the first passionate embrace with your spouse and she will also follow you to the abode of your ancestors."

Pandu regretted his folly. He cursed himself and his luck, and wailed bitterly.

Pandu did not see any wisdom in going back to Hastinapur. He decided to lead the life of a recluse and live on alms. Therefore, he asked his wives Kunti and Madri to go back to Hastinapur. "Life has no meaning for me now. I have decided to lead the life of a celibate, spending the time in penance and subsisting on forest fruits and roots. Therefore, I request you to go back to Hastinapur," Pandu told his queens.

The queens refused to go. "Our life is tied to yours. How do you expect us to leave you alone? As your wives we are tied to a common fate. What you command of us is a fate worse than death for a wife, whose husband is still alive," said Kunti and Madri.

The king and the queens discarded their royal robes, distributed their jewellery and silks among the brahmins and instructed the weeping attendants to go back to Hastinapur. Pandu, along with Kunti and Madri, went deep into the forest and arrived at Shatashringa, the mountain of a hundred peaks inhabited by the Siddhas and Charanas.

Pandu settled there with his wives and involved himself in deep meditation and penance. Soon the sages and rishis living there developed a deep bond of compassion with the reclusive king who had renounced his royal world to be with them.

One day, Pandu made a vain attempt to join a group of rishis embarking upon a tough journey to the high mountains. The rishis were going for a *darshan* of Lord Brahma who was expected to be present on a high mountain peak. When Pandu expressed his desire to join their retinue, they disapproved of his idea as his wives could not undertake the difficult journey through the icy peaks and deep gorges. The reason Pandu wanted to go was to seek the blessing of Lord Brahma to undo the curse upon him, so that he could have children. One of the rishis informed Pandu that he could see that children were ordained for him through his wives. Pandu felt reassured and happy.

Coming back to his wives, Pandu said, "A sonless man is deprived of heaven. Shashtras permit a woman to have children through socially equal or superior persons. Neither I nor my ancestors will know any peace should I die without a son."

His wives were aghast at the thought of having to procreate through the medium of anyone other than their husband. They knew Pandu, being under the curse, was helpless.

Kunti had not disclosed to anyone the boon she had received from Durvasa. It was now the time to disclose the greatest secret of her life. She disclosed it to Pandu. Pandu smiled, as a new hope just discovered would light up the darkest forlorn corner of his heart. Using the boon bestowed upon Kunti, he could be blessed with divine sons. Pandu persuaded Kunti to invoke the Gods of Dharma, Vayu and the king of the Gods, Indra. The efficacious incantation instantly brought the Gods invoked in that order.

The child born with the blessing of Dharmaraj was called Yudhishthira. Pandu was told by an unseen voice, "Your son will be the most virtuous of men and will rule the earth. He will never speak untruth." The same incorporeal voice said of the second child, "This child will be second to none in strength. He will be called Bheema."

Not long after, infant Bheema was happily frolicking in the lap of his mother, when he accidentally fell down a steep rocky cliff. The devastated mother rushed her way through the rocks only to find the healthy unscratched infant gurgling merrily amidst shattered rocks that lay crushed under him.

The third son to Kunti was born with the blessings of Indra, the God of the celestial beings, and of rain and thunder. The baby was born when the constellation of Phalguna was rising. The invisible voice was heard amidst the rumbling thunder, "This son of yours, like Indra, will be invincible in battle. He will defeat all his foes and restore the kingdom!"

Madri, who had no sons, spoke her heart to Pandu, that she wanted children as well. She was not sure whether Kunti, being a co-wife of Pandu, would be willing to comply with her wishes. Therefore, she wanted him to intervene on her behalf. Pandu urged Kunti to help Madri have a baby as well. Kunti gave Madri the mantra and she invoked Ashwinis, the twin-Gods of medicine, through whom she had beautiful twin sons, named Nakula and Sahadeva.

With five sons, Pandu was a happy and satisfied man now.

Pandu was leading a reclusive but happy life in the forest with his two wives and five sons. It was sixteen years ago, that he had taken to the forest life. His third son, Arjuna, had grown up into a handsome boy of 14 years. It was his birthday. A serene atmosphere marked the day when the brahmins were invited for a feast. The queens were dressed in their finest clothes. Madri, the younger wife, looked exceptionally beautiful that day. Madri had inadvertently instigated the cursed king, who was now under the spell of uncontrollable desire. Madri was in her senses and did her best to soothe the flared desire of Pandu. But Pandu was trapped in the deadly web of fate. Sage Kindama's curse proved true. Pandu died in the arms of Madri, who wailed helplessly.

Kunti and the other rishis rushed towards the crying Madri only to be shocked at the sight that awaited them. Kunti too began weeping loudly, even as she consoled a distraught Madri. She fell into a swoon and was brought to her senses when Madri sprinkled water on her face. The two of them embraced each other and wept bitterly.

The young princes too were shocked at the untimely death of their loving father. The learned sages of the Shatashringa, who had trained and tutored the young princes, consoled them. Kunti offered to embrace the funeral pyre along with Pandu's dead body. However, Madri insisted that she wanted to follow her husband to the abode of death. She insisted on her demand saying she had been the cause of her husband's death and therefore should be the one to die. "Moreover, I cannot be impartial towards your children, while you are endowed with the great ability to nurture my children as your own. Therefore, you must stay alive for the sake of the children," said Madri to Kunti, and that was the last word on the subject. Madri mounted the pyre along with the dead body of Pandu. Soon, the flames engulfed them.

Kunti Returns With The Young Princes

Kunti was now left alone with the five young princes. The sages and rishis of Shatashringa advised Kunti to return to Hastinapur along with the five young princes. The sages escorted the mother and her five young sons to Hastinapur along with the last remains of the royal couple.

When the small royal entourage entered the capital, citizens poured in to have a glimpse of the princes. The Kuru elders received them warmly with all due honours. The wisest sage in the group spoke to Bhishma, "The Kuru king abandoned the world to lead a celibate life. But gods gave him five children. Pandu died seventeen days ago and Madri followed him on the funeral pyre. Perform the last rites of Pandu and enthrone his eldest son Yudhishthira."

Bhishma and Dhritarashtra performed the last rites of Pandu and Madri on the banks of river Ganga. The brahmins were sumptuously fed and given large donations.

Vyasa arrived in Hastinapur soon after the mourning period was over. He headed straight to Satyavati's chamber. "Mother dear," he said, "the coming days are ominous for the Kuru dynasty. You would not be able to bear the difficult times ahead leading to the end of the Kuru dynasty. So, I have come here to request you to spend your days in peace in a forest retreat."

Satyavati had no desire to live in Hastinapur. She was especially compassionate towards Ambalika, whose husband, as well as son had died. She asked Ambalika to accompany her for quiet meditation in the forest. Ambika, Dhritarashtra's mother refused to live in Hastinapur without her sister and mother-in-law. The three queens left the city forever. Satyavati died peacefully in the forest and was lucky not to live long enough to see the destruction of Kurus.

The Royal Intrigues Begin

The five Pandava brothers along with their mother Kunti came to live in Hastinapur. They adapted well to the life in the palace. Their manners were pleasing and noble. Kuru elders loved them. But the rivalry between the cousins could not remain unnoticed by their elders. Duryodhana and his brothers considered the presence of the Pandavas a trespass in their private fiefdom. Duryodhana especially disliked Bheema. Of all the young princes, Bheema was the most powerful, and was ever the victor in all the sports and contests.

The young princes were trained to throw the stone, cast the noose; they practised wrestling and boxing. As they grew up, they learnt to mark the young calves, count and brand the cattle.

Bheema, unlike the other Pandavas, made Kaurava brothers the butt of his jokes. He did not miss a single opportunity to humiliate them, as he was strong enough to fight a couple of Kaurava brothers single handedly.

Dhritarashtra, the blind father of a hundred sons, was also blind to the follies of Duryodhana, his eldest son. He had been ruling over Hastinapur since Pandu retreated to the forest.

Dhritarashtra had been anointed the king in Pandu's absence temporarily, but his long association with the throne had fired a desire in his heart never to abdicate the throne, while Duryodhana considered himself the rightful heir to the throne.

Dhritarashtra, who was not absolutely blind to reason, was often indecisive. It was his brother-in-law Shakuni, who was the real villain of the piece. He was quick to concoct evil game plans and was even quicker at melodramatic exaggeration. Instigated by Shakuni, Duryodhana considered himself the rightful heir to the throne. He could convincingly pass off this message to Dhritarashtra, who according to them should have been the original king of Hastinapur, had he not been blind.

Duryodhana had a one-point mission. "I will finish off Bheema. He is the only thorn in my way. The other Pandavas will be fangless in the absence of Bheema. That will leave my suzerainty uncontested."

Duryodhana was discreet enough to make subtle deadly game plans to kill Bheema without being spotted. He had a great pavillion constructed in Parankoti near the bank of river Ganga, where he invited the Pandavas for a picnic.

Bheema's gluttony was well known. Duryodhana targeted his weakness for food and had a sumptuous meal with a variety of dishes prepared. Bheema was sure to fall in the trap. Duryodhana, in the best traditions of hospitality made special care to personally serve Bheema, helping after helping. The other Pandavas having finished their meal, went out on a stroll even as Bheema was still helping himself. After finishing his meal, Bheema, feeling lethargic, dozed off on the sandy banks of Ganga.

Duryodhana emerged out of his hiding as he noticed Bheema lying unconscious. He noted with satisfaction that the poison was working on him. He threw Bheema in the river, with the help of his brothers. Everyone returned to Hastinapur leaving

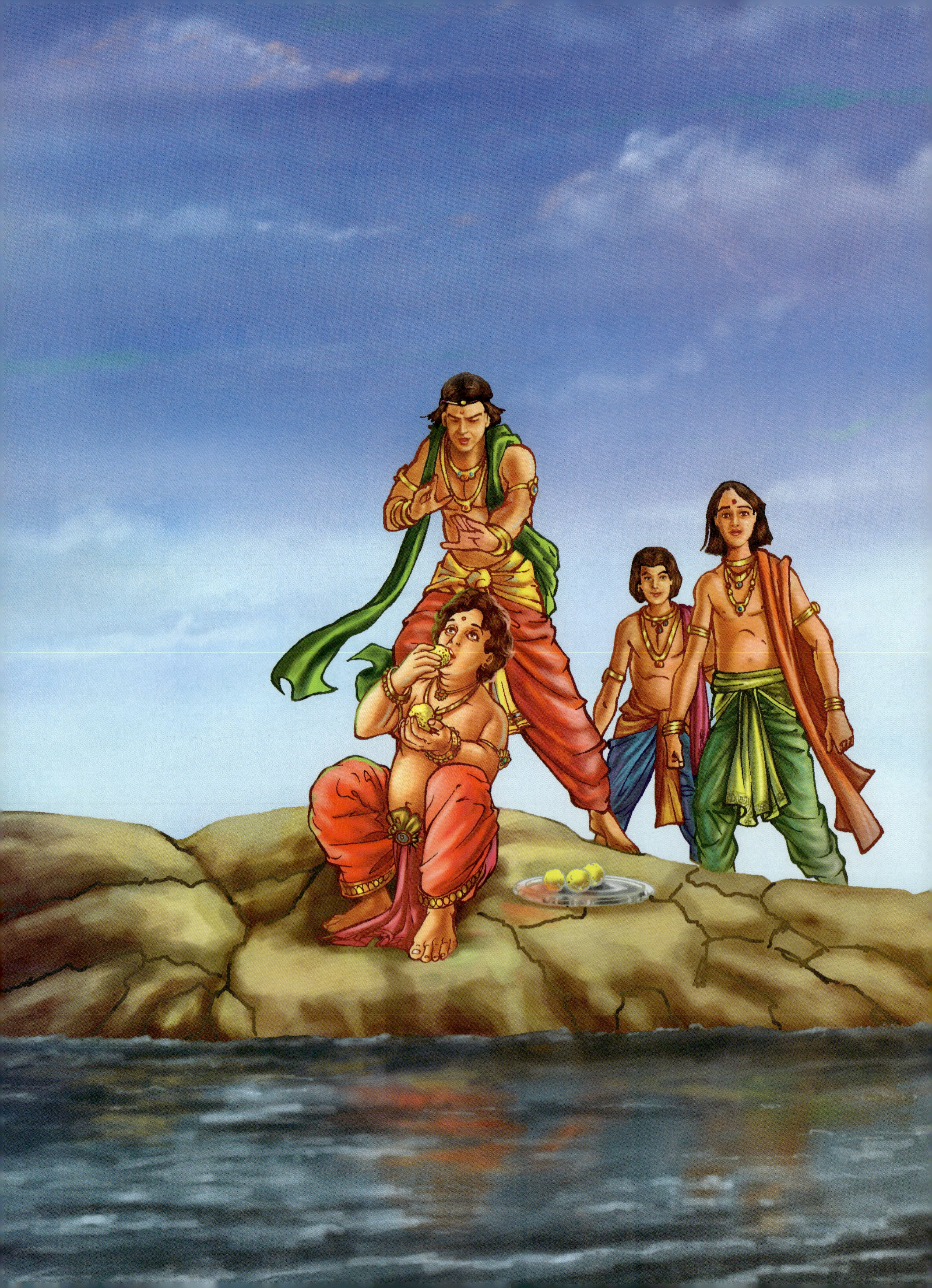

Bheema drifted with the current and sank into the kingdom of the Nagas. A group of snakes pierced their fangs into his body. He remained not only unaffected, but to the surprise of the venomous snakes, he regained his consciousness. The poison in his body had been neutralised by the venom of the snakes. Bheema disentangled the snakes around his body and killed some of them. The others slithered away fast to their king, Vasuki, and narrated to him, with horror, the events they had just witnessed.

Vasuki, the *nagaraja*, along with a group of his counsellors, came to see the wonder boy. Aryaka, Kunti's great grandfather, was one of the ministers with Vasuki, who recognised Bheema and told Vasuki about him. Vasuki knew instantly that Bheema had met with treachery and was pleased with the bravery of the boy. The Naga king offered Bheema precious gems, but Aryaka intervened to offer even greater rewards.

Bheema to his fate, while the Pandavas noted the absence of Bheema with concern but dismissed their worries thinking he might have left before, unnoticed.

"If you desire to reward Bheema, give him *rasakunda*, the nectar of strength, which he will not get in the world of men," pleaded Aryaka to Vasuki. Vasuki offered Bheema bowls of *rasakunda*, without even a second thought. "Drink the nectar," Vasuki urged Bheema, "each bowl you drink will give you the strength of a thousand elephants." Bheema drank eight bowls of the potion of strength as the Nagas watched him in awe. For eight days, Bheema remained in the world of Nagas.

Meanwhile, the absence of Bheema caused great worry to Kunti and her sons, who suspected foul play by Duryodhana. Kunti let out her worries before Vidura, who advised her to maintain a dignified calm, as her allegations could permanently create a schism in the Kuru clan. Moreover, according to Vidura, an open allegation against Duryodhana will only prompt him to adopt more secretive and malicious designs.

When Bheema expressed his desire to go back on the eighth day, the Nagas escorted him to the surface of the river. Bheema rushed straight to Kunti's apartment in the palace and told her all that had happened to him. Kunti wept even as she embraced Bheema. Next, he touched the feet of Yudhishthira. The Pandavas were happy to find one of their missing siblings back in their fold. "Don't discuss the poison episode with anyone, but we should remain more cautious in future," Yudhishthira cautioned Bheema.

Duryodhana was livid with rage on coming to know of Bheema's escape. He was more determined in his resolve to do away with the Pandavas. He was quiet and cautious, waiting for the right opportunity to strike.

Dronacharya Arrives

Kripacharya, Sage Sharadvata's son, was appointed to teach and train the young princes. Soon, the princes outgrew the lessons that Kripacharya had to offer. Bhishma began looking for a more learned guru.

One day the princes were playing when their ball fell into a well. The princes were watching helplessly when they noticed a tall, dark and lanky brahmin watching them with amusement. "Shame on you, O, kshatriya princes," the brahmin said, "You can't even get a ball out of a well!"

"Can you?" the princes asked the brahmin in amusement. "I can not only get your ball out of the well, but even this ring!" the brahmin said, taking the ring out of his finger and throwing it in the well.

The brahmin plucked a few blades of grass and chanted mantras over them. The blades of grass turned stiff and reed-like. The brahmin aimed at the ball and the swift reed pierced the ball. Then he threw more reeds, which stuck successively one above the other till the last one touched the top edge of the well. The ball could now be pulled out easily. The brahmin unslung his bow, fitted an arrow into it and shot inside the well. The arrow brought back the ring in a sharp trajectory. The princes bowed before the brahmin and requested him to teach them the art of warfare.

When the boys described the skills of a stranger, who had helped them extricate the ball from a well, Bhishma immediately understood. It could be none other than Dronacharya. Bhishma guessed Drona could be found at Kripacharya's house. He was right. Drona met him right at the doorsteps of Kripa's house.

The two needed no introduction. "What brings you to Hastinapur?" Bhishma queried.

"I am here to find some disciples and earn a fortune," Drona replied.

"That is strange. A brahmin seeking fortune!" Bhishma wondered.

"There's no surprise in it. I have my reasons for seeking wealth," Drona's countenance grew serious. The reason that Drona gave was truly touching.

"I studied the art of warfare at Rishi Agnivesha's ashrama. I didn't introduce myself as Rishi Bharadwaja's son to him. Drupada, the prince of Panchala, also joined the ashrama. We became very good friends. Drupada always reassured me of his friendship and promised to share his wealth and happiness when he succeeded his father as the king."

"After my education was over, I married Kripi. When my son Ashvathama was born, my happiness was complete. I needed neither fame nor money. I was happy and satisfied with my world," Drona told Bhishma.

"One day I found my son crying. Unlike other children, he had never tasted milk. I, being poor, could not afford milk for him. One day I found him drinking rice powder mixed in water which his friends had given him to drink. He thought, it was milk. He was happy and enjoyed his drink even as his friends made fun of him. I was touched by the sight and decided to earn a fortune," Drona said.

"That was when I was reminded of Drupada, who was now the king of Panchala. Taking Kripi and Ashvathama along, I went to meet the Panchala king. Leaving Ashvathama and his mother outside, I went in to meet my friend Drupada. I reminded him of our friendship and his promise. But I was completely shocked at his response. He was cold and egoistic. 'Are you in the right frame of mind?' he asked coldly, 'There can be no friendship between a king and a poor brahmin. I do not remember promising to share my kingdom and wealth with anyone. However, as you have come to me, you can have food and shelter for the night.' The insult was too much for me. I left Panchala immediately and came to Hastinapur. I am here to teach the princes and earn a fortune," Drona said with determination.

"It will be our privilege to have you as the tutor and not the other way round. You will not lack anything you want in Hastinapur," Bhishma reassured. Drona's fame as rishi Bharadawaja's son, Parshurama's disciple, and his mastery over weapons had escaped none. Bhishma knew his worth more than anybody else.

The next day, the young princes stood before their tutor and bowed humbly to him, ready to receive the training. Drona quickly surveyed the group of princes and asked, "I am going to ask for my *gurudakshina* at the end of the training. Who amongst you can give me what I ask for?" While the other princes remained silent, a voice in the group spoke, "I will." It was Arjuna. Drona had already chosen his favourite disciple.

The Bird's Eye

Young princes from far and near kingdoms came to Hastinapur to receive training from the most reputed master in the art of warfare. Drona trained them in every subtle nuance of the art of warfare. They were taught horse riding and elephant riding, lancing and swordsmanship, hand to hand combat, defence and attack, wielding mace, bowmanship and every other aspect of war. Amongst the princes, Adhiratha's son Karna was also receiving training under guru Drona.

Karna felt jealous of Arjuna and always spoke ill of him. Dronacharya advised him a number of times not to feel jealous of Arjuna or speak ill of him. But Karna, instigated by Duryodhana, refused to mend his ways.

During the course of training, Dronacharya decided to test the skills of his students. He had hung an artificial bird from a tree, which was the target. He explained to the assembled boys, "The head of the bird over there is your target. I will call each of you, one by one, here. You will shoot only when I command you to do so."

"Come here, Yudhishthira," Dronacharya commanded. As Yudhishthira came, he asked him to sling an arrow to his bow and aim at the bird. "Don't shoot, till I ask you to do so," Dronacharya warned. "What do you see?" asked the guru. "I can see the tree and the bird, the bow and the arrow, my arm and you," Yudhishthira replied.

"All right, you can go now," Drona said coldly. Next, he called Duryodhana. One by one he called all the princes except Arjuna. All of them, including Karna, gave more or less the same reply to his question. All of them were asked to go back to their place without trying their skill in shooting.

Finally, Dronacharya called Arjuna. As he aimed at the bird, his guru asked, "What do you see? Do you see me, your companions, or anything else?"

"I can't see anything except the bird's eye," replied Arjuna looking straight at his target.

Drona's face cheered up. "Shoot now," he commanded. The bird's head dropped to the ground in an instant.

"You all have learnt nothing. Only Arjuna amongst you is my worthy disciple," Drona chastised everyone and praised Arjuna. Drona then embraced Arjuna and said, "I have made you the best bowman in the entire world, but you must promise me one thing."

"What?" asked Arjuna.

"That if ever I come against you, alone or with many, you will fight to win," said Drona.

"I promise," replied Arjuna.

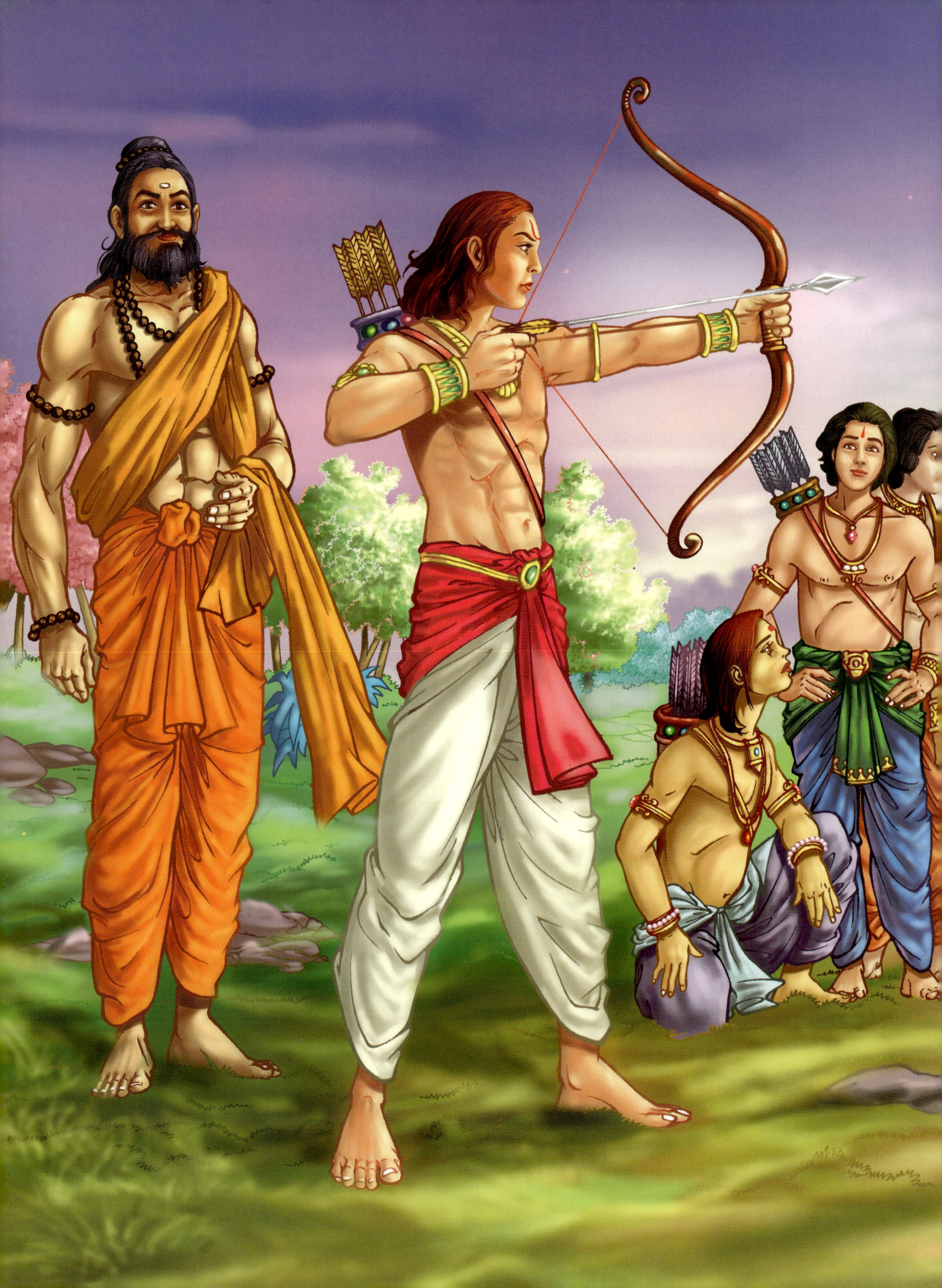

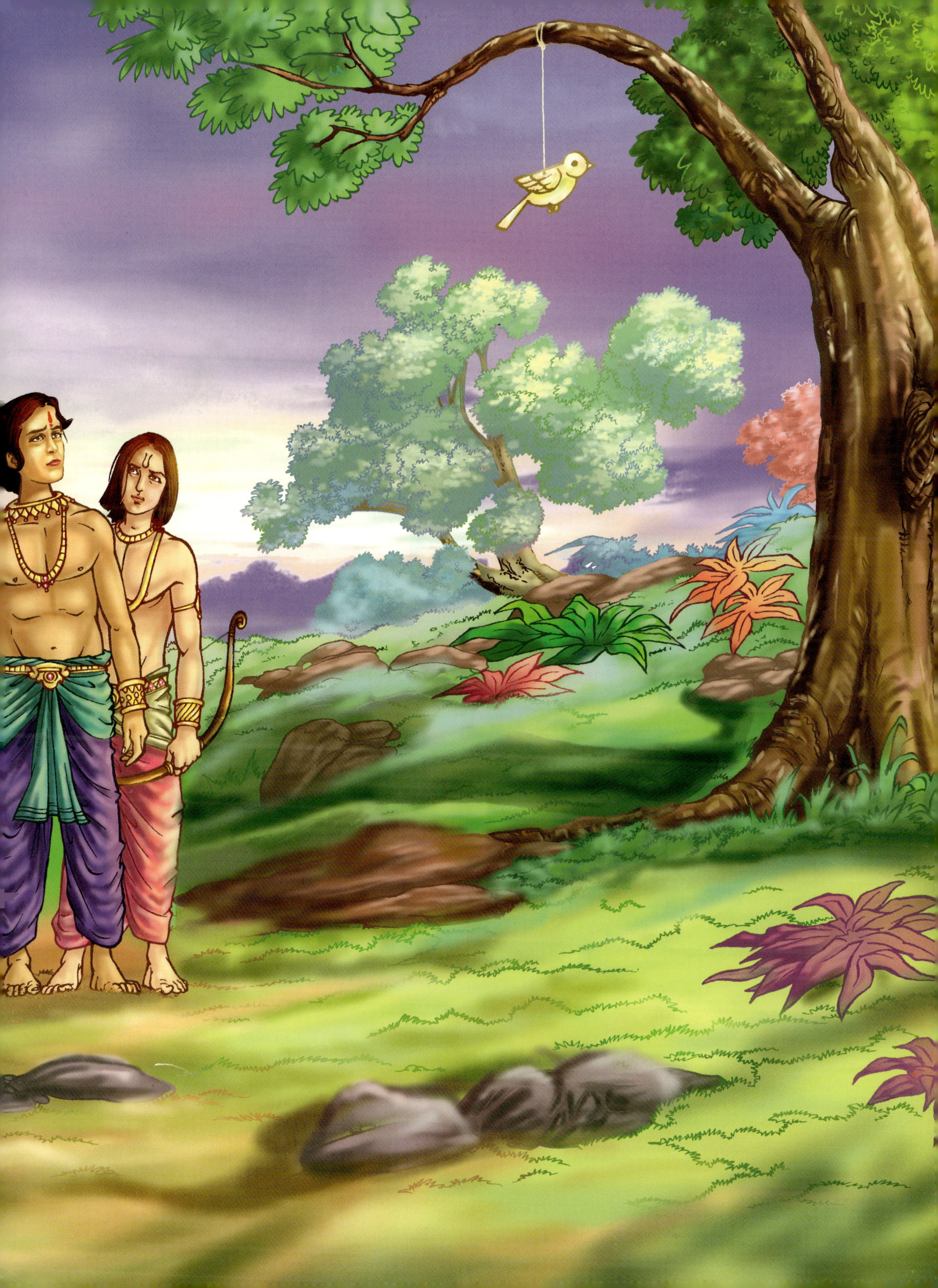

The Guru's Foul Play

There was, however, a better warrior than Arjuna. Ekalavya, son of Hiranyadhanush, the king of Nishadas, was indeed superior, as became evident accidentally one day.

The young princes, just before graduation, had gone on a hunting spree, not forgetting to take their dog along. Running ahead of the princes, the dog saw the dark Nishada boy and began barking ceaselessly. Ekalavya was practising bowmanship and did not want to be disturbed then. He tried to shoo the dog away, but the dog persisted with its barking. A trifle irritated, Ekalavya shot several arrows, one after the other into the open jaws of the dog, without hurting it. The bark turned into whine as the dog ran to its masters. The princes were amazed at the tremendously high level of skill showed by the marksman. Dronacharya was more worried than amazed. An anonymous archer lurking in the forest was in all likelihood going to surpass Arjuna in his skills. Drona and the princes followed the trail of the dog till they saw the Nishada boy absolutely involved in his practice.

"Well done boy! Who are you?" asked Drona. "Ekalavya, son of Hiranyadhanush, king of Nishada. The same Ekalavya, whom you refused to teach and take into your fold at the behest of your princely disciples," Ekalavya replied.

"Well, in that case may I know who is your worthy guru?" asked Dronacharya, puzzled. "You! Who else but you can be my guru?" Ekalavya replied, pointing at the wooden statue of Drona, which had been the source of his inspiration, lesson after lesson.

Dronacharya was even more puzzled now. He thought for a while and said, "I am honoured to have been considered as your guru. But if I am your guru, I have every right to claim my *gurudakshina*. Will you give me what I ask for?" asked Dronacharya cunningly.

"By all means. You have only to state it and it will be yours," said Ekalavya confidently.

"In that case, give me your right hand's thumb," said a distant and cold Dronacharya, even as the young princes stood stunned in silence.

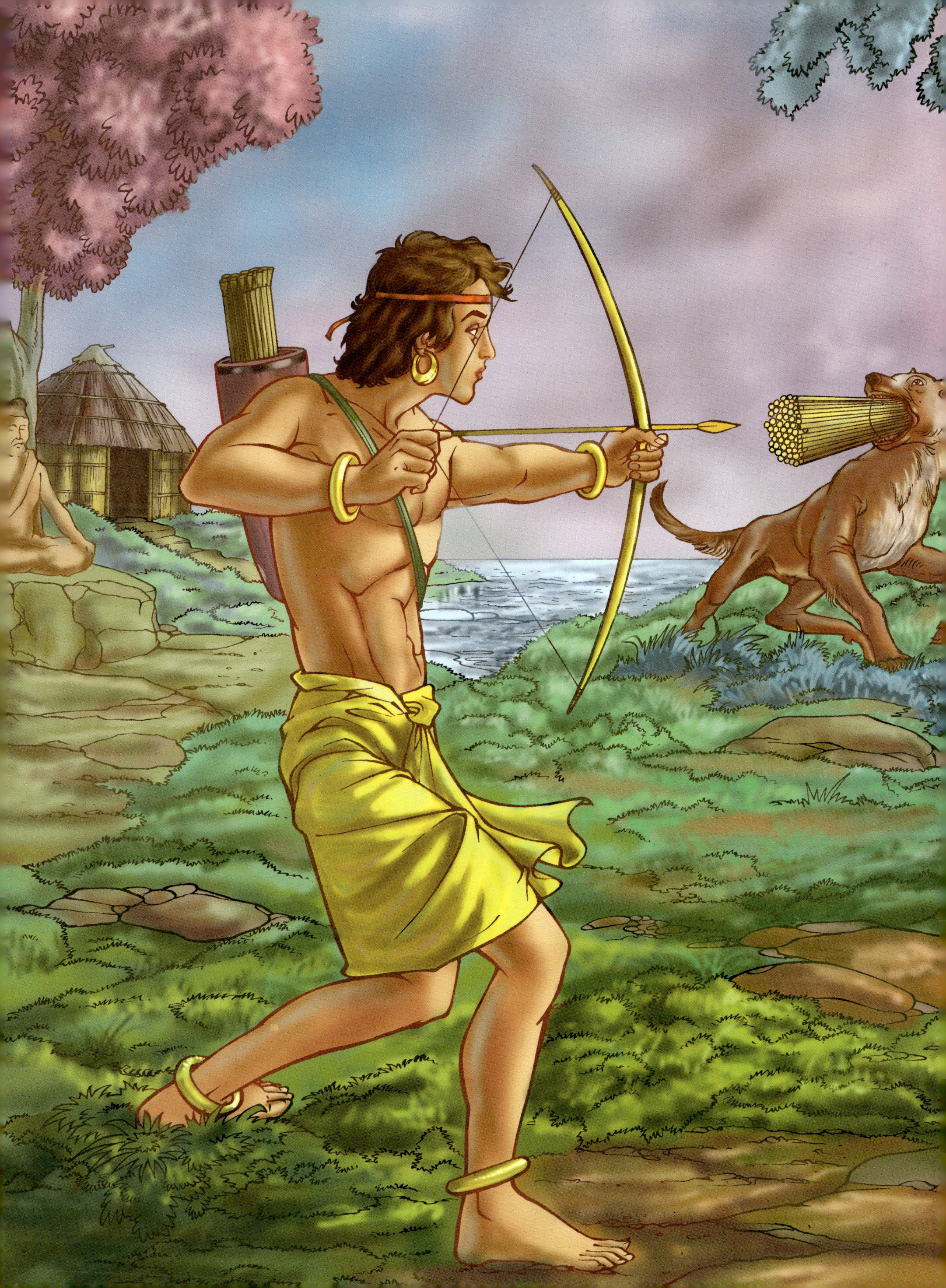

Ekalavya didn't even stop to give a second thought to his guru's command. Using a knife, he quickly struck off his thumb and offered the dismembered part to his guru. Drona, quiet, speechless and thoughtful, accepted the offering and moved out of the glade with the young disciples, leaving Ekalavya alone to his fate.

The Kuru princes were about to graduate. Drona had planned a grand competition on the occasion. The Kuru elders gave Drona the permission to hold the same in any way he wished. Pavillions were erected, colourful tents were spread, enclosures were made for the royal ladies and a dais was constructed for Dhritarashtra and Bhishma. Finally, astrologers were consulted for an auspicious day.

On the auspicious, bright and clear day, Drona entered the open arena followed by the princes. The spectators were thrilled to watch the chariot racing, equestrian skills and combats with the mace. Vidura described in words the grand spectacle to the blind Dhritarashtra, who was too keen to hear about the proceedings.

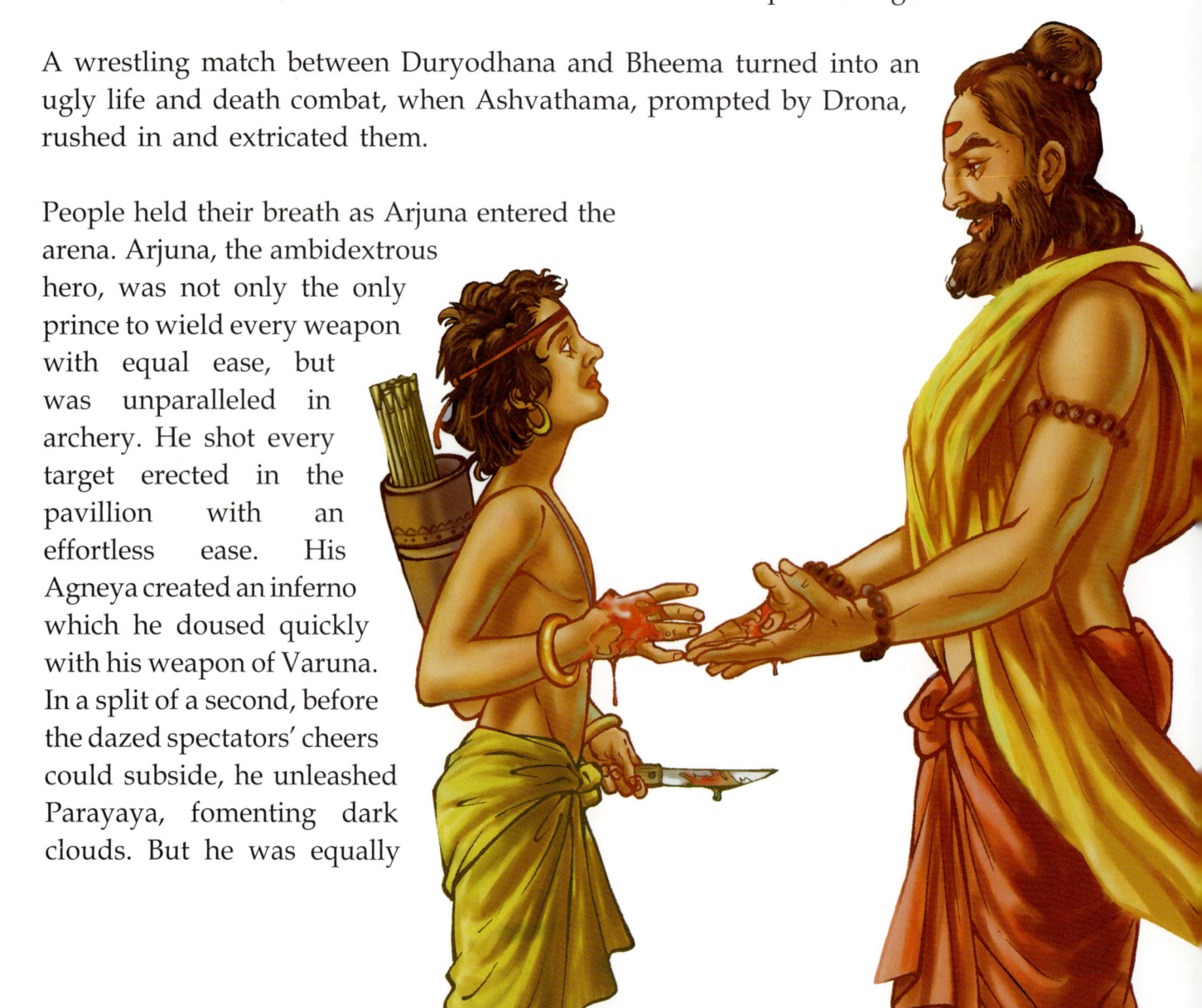

A wrestling match between Duryodhana and Bheema turned into an ugly life and death combat, when Ashvathama, prompted by Drona, rushed in and extricated them.

People held their breath as Arjuna entered the arena. Arjuna, the ambidextrous hero, was not only the only prince to wield every weapon with equal ease, but was unparalleled in archery. He shot every target erected in the pavillion with an effortless ease. His Agneya created an inferno which he doused quickly with his weapon of Varuna. In a split of a second, before the dazed spectators' cheers could subside, he unleashed Parayaya, fomenting dark clouds. But he was equally quick with Vayavya, whose strong winds made the clouds disappear. Antardhana, that created an illusion of a thousand Arjunas shooting the targets accurately even as the spectators and every other object vanished for sometime, was the best piece of event, leading to the grand finale.

Just then, a young warrior with golden earrings entered the arena claiming that he could do all that had just been demonstrated. Raising his bow, he cumulated one of the feats just displayed and looked at Arjuna with a hint of challenge. The young man as resplendent as sun declared, "I want to meet Arjuna in a one-to-one combat."

Arjuna was least interested in meeting the challenge and dismissed him contemptuously, alleging him to be an outsider who had no business to be there. The young man was Karna, not a prince but son of a low caste suta. When challenged again, Arjuna look up his bow.

Before the two aggressive warriors could enter into a combat, Sage Kripacharya rose up. "Young man, you are going to fight a Pandava, a Kuru, Pritha's youngest son, Partha. Reveal your ancestry and the royal house you belong to. Princes do not enter into a man-to-man combat with ordinary men."

Karna had no answer and he bowed his head, unable to bear the humiliation. Before Karna could retreat with the burden of insult, Duryodhana announced, "Royalty belongs to one by birth or heroism. This young warrior is a true heir. I offer him the kingdom of Anga right now. The priests will anoint him the king right here. Look at his natural armour. Look at his resplendent face. He is no ordinary mortal but truly a king. This hero deserves to be the king not only of Anga but of the whole earth."

The Pandavas were apprehensive of Karna's friendship with Duryodhana but Kunti rejoiced. Her first born deserved the honour she never could give him.

Dronacharya's Revenge

After the tournament, a relaxed Drona summoned his disciples and said, "Your training is over. The time has come when you must give me my *gurudakshina*. I will have more than my share of *gurudakshina*, when you capture Drupada, the king of Panchala, and bring him to me."

Taking the wish of their guru as his command, the Kaurava and Pandava princes at once armed themselves and headed for Panchala with Drona to head them. His students laid a siege on Drupada's capital and routed Drupada's army.

Nonetheless, Drupada being protected by the best amongst the troopers and no ordinary warrior himself, eluded capture. Arjuna realised that Drupada could be captured only when distracted from his main forces. He asked the Pandavas to follow him as he stationed himself a mile away from the actual battle scene.

The Kauravas could not confront the Panchala might, invigorated after reinforcement. The Panchala generals next focused their attention on the Pandavas, after having broken the ranks of Kauravas.

As the Panchala army approached them, they waited for them to reach within the shooting range of arrows. Bheema, the mightiest warrior, waded through the Panchala army wielding his mace and killing anyone who came within the range of his mace, even as Arjuna and the other Pandavas raced through the path carved by Bheema.

As his chariot came parallel to Drupada's, Arjuna jumped into the Panchala king's chariot wielding a naked sword. Drupada had been captured. "Here's your *gurudakshina*," said Arjuna presenting the proud king to Dronacharya.

"Remember me?" Drona threw a piercing glance at the humbled king, who didn't look up, weighed by the burden of shame.

"You said, friendship can only be between equals. Now I am your equal. Your kingdom is mine. Your life is now in my hands, but I will spare it for old friendship's sake. I will also give you half the kingdom. The land to the south of Ganga will be yours, and that to the north, mine," Drona was bitter, sarcastic and generous at the same time.

Drupada or Yagyasena was a strong kshatriya king. The Pandavas having humbled him established their superiority over the Kauravas once more. Bhishma was highly pleased with them. The Pandavas, because of their intrinsic worth, were also popular with the common men. Duryodhana was not popular with the common men who favoured Yudhishthira as the crown prince over Duryodhana.

Bhishma called a meeting of the counsellors in the court to discuss the issue of succession. Yudhishthira was favoured for his qualities and strength of character. Much against the innermost wishes of Dhritarashtra, he had to declare Yudhishthira as his regent and crown prince.

Duryodhana decided that he would not let that happen at any cost.

Duryodhana's Evil Designs Fail

Duryodhana had the ambition of inheriting the crown. However, his ambition was thwarted when Yudhishthira was declared the crown prince of Hastinapur. Duryodhana felt the crown slipping out of his hands, and felt the ground slipping from under his feet.

In the meanwhile, the Pandavas were proving to be brave, virtuous and popular. Within a short time, Yudhishthira, the eldest son of Kunti, with his good behaviour, sagacity and discernment, surpassed his father, Pandu, in fame.

Bheema, the second Pandava, took lessons from Balarama in wielding the sword and the mace, and in steering the chariot in the battlefield. Arjuna was renowned for his qualities of marksmanship, agility and proficiency with diverse weapons. He was considered unrivalled by his tutor Drona. Sahadeva learnt all the precepts of morals and manners from Drona. Guru Drona was considered akin to Brihaspati, the Guru of the Devas, in spiritual lore. Nakula earned fame as a wielder of unusual weapons.

Although Dhritarashtra celebrated with the Pandavas, inwardly his feelings went with Duryodhana. He was advised by his evil minister Kanika, who was always scheming against the Pandavas. Meanwhile Duryodhana was looking for a chance to eliminate Pandavas forever. He had three confidantes who were the instigators as well as the collaborators in his evil designs.

Pandavas, however, never cared about the plans made against them. They were gaining popularity as great warriors. Indeed, Arjuna and his brothers became mighty enough to slay Sauvira, who during his three-year-long Yajna had kept even the invading Gandharvas at bay. Arjuna vanquished the Yavana king, who even Pandu, in days gone by, could not.

Then Vipula, who had shown scant respect for the Kurus, was also slain. Later, Dattamitra, who was renowned for his power in battles, was also subdued. Arjuna, in his single chariot and with Bheema in support, routed the kings of the east and their ten thousand chariots. In the same way, he conquered the south and brought ample booty to the land of Kurus. The Pandavas, having subjugated all other territories, extended their empire.

However, Dhritarashtra was not very comfortable with the tidings of the gainful might of the Pandavas. Deeply distressed, he summoned Kanika, the counsellor well-versed in the science of politics, and said, "The star of the Pandavas is on the rise, they are very successful. Should I have them as allies or as rivals? I shall abide by your counsel."

Kanika replied, "Listen to me O king, and do not be vexed with what I have to say. The might of kings must be made explicit with hands ready to strike. Slay your foe with gifts and camaraderie. Kill him with discord or with force." Then Dhritarashtra asked, "How is an adversary demolished best? By concord, by propitiation, by discord or by aggression?"

Kanika was a clever advisor. He replied, "Listen, O King to the tale of the clever jackal who was a past master in art of diplomacy. Supreme in self-interest, he lived in a forest with his four friends — tiger, mouse, wolf and mongoose. One day they saw a beautiful and agile stag. They ran after this prized beast of prey, but could not seize it, as it was quick and sprightly. The four friends were disappointed. Therefore, they conferred amongst themselves.

The jackal said, 'O tiger, you have failed to get the stag because he is young, smart and strong. I have a plan. Let the mouse nibble away his feet when he is asleep. The stag with the gnawed feet can then be felled by the tiger. And then all of us shall feast on him.'

They did as they had planned. The mouse nibbled the feet of the stag and the tiger killed it. The jackal was clever and smart. When he saw the freshly slain stag, his mouth watered. He said, 'I shall keep a watch over it till you come back after your ablutions.' The others were assured that their dead prey would be safe. They therefore sauntered to the river nearby and the jackal stood there deep in thought.

The mightiest amongst the four, the tiger was the first to return. He found the jackal brooding and asked, 'How is it that you who are so clever, look vexed? Come, let us feast on the flesh of our prey.'

The jackal replied, 'O mighty one, the mouse claims that his might felled the stag. And it is due to his might that you will get your food. His behaviour and boastful words towards you have made this meal distasteful to me.' The tiger felt humiliated listening to these words and decided to prove his worth. He said, 'If those are his words, I shall kill my prey with my own hands and then eat.' The tiger then left hurriedly on his mission.

When the mouse reached the spot, the jackal said to him, 'Listen to what the mongoose has said to me: this carcass is poisoned by the tiger's claws. I will not eat it. Instead, O jackal, if you permit, I shall make a meal of the mouse!'

The mouse was scared when he heard what the jackal had just said, and scuttled off. Next, it was the turn of wolf. When the wolf arrived, the jackal said to him, 'The king of beasts is set against you and he is coming here with his mate. It portends ill for you. Now you may do as you please.' The wolf did not have the courage to stay to relish his meal. He too left the place.

Finally, the mongoose came. To him, the jackal said, 'I have driven away the others with the might of my arms. Fight with me and then eat this flesh.' The mongoose replied, 'When you have overcome the fierce tiger, the wolf and the mouse, what match am I for you?' So saying, he scampered away fearing the might of the jackal. The witty jackal had the feast all to himself."

Kanika said to Dhritarashtra after narrating the story, "You're a king with ample resources, but the Pandavas are men of might. Protect yourself from them. Shape your conduct to safeguard yourself and your children from the Pandavas. Act in accordance with polity so that you do not have to repent."

The men and women of Hastinapur, who were witnesses to the deeds of the Pandavas, spoke openly about their excellence. Inside the assemblies or outside in the streets, the citizens took the name of Yudhishthira as the most promising ruler for the kingdom.

Common citizens were of the opinion that if Dhritarashtra could not reign earlier because of his blindness, he should not be made the king even now. The other alternative was Bhishma, the honest one, but he was compelled by his vow. The choice therefore, naturally, fell on the first Pandava. He was popular amongst the citizens and therefore they decided to install him on the throne. He was young, truthful, virtuous and a favourite with the elders.

Duryodhana heard the common discussion that was going on in the capital and was sorely vexed by the preference shown for Yudhishthira. Being intolerant and jealous by nature, he went to Dhritarashtra, his father, and said, "O father, casting you and Bhishma aside, the citizens would have Yudhishthira for their king. Bhishma will approve of this because he is under the vow. Earlier, Pandu acquired the kingdom by virtue of his excellence and you could not inherit the throne because of your blindness. We, along with our children, shall remain the lowly ones in the royal line. O king, we shall be the ones spurned by the world. If Pandu's son acquires the kingdom as an inheritance from Pandu, then the sons born in his family will claim the throne thereafter. The citizens are out to cast us into difficult times. If sovereignty had been yours, we would have inherited it even if the subjects were not in favour."

Duryodhana was assisted by three confidantes. They were Shakuni, Karna and Dushasana. They incited him to take recourse to evil designs, whenever they got an opportunity to advise him. Even as the king was left to be tormented by conflicting emotions, Duryodhana went ahead to consult Karna, Shakuni and Dushasana. They always told him what he wanted to hear. The evil coterie made a very dangerous plan to burn the Pandavas alive.

Plot to Eliminate Pandavas

"Father, if an excuse is found to get the Pandavas out of Hastinapur, we shall have enough opportunity to do something," suggested Duryodhana to the king. "Send them away to Varnavata and we may be able to execute our plan," he added.

Dhritarashtra was in a dilemma. He made a weak attempt to resist the demand of his son. He pointed out that Pandu never denied him anything. He gave him the kingdom he conquered. Dhritarashtra added that Yudhishthira was just and noble. People loved him and he could not be exiled, nor deprived of what lawfully was his. No one would forgive them for their cruel act.

Duryodhana craftily countered the arguments of Dhritarashtra. He reminded his father of the consequences of not sending them away. It meant a clear doom for them. Duryodhana further pointed out that once the Pandavas were out of the way, they could easily buy the goodwill of the people. They already controlled the treasury with him as the king.

The ministers were loyal to him, they had the upper hand. "If they could be sent on any pretext," Duryodhana said, "the throne will be mine. They can return after that."

Dhritarashtra was still in two minds. He too wanted his son to succeed. "But I have never voiced the sentiment, it is too sinful," he feared, "Bhishma, Drona, Vidura will never allow that to happen. They will kill us for our crime."

Duryodhana was too stubborn to give up so easily. He countered, "Bhishma will stay neutral and side with you as you're the king. Drona and Vidura will equally have no choice but to side with you. You have simply got to persuade Pandavas to make a trip to Varnavata to see the town and meanwhile, I'll set about buying the goodwill of the citizens."

Dhritarashtra gave his silent assent to the proposal. Their chance came one day before the festival of Pashupati Shiva. Everyone was present in the court. Dhritarashtra's ministers, prompted by him, began praising the charms and beauty of Varnavata.

Dhritarashtra suggested to the Pandavas that they should make at least one visit to Varnavata. "It is a delightful city and the celebrations there on the occasion of the fair are bound to be spectacular. Varnavata is surrounded by groves and woods, you'll find it utterly charming. My son! You're the crown prince of the kingdom. The royal participation in the annual fair there is a must. So, go there along with your mother and brothers. Go, my sons, and have a nice time."

Varnavata was a town on the bank of Ganga located at a distance that could be covered in eight days from Hastinapur. This town was a part of the Kuru kingdom and the people of Varnavata were eager to see their crown prince.

The righteous Yudhishthira was gentle and peace loving but not witless. He was suspicious about Dhritarashtra prompting them to head to Varnavata. However, out of respect to the king, he could not refuse to go.

Vidura accompanied the Pandavas out of the city. He stopped at the outskirts and spoke to Yudhishthira, drawing him aside, in a hush-hush tone in the language of the Mlecchas. Only Yudhishthira understood this tongue.

Vidura sounded serious. He spoke cryptically, "He who knows that the enemy is scheming, takes suitable measures to protect his own interests. This is what the science of politics says. Directions lie in the stars; let them guide you. One who is in control of the five senses can't be defeated. You should know that there are weapons other than the actual weapons, and they can destroy as effectively. Creatures of the forest know that straw and wood burn."

Yudhishthira, who had a keen insight, understood every word that Vidura said. When he had left, Kunti asked Yudhishthira what Vidura had told him. Yudhishthira told her, "He said, the palace for us in Varnavata will be enflamed and advised me to be like a fox who has more than one exit in its burrow." Both Kunti and Yudhishthira decided to keep the information a secret for the time being.

The Palace Burns

The citizens of Varnavata welcomed the Pandavas enthusiastically. Purochana escorted them to the palace which was named the Blessed Home. When the Pandavas entered it, Yudhishthira observed the palace very closely, especially its walls and pillars. Drawing Bheema aside, Yudhishthira remarked, "This palace looks quite different from what it actually is. The artisans and masons must be commended for the wonderful job they have done, for this house will burn like straw. No one can guess that the house is actually built of hemp, bamboo and shellac while it appears to be solid stone and brick. Vidura rightly warned us that Duryodhana wants to kill us in the blazing inferno."

Bheema's blood boiled on hearing what Yudhishthira said. However, he kept his cool and asked, "If that's the plan of Duryodhana, then why should we stay here? Let's get out of this place." He offered a practical solution.

Yudhishthira thought otherwise. He suggested that if they left the place, the Kauravas would be more careful in maintaining the secrecy of their next plot, which would be to the disadvantage of the Pandavas. So, they should stay there and make counter-plans.

A little while later when they had settled, a man who appeared cautious and secretive came to see the Pandavas. The Pandava brothers eyed him suspiciously. After introducing himself as a miner, he revealed the purpose of his coming there. He was sent by Vidura to counter Purochana who had plans to burn the house on the last day of the dark fortnight. The miner could notice scepticism on their faces. To prove his point he referred to what Vidura had spoken to Yudhishthira in his Mleccha tongue.

The Pandavas were convinced about the truth in the words of the miner. Yudhishthira apologised to him for not being cordial to him. He showed him around the palace. After surveying the whole place, the miner remarked that an underground tunnel leading to the forest was required to be constructed.

The Pandavas went out of the palace every day, on riding or hunting expeditions, to familiarise themselves with the terrain. At night they all slept in one chamber with their weapons by their side. The entrance of the tunnel was made in the chamber of the Pandavas. The miner did a very neat job in making the tunnel and covering the entrance.

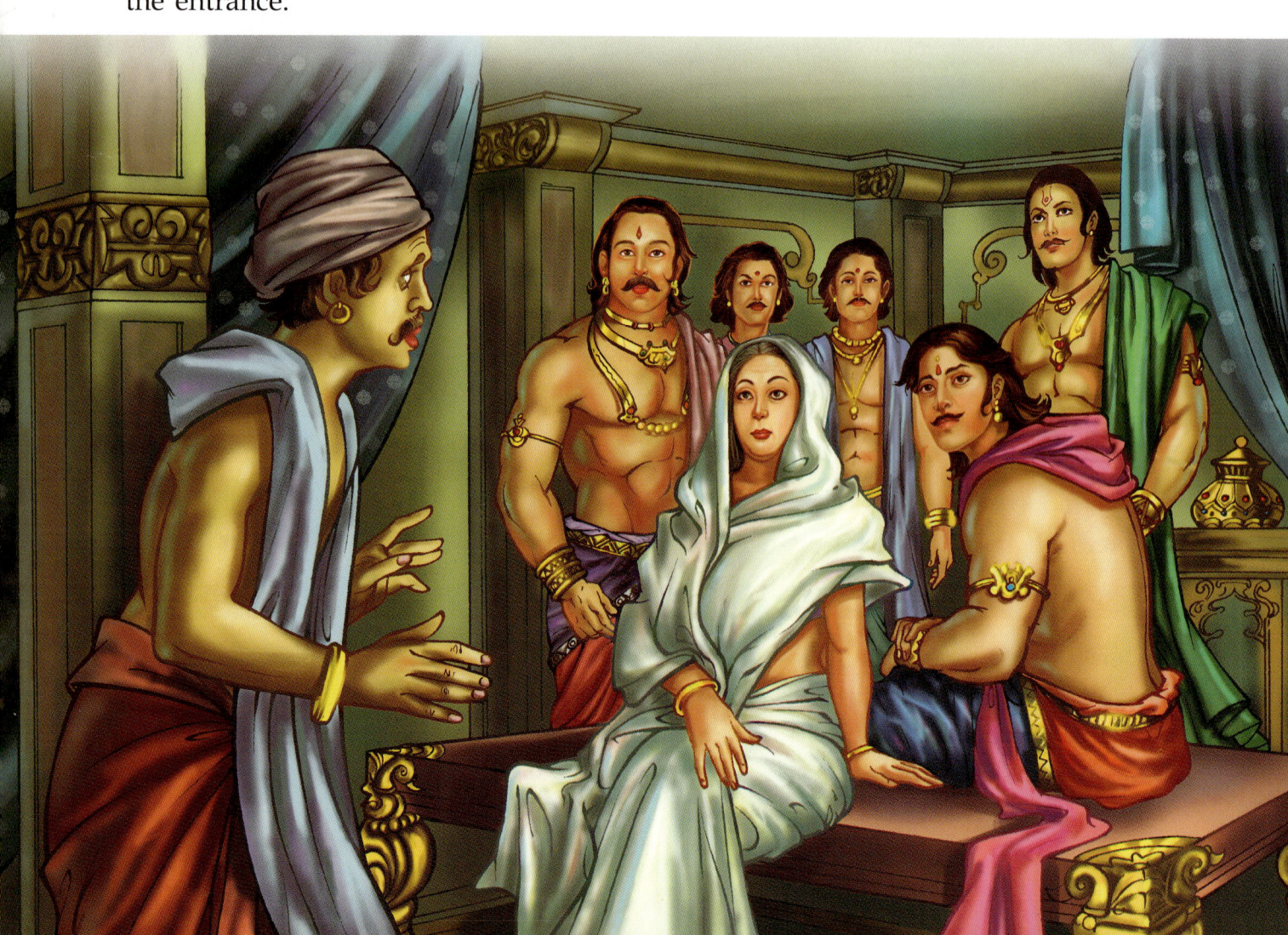

Purochana did his best to lull the Pandavas into complacency, believing that they were unaware of his intentions. Before he could strike, Yudhishthira alerted the Pandavas. He informed them that it was time for them to leave.

As Bheema touched the flaming torch along the pillars and walls, the hissing and blazing fire engulfed the palace quickly. The Pandavas including Bheema, escaped safely through the tunnel.

The Pandavas emerged out of the tunnel in the forest, and were heading towards the river, when a man stood before them. He introduced himself as a messenger of Vidura. He conveyed Vidura's message to them, "Vidura has told me to inform you that like a fox, a man should have many exits in his house so as to face any unexpected danger." He then asked them to follow him. Pandavas followed him down to the river. Wading through knee-deep water, he dragged a boat out of the reeds and beckoned them to step in. He was in a hurry to safely get them to the other side before dawn.

The Pandavas were safe but exhausted. Having escaped the fire, they were still apprehensive of the dangers lurking ahead. It was Bheema's duty to ensure everyone's safety. Bheema hoisted Arjuna and Yudhishthira on his shoulders, balanced the twins on his hips, and with Kunti in his arms, he waded through the forest as a mighty ship makes way through the high tide.

After a while, Kunti felt thirsty, and everyone wanted to rest. He set them down under a large banyan tree and went to fetch water for them. Bheema discovered a large lake nearby from where he got water for everyone. Soon his brothers and his mother went to sleep while Bheema guarded them.

Bheema Slays Hidimb

While the Pandavas lay sleeping in the forest, a rakshasa named Hidimb could smell the sweet scent of human flesh. He asked his sister Hidimba to find out the men in his territory and kill them.

Hidimba too could smell human beings and followed the direction of the smell. She was about to attack the sleeping Pandavas and their mother Kunti, when she noticed Bheema. She was enamoured by the handsome Pandava. She promptly dismissed her brother's command and instantly transformed herself into a beautiful damsel. Then she walked up to Bheema and bowed to him in respect. "Who are you? And who are these people sleeping here?" she asked, and informed him at the same time, "My brother, a rakshasa, is the lord of this forest. He has sent me to kill you all. Accept me and I'll carry you and these people to safety."

Bheema remained unaffected by the threat while Hidimba was getting restless, "Wake them up and I'll get everyone to safety before my brother arrives." Bheema, however, was not the one to feel threatened by a rakshasa. Moreover, he did not want to disturb the sleep of his mother and brothers.

Soon a monstrous form charged out of the bushes. Hidimba stood still. He roared with bestial fury, when he noticed his sister in an attractive human form in conversation with Bheema. "What attraction did you find in this puny human being that you disobeyed my orders? Just wait, I'll kill him first and then you!" And the rakshasa with his blood shot eyes, gnashed his teeth.

Bheema rose up casually. "Why disturb my brothers and mother?" he asked. "I can give you a good fight, but away from here. As for killing your sister, it's not right to kill women. Moreover, your fight is with me." As Bheema moved a little away from his sleeping family, the rakshasa charged at him.

Soon the two combatants were grappling with each other. The thud of blows and muffled grunts woke up Kunti. She noticed a beautiful young woman there. "Who are you?" she asked surprised.

"I am a rakshasa's sister," replied Hidimba. "My brother ordered me to kill you all, but when I saw your son, I changed my mind. I wanted to take you out of this place, but your son didn't want to disturb your sleep. Right now, he is fighting with my brother over there." Their conversation woke up every one else. The brothers saw the two combatants grappling at a distance. Arjuna cheered Bheema, "I am awake, Bheema!" "Stay where you are and watch some fun!" Bheema responded.

Arjuna waited with bated breath for Bheema to finish off the rakshasa, but the combat was prolonging too long for his patience. Arjuna wondered, "Why is he playing with the rakshasa? Doesn't he know a rakshasa's powers become twice as much at twilight?" "Bheema!" he shouted, "You've had enough of play now. Just finish him off!" At the command of Arjuna, Bheema lifted the giant, whirled him around for a while and then with a mighty roar flung him down. The rakshasa died.

From there, they decided to move ahead to a small town not far away where they could lie low without the fear of being detected by Duryodhana. As they set out, the beautiful Hidimba followed them. Bheema heard the sound of her trinkets, and turned around to find Hidimba following them. Bheema harshly told her to go back as men and rakshasas had nothing in common. Hidimba went forward and touched Kunti's and Yudhishthira's feet and entreated, "You surely understand a woman's love. I've deserted my family for your son, chosen him as my lord. My life will become meaningless if he rejects me."

Yudhishthira was sympathetic towards her when she appealed to him to allow Bheema to go with her. She promised to return him before nightfall. Yudhishthira and Kunti encouraged Bheema to go with her. Bheema finally agreed.

Hidimba leaped into the sky together with Bheema and came to a mountain glade of impeccable natural beauty. The two spent some time there. In time Hidimba conceived, and gave birth to a son. In moments, the child became a full-grown youth with the strength of a rakshasa and the power to change into any form at will. The young man bowed and touched his parents' feet. Hidimba was very pleased to see her son. "His head is as smooth as a clay pot," she remarked fondly. "That's what we shall call him — Ghatotkacha," replied Bheema.

The mighty son soon mastered the secrets of wielding weapons of all kinds. Hidimba had promised to return Bheema to his family. She kept her promise. The Pandavas were overwhelmed with joy on receiving Bheema and his son Ghatotkacha. Finally, taking leave of his father, uncles and grandmother, Ghatotkacha said, "I and my mother must return now." And he politely touched their feet to take their blessings. Turning to Bheema, Ghatotkacha said, "Dear father, I'm leaving now but I will appear whenever you remember me."

As soon as Hidimba and her son Ghatotkacha departed, the Pandavas too left the place. They went from forest to forest in the garb of ascetics. They had grown long matted hair and put on the clothes of ascetics. Bheema, strong as he was, carried Kunti over rough terrain and whenever possible, they stayed in the retreats of ascetics where they spent their time listening to discourses on the Vedas and Vedangas.

Bheema Slays Vakasura

One day as they were passing through a forest near Panchala, they came across honourable sage Vyasa. The Pandavas greeted him and touched his feet reverently. Sage Vyasa blessed them. The great Sage Vyasa consoled them saying, "The suffering you're going through is a part of your destiny. Be patient, my children! Every dark cloud has a silver lining. Keep patience when you are in adversity. Rest assured prosperity must follow it. I love you and Dhritarashtra's sons equally, but the young and unfortunate touch a person's heart. That is why, I sympathise with you."

Sage Vyasa advised the Pandavas to go to a nearby town called Ekachakra and stay there in peace. "Stay there till I come, and keep your disguises," he advised the Pandavas. He accompanied the Pandavas to the outskirts of the town. Before departing, he revealed to Kunti, "Don't worry about your sons; they are brave, valiant and kings among men. They will rule their father's kingdom." To the Pandavas, he advised, "Adapt to the circumstances and the ways of the people you live with and you will succeed."

The Pandavas reached Ekachakra and started living there with a brahmin family. They were disguised as brahmins. They led a quiet life, doing nothing to draw attention to themselves. During the day, they would go begging in the town and come back at dusk with alms and food to hand over to Kunti. She would divide the food into two halves, one part was given to Bheema, and the other part would be equally divided amongst the rest of them. A little portion would go to her.

One day, when the brothers had gone out on their morning begging rounds, Kunti heard the wife of the brahmin crying. She wondered what grief could be the cause, so she listened at the door of their room.

The brahmin was saying to his wife, "This worldly life is full of sorrows. I told you long ago, that we should leave this city and find a living elsewhere. Now look what has happened! One from our family must die today. If I were to die, I fear that you will not survive without me for long. If both of us are dead, I shudder to think what the fate of our two orphaned children would be. I feel that the only recourse is for all of us to commit suicide!" The wife of the brahmin, who was crying, said, "I cannot think of a life without you. How will I be able to bring up our children? It is best that I die, for then you will be able to remarry. My only hope is that the woman you marry will be kind to our children. Let me drive the food-cart today!"

The daughter of this couple, seeing both her parents struck with grief, interrupted her mother and said, "If either of you dies, we will be orphans. In any case, a daughter does not belong to her parents, but to her husband's family. Since you would have parted from me anyway at my marriage, I am the best person to die. Let me go and face my fate at the hands of the asura." At this moment, their son, a young boy, shouted, "No need for anybody to die. I will go and kill this asura!" and started prancing about. Even in this moment of grief, this childish gesture brought a weak smile on the faces of rest of his family.

Kunti judged that it was time to interrupt this family conference and entered the room. She asked the brahmin what was the matter, why all this talk of death and grief? And who was the asura they were talking about?

The brahmin said, "There is an asura by the name of Vakasura, who lives near our city. He had made a habit of coming into the city, indiscriminately killing and eating people, whenever he happened to be hungry. We used to live in constant terror. Our town elders, driven to desperation, entered into a pact with the asura. According to this, we are spared of his attacks, but this truce came at a high price. Every day, we have to provide him with a cart-load of food, driven by someone from the city. The asura eats all the food, the bullocks drawing the cart and the driver. It was decided that each family will provide that unfortunate victim, by turns. Tomorrow it is the turn of our family. That is why you heard us crying on our fate and resolving to commit suicide."

Kunti thought for a while and said, "Let me propose a way out of this. Since you have been kind enough to offer your hospitality to us, let me repay the favour. I shall send one of my five sons to drive the cart."

The brahmin was aghast. He said, "I cannot possibly allow you to do such a thing. It has been said that guests are like the Gods. Anyone who knowingly subjects his guests to danger is sure to rot in hell for all eternity."

But Kunti insisted that her son would go. "My son Bheema can kill great and mighty rakshasas effortlessly. His strength is extraordinary. And I'm telling you all this in strict confidence. Let no one know about it."

The brahmin and his family felt reassured on hearing the words of Kunti. Then Kunti went to Bheema and told him about the menace of Vakasura and that he was expected to deal with him. Bheema was only too happy when he came to know that he was expected to meet the challenge of Vakasura.

When Yudhishthira and his three brothers returned home with alms in the evening, Kunti gave each of them his share. After the meal was over, she told them the entire story.

Yudhishthira felt deeply concerned for his brother, and looked at his mother Kunti in exasperation, "Mother dear! I love my brother Bheema no less than any one else. How could you do something so thoughtless? Why did you offer to send Bheema for someone else? Isn't it due to him that we are safe? That we sleep in peace? That we're hopeful of regaining our kingdom?"

Kunti heard the words of Yudhishthira with utter calm. Addressing her first born, she replied in a very composed tone, "You need not worry about Bheema, my child. My son, we owe a lot to this family. This generous brahmin has given us shelter and has kept us safe from Dhritarashtra's sons. If we don't do anything, the entire family will be eliminated. We are kshatriyas and it is our duty to protect them. I know, more than anyone else, the physical strength of my son Bheema. He killed the rakshasa Hidimb, brother of Hidimba. Have you forgotten that even as an infant, he slipped out of my hands and fell on a rock breaking it into pieces?"

Further, to console Yudhishthira, Bheema said, "Dear brother! I'm fortunate in having you as my elder brother. But don't worry about me. I have yours as well as our mother's blessings with me. I am confident of slaying that wicked rakshasa Vakasura."

Yudhishthira felt reassured. He knew Vakasura could not harm Bheema, but he now worried that if Bheema's strength became known after his brush with Vakasura, Duryodhana's men would easily locate them. But Kunti allayed his fear and informed that the brahmin had given his word that he would not disclose anything relating to Bheema and Vakasura.

The next day Bheema marched ahead to meet the challenge of Vakasura, riding a cart full of rice and two buffaloes following behind. He found the rakshasa's den but no one responded to his calls. He settled down to eat whatever there was in the cart, shouting and yelling the rakshasa's name intermittently.

When he was almost through, he heard the sound of gigantic footsteps. Vakasura was a monstrous red-eyed giant, whose footsteps made enormous craters where he trod. The sight of Bheema nonchalantly eating away the food made him furious.

"You fool! Your time is up. Now you'll go to the abode of Yama!" Saying so, Vakasura charged at Bheema, uprooting a tree with one hand.

Bheema was still as casual as before. He dusted his hands very calmly and got out of the cart to take on the might of Vakasura. The next moment Vakasura was fighting for his life. Bheema uprooted a tree and hurled it at Vakasura. Vakasura caught hold of Bheema's arms, but Bheema extricated himself easily and charged Vakasura with

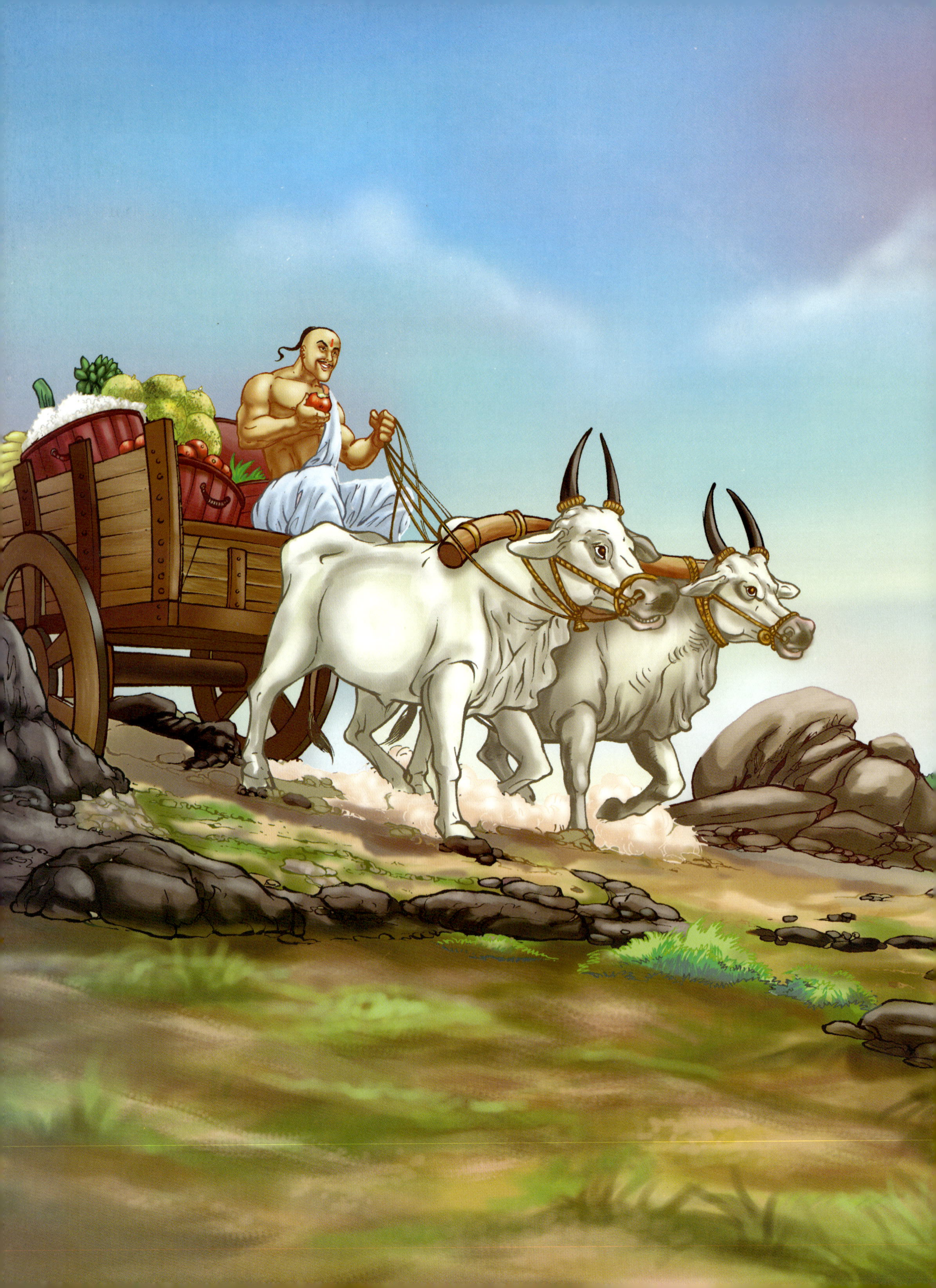

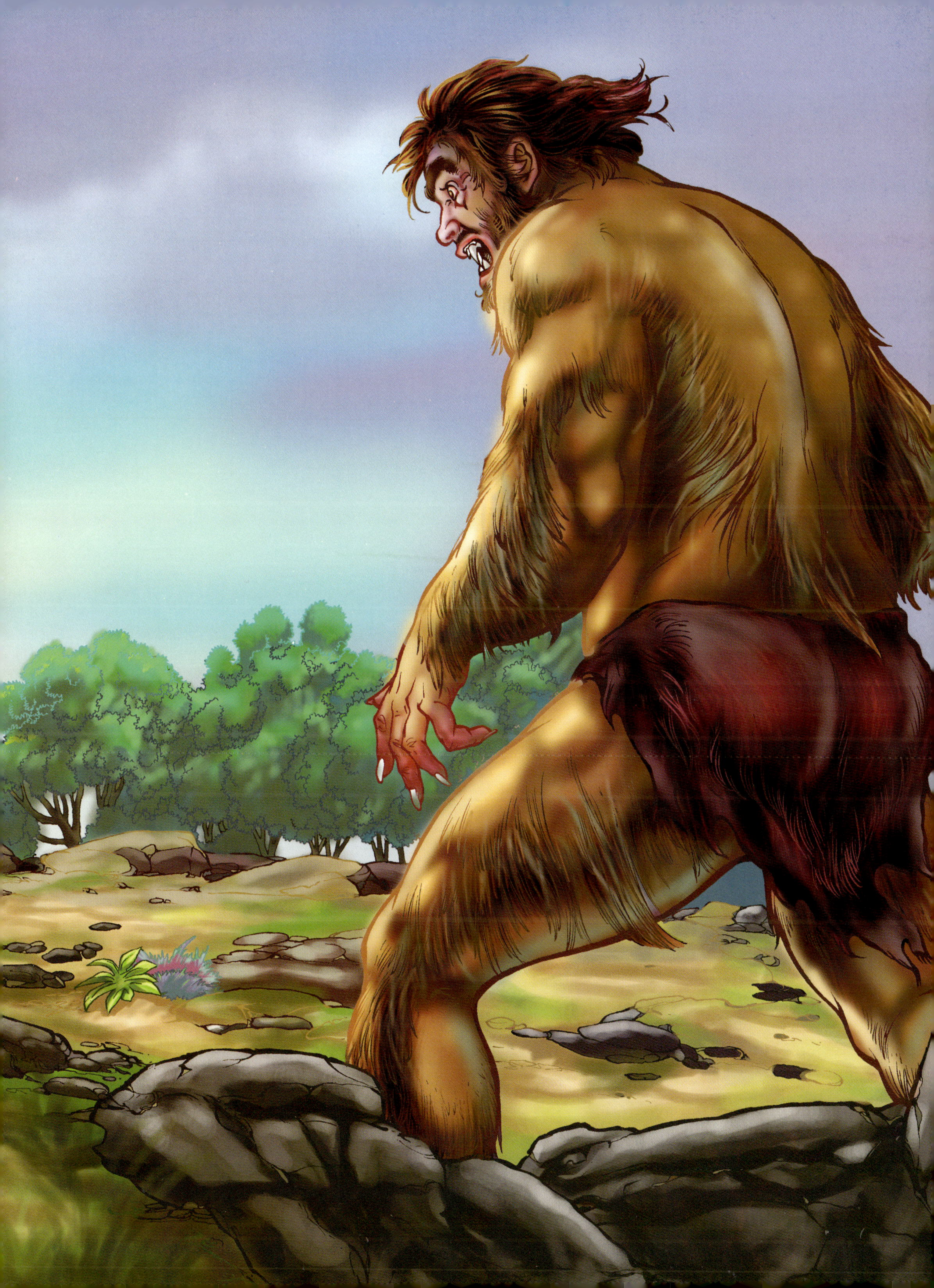

the branch that he had torn out from a huge tree. The earth shook as the two giants grappled with each other and hurled uprooted trees at each other. Finally Bheema pinned down the rakshasa to the ground and finished him off.

Bheema carted Vakasura's dead body to Ekachakra and left it there on the roadside for public view. He went inside the brahmin's house and had a sound sleep.

When the citizens of Ekachakra noticed the dead body of Vakasura lying unattended on the roadside, they were all pleasantly surprised. The brahmin whose turn it was to go to Vakasura, said some divine being took the food cart from him and went to kill the demon.

Vakasura's annihilation was no ordinary news. Anybody hearing about it could easily guess Bheema's involvement in it. Therefore, Kunti advised her sons to move out of Ekachakra as there was every possibility of their being discovered there.

Arjuna's Combat With Gandharva Chief

They left the town taking leave of the brahmin family with whom they had been staying. By nightfall, they reached the bank of the Ganga. Suddenly they saw a chariot advancing towards them. The warrior in the chariot shouted at them, "Stop whoever you are! How dare you come towards the holy river Ganga at this odd-hour? Who are you? Don't dare bathe in this river! Get away from here or you will be killed right here and now."

The Pandavas wondered about the warrior, who had just challenged them. That warrior was Angarparna, the chief of Gandharvas. He was frolicking in the water in the company of his wife. When he saw a group of brahmins and their mother approaching them, he came out, mounted his chariot and challenged the Pandavas.

Arjuna replied, "Honourable sir! We did not know that the heavenly beings come to this river for bathing at night. But that is not the way to talk to a kshatriya warrior. The divine river Ganga belongs equally to all. No one should claim an exclusive right over her."

The words of Arjuna were enough to infuriate the Gandharva, "I am Angarparna, who is well known for his valour and physical strength. The forest in this area near the river belongs to me. No one, including the heavenly beings, can come here without my permission. It's your last chance to go back and save your life."

It was now Arjuna's turn to retort sharply, "It isn't befitting for a celestial being to indulge in false pride. Also, it is foolish to consider others inferior and weaker. The universe still has mighty warriors to take on haughty beings like you. It seems you have not come across a true warrior. I challenge you to face me."

Angarparna instantly flew into a rage and drew out his sword. He attacked Arjuna, who defended himself with a burning torch, shouting, "Save yourself, O, Angarparna. So far you have not come across a real warrior. Here is your chance."

Saying so, Arjuna chanted an incantation on the torchlight and hurled it at Gandharva. The missile set fire to the chariot and Angarparna had no option but to jump out of it. In the combat that followed, Angarparna was severely wounded. He lost consciousness. Arjuna caught him by his hair and dragged him to Yudhishthira.

Angarparna's wife could not bear the miserable plight of her husband. She came begging to Yudhishthira and requested him to spare the life of her husband. Kunti requested Yudhishthira to spare the life of Angarparna saying that it did not add glory to her warrior sons to kill someone who had been defeated and insulted before his wife.

Yudhishthira obeyed his mother. Angarparna also regained his consciousness by now. Arjuna addressed Angarparna. "It is due to my respected mother that you are free today. Let this be a lesson for you to never boast about yourself in future. Now you can leave this place."

Angarparna was full of gratitude for his life having been spared, and offered Arjuna a gift, "I wish to offer you the gift of divine insight called *Chakshushi*. It'll allow you to see any thing at any place and any time. I also wish to offer you one hundred divine horses. They can put on any colour and run at any speed their master wants."

The Pandavas thanked Angarparna and said that although they felt lucky to receive the gift of divine sight, they were not in a position to keep the horses. However, they promised that they would accept the horses when needed.

Finally, the Pandavas and Angarparna parted ways amicably. Angarparna and his wife proceeded to their heavenly abode on a chariot. The Pandavas continued their journey.

Sage Vyasa had asked them to move to Panchala. Kunti expected better luck for themselves in Panchala, and therefore urged her sons to proceed towards the place. On the way they came across the hermitage of Sage Dhaumya. They requested the Sage to be their family priest. The Sage gladly accepted their offer. From there, as the Pandavas proceeded towards Panchala, they met some brahmins, who asked them where they were coming from and where they were proceeding to, and who they were.

The Story of Drupada's Children

The Pandavas told them that they were five brothers and the lady with them was their revered mother. They also disclosed that they were coming from Ekachakra and heading for Panchala. The brahmins requested them to join their company as they too were going to Panchala to witness the Swayamvara of Panchali (Princess of Panchala).

The birth of Panchali, also known as Krishna Draupadi, had taken place in strange circumstances. When Dronacharya had been insulted by King Drupada, he took a severe revenge and had him defeated and humiliated. The king took this disgrace to heart. So he decided to have a son who could avenge his disgrace.

King Drupada approached two sages, who were descendants of Sage Kashyap. He wanted these two sages, Yaja and Upayaja to perform a Yajna for him so that he could be blessed with a son strong and brave enough to kill Dronacharya. The sages readily agreed to perform the Yajna. When the Yajna was over, the sages offered the queen, the *prasada*. Since the queen was chewing betel leaf, she asked the sages to wait for sometime.

One of the sages consigned the *prasada* to the sacrificial fire, saying, "The *prasada* of a duly performed Yajna does not wait for anybody." As soon as the *prasada* was consigned to the flame, the fire leapt up and a prince emerged out of the sacrificial fire. He appeared to be a warrior having a bow, a quiver of arrows and a spear. He uttered a roaring war cry, as if to challenge his enemies.

The other sage also put the *prasada* in the Yajna fire and in an instant, a princess came out of the fire. She had a darkish complexion, but was extremely charming. She possessed large dark eyes, long black curly hair, a swan-like neck, bow-like brows and her gait was majestic and graceful.

As soon as the princess emerged out of the sacrificial fire, a divine broadcast was heard, "Name this girl Krishna. Her birth is with a purpose to cause destruction of those who are evil and anti-religious."

It was decided to name the prince Dhrishtadyumna as he appeared to be stubbornly bold (Dhrishta) and also possessed heavenly brightness (Dyumna).

Arjuna Hits The Fish's Eye and Wins Draupadi

On arriving at Panchala, the Pandavas took shelter at a humble potter's house. The unsuspecting potter family thought them to be what they appeared — poor brahmins living on alms.

The city hummed with activity. Bright and colourful pavillions dotted the city. An amphitheatre enclosed within high walls and surrounded by gardens and groves, was the venue of the Swayamvara.

Drupada, the king of Panchala, was not quite happy. He had always wanted Draupadi to marry Arjuna because with Arjuna as his son-in-law, Drona's bitter enemy could be contained. Drona would not think of harming his beloved pupil's father-in-law.

However, Drupada determined that the man who married his daughter should be as formidable a warrior as Arjuna. So, he got a mighty bow made, which only Arjuna could have strung with ease. On the ceiling was a revolving ring to which was attached a toy fish, while a pan full of oil was placed below.

The condition of the Swayamvara was announced. The archer participating in the Swayamvara had to aim at the eye of the revolving fish while looking at its reflection in the pan full of oil. The archer who could shoot at its eye would be the winner. He would win the hand of his daughter.

The pavillions were packed long before the auspicious hour. Spectators and prospective bridegrooms waited with bated breath for the event to commence. The seating arrangement was in the shape of a dolphin. The suitors sat towards the top while its central part formed the dais. Several arched gates were constructed. Fragrant flowers decorated the archways and spread a pleasant smell in the air.

Among the kings present there, were Duryodhana, Dushasana, Karna, Shakuni, Krishna and Balarama, cousins of the Pandavas, and Jarasandha, the king of Magadh. One side of the enclosure was reserved for the brahmins, where the five Pandavas dressed as brahmins took their seat unobtrusively.

The princess of Panchala was asked to get ready to be in the Swayamvara hall. Soon, she entered the hall. The hush as she entered the room was palpable. Bugles and drums started playing as the announcement of her arrival was made. The gathering, including kings, princes, saints, sages and the brahmins, cheered the announcement.

The Pandavas, although very much present in the hall, remained unnoticed. However, Krishna and his elder brother Balarama did not fail to notice them. Krishna, Kunti's nephew, the younger son of her brother Vasudeva, idly glanced around. He spotted the unusually muscular brahmins. He did not believe the story of Pandavas' death and his gaze sharpened as he noticed the bow-string marks on their shoulders.

Casually glancing at the five young men, Balarama too felt sure about the presence of the Pandavas. Nobody else, however, could notice the presence of the Pandava warriors, as they were completely absorbed in the events in the arena.

Meanwhile, Draupadi looked like a heavenly nymph standing by the side of Dhrishtadyumna. She attracted everyone's attention even as Dhrishtadyumna invited the suitors to come one by one and participate in the shooting trial. As the event began, a number of princes came forward to try their luck. But none of them could so much as pull the string on the bow. Tension mounted visibly and the warriors looked with veiled consternation at the great bow. Each one thought he would succeed where others would not.

After Duryodhana and Dushasana failed to string the bow, it was now Karna's turn. He rose and walked into the arena. His golden armour shone brightly and his earrings dazzled. He was a master archer with a perfect aim. He picked up the bow effortlessly and in one move strung it dexterously. He placed an arrow against the bow-string and pulled it back, about to shoot. Suddenly some of the princes objected, "How can the son of a charioteer participate in the Swayamvara meant only for princes?"

Panchali understood what the commotion was about. She raised her head and looked contemptuously at the great archer. "I'll never marry the son of a charioteer," she spoke slowly and clearly to her brother.

Karna bore the humiliation stoically, and with a grim laugh, threw the bow down. He retreated to his seat. The others who followed him, including Shishupala, Shalya and Jarasandha, did not meet even half as much success. Almost all the renowned warriors tried their luck and failed. Drupada and his son Dhrishtadyumna were worried now, as the challenge in the Swayamvara seemed to remain unconquered. Drupada thought that if Arjuna was here, he could have certainly performed the feat quite easily.

Arjuna, feeling the archer's itch, rose when all the kshatriyas had tried and failed. The kings laughed aloud when the bare bodied brahmin picked up the bow. The brahmins themselves were no less amazed to see one of their caste aspiring to beat the kshatriyas at their game. "Stop him before he brings disgrace to our community," some of them murmured. "How will he do, what the valiant kshatriyas have failed to do?" others wondered.

However, there was a group of ascetics who thought otherwise. They thought him to be daring. "He will bring us glory. Just notice his confidence. See his physical build," they whispered. The others conferred, "Yes, it appears no prince present here can match him in any respect. Let us wait and watch."

Arjuna stepped ahead, and raising the bow, strung it gracefully. He cast a glance at the audience including the brahmins. The brahmins cheered him loudly. King Drupada, his son Dhrishtadyumna and daughter Draupadi wished the young brahmin to succeed so that the despair of unsuccessful Swayamvara would turn into a happy ending.

Arjuna took a deep look into the pan of oil. He finally shot his arrow taking an aim at the eye of the fish. In a flash, the arrow hit the target. The gift of *Chakshushi* that the Gandharva king had given him once could not have been made a better use of, at a more opportune moment.

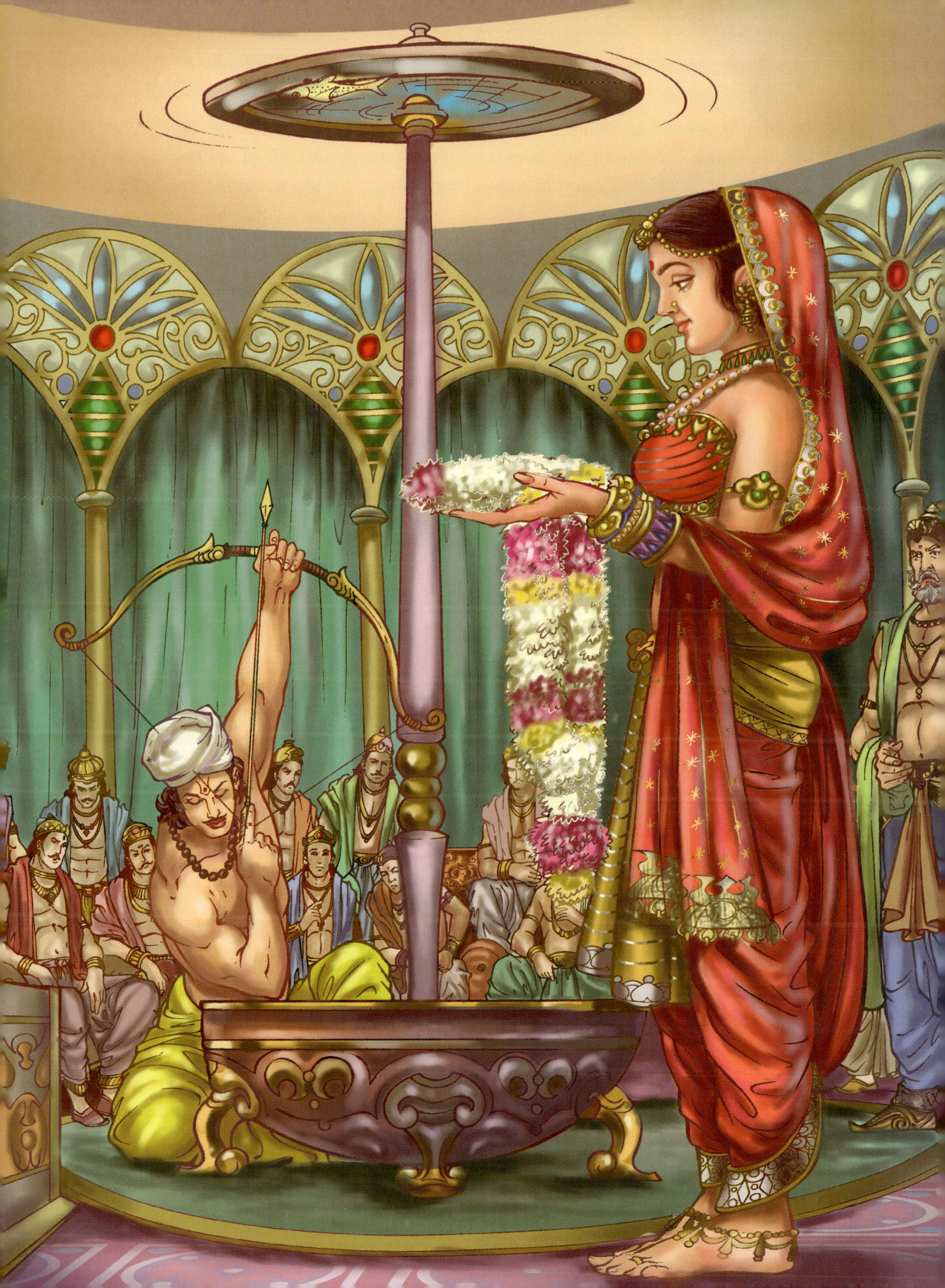

The brahmins applauded the feat with uncharacteristic abandon. The Panchala princess was enlivened with joy. But the kshatriya princes doubted the skill of the young brahmin. So he shot another arrow, which pierced the previous arrow and hit the eye of the fish again. The princes and kings stared incredulously with mouths agape. King Drupada carefully observed the young brahmins. Hope surged in him. Perhaps, the prophecy of his priest that Pandavas were not dead, was true.

When the target fell, Draupadi looked up and looked into the eyes of the young brahmin. Their eyes met. She felt wonderful. A beatific smile greeted the young brahmin as she was accosted by her brother to welcome him with the bridal garland. Shyly she placed the bridal garland around his neck. The princess had chosen her lord. The kshatriya kings were disappointed. The disappointment was mingled with humiliation, and they were infuriated. The infuriated princes rose up in a body. They openly blamed King Drupada and his son for allowing a brahmin to be a suitor, thereby causing humiliation of the kshatriya princes. "A Swayamvara is for kshatriyas only," they complained to Drupada. "A brahmin cannot participate in an exclusive kshatriya affair. Draupadi must choose one of us," they insisted.

Without waiting anymore, the princes got up, led by Shalya and drew their swords and made attempts on the lives of king Drupada, his son and the daughter Draupadi. They also made an attempt to kill Arjuna, but Bheema leapt down from the stands with a mighty roar. Uprooting a thick post, he charged at the princes. Shalya advanced towards him but the mighty Bheema lifted him, and then flung him down on the ground. The other kings surged back as the Pandavas fell on them. The two brothers valiantly fought the mob of discontented princes and compelled them to run for their lives.

Krishna was watching the commotion with a touch of amusement. As he saw Bheema uprooting the post, he drew Balarama's attention to it. "That's Bheema for sure. Only he can uproot a post with a little jerk, and the other one is Arjuna. Only he could have shot that target. I am happy that our aunt Kunti and her sons escaped the fire in Varnavata," said Krishna.

The brahmins rushed to assist Arjuna and Bheema and joined the fray. "We're with you!" they shouted to Bheema and Arjuna as they hurled their water pots and staffs at the kshatriya princes.

In the melee, Karna rushed to the rescue of his beleaguered friends. He challenged the brahmin archer to face him in the skill of archery. Arjuna held his bow and slung the quiver of arrows on his shoulder. The other brahmins with their tridents stood by Arjuna. He reassured them and advised them not to worry about him, as he alone was more than a match for them all. Arjuna quickly pierced the array of princes with his volleys of arrows.

Next, Arjuna turned to Karna and shot arrows at him, which he found difficult to contain. Karna understood that he was not facing any ordinary warrior. He was highly impressed with the extraordinary skills of the brahmin archer. Karna asked with amazement, "Who are you? No one with the exception of Arjuna had the skills in archery to face me. You have successfully beaten me in my game. Who are you, if not Lord Indra or Lord Vishnu himself in disguise?"

"I am but an insignificant brahmin who mastered the skills in archery with the blessings of my guru," replied Arjuna.

The kshatriya princes, on witnessing the prowess of the two Brahamins were compelled to revise their opinion about them. "They are trained kshatriyas," some of them expressed their opinion, "Karna and Shalya could not have been overwhelmed under ordinary circumstances."

The crowd of kings and princes made way as Arjuna and Bheema moved away from there. Krishna stood up to address the princes, "This fight is futile as Drupada's daughter has been fairly won."

The confusion amongst the crowd gave Arjuna and Bheema enough opportunity to slip away along with Draupadi. The five brothers and Draupadi were on their way to the potters' house.

Kunti was getting worried as the Pandavas had still not arrived, and it was getting dark. She anxiously gazed at the darkening sky. She feared Duryodhana's men would be all around, looking for them.

The Pandavas were enthusiastic, having been successful in the court of Panchala. They were oblivious to the fact that Draupadi's brother Dhrishtadyumna was secretly following them to gather more information about them.

The Pandavas wanted to give their mother a surprise. Arjuna was the first to enter the house with Draupadi. "Here is the alm I received today, mother," he said jubilantly. Kunti, busy in her chore, responded without looking up, "Share it amongst the five of you and enjoy."

But when Kunti looked up to find a beautiful bride bedecked in expensive clothes and jewels, her eyes widened with disbelief. She was aghast at what she had said just then. "Oh, what have I done!" She cringed in horror at the import of her words. Before long, Yudhishthira told her all that had happened.

Yudhishthira, turning to Arjuna, counselled, "She rightfully belongs to you as you have won her in the Swayamvara." Arjuna refused, "How can I marry when my elder brothers are still unwed? It's against the injunctions in scriptures. Moreover, how can I let our mother's word be untrue?"

Others waited for Yudhishthira to settle the issue. Yudhishthira could notice that all his brothers were mesmerised by the beauty of Draupadi. He guessed if Draupadi was wedded to only one of them, she could be a cause of friction amongst the brothers. He wanted to avoid such a situation from arising in future. "Draupadi will become our common wife," pronounced Yudhishthira in the end.

Draupadi too concurred with the decision. She wanted to assuage the guilt and worry of her mother-in-law. "Don't worry mother! It's the destiny that rules. Whatever has happened has been according to the will of the almighty. I am destined to be the common wife of five brothers, according to a boon given to me by Lord Shiva in my previous life."

Lord Krishna and Balarama, who had followed them to quench their curiosity, saw them enter the potter's house. A little later, both of them entered the house and touched the feet of their aunt, Kunti, and asked what was it that worried them. She told them how indiscreet she had been in using the words, and the consequence of her words. They consoled Kunti and Lord Krishna corroborated the story of Draupadi's boon.

Kunti expressed her desire to hear the story in greater detail. Lord Krishna willingly obliged and told Kunti how Draupadi had undergone a severe penance in her previous life to appease Lord Shiva. She wanted Lord Shiva to bless her so that she got a husband who would possess five different qualities. But she got a boon instead that she would marry five men at a time, each of whom would possess one of those five different qualities.

Kunti was a satisfied mother and mother-in-law now, and Draupadi was a happy wife of the Pandavas.

The Return of The Princes

Lord Krishna and his elder brother Balarama were not the only ones to follow the Pandavas. Dhrishtadyumna, determined to discover the true identity of the brahmins, had also followed them. He hid himself in their chamber. He observed Kunti serving food and noted that Bheema received the largest share. He noticed his sister lying at their feet at night. He carefully listened to their conversation. He heard them discuss wars, weapons, strategy and statesmanship, subjects dear to a kshatriya's heart. He did not hear a word of the Vedas or the Shastras, penance or piety, much as he had expected from brahmins.

Dhrishtadyumna was convinced, after listening to the conversation, that his sister had been wedded in a royal family of kshatriyas. Slipping away before dawn, he went straight to his father.

The Panchala king had been waiting anxiously to hear from his son. "I only hope the man who won Panchali has a respectable origin," he sighed anxiously. "Oh, my son, how sincerely I wanted Arjuna as a groom for my daughter, but that was not to be."

Dhrishtadyumna smiled, "That's what has happened, father. I spied upon the brahmins and followed them to their resting place at a potter's house. What I saw has filled me with joy. The five brahmins are, in fact, the five Pandavas. None of the five resembles a brahmin even remotely. These men are muscular and strong and have the warriors' graceful, lithe walk. They speak not about Shastras or Vedas but about weapons and warfare! No brahmin can pull off a post as that brahmin did yesterday in the skirmishes."

Dhrishtadyumna continued enthusiastically even as Drupada's eyes shone with hope. Describing the mother of the five brahmins, Dhrishtadyumna continued, "She's more regal than any lady I've seen. They are certainly not brahmins father, but the five Pandavas and their mother Kunti. They have, for sure, escaped the inferno!"

Drupada was extremely happy to learn that the Pandavas were alive, but he had to ascertain what his son had just reported. He summoned the family priest. "Go to the potter's house and bring me all the information you can about those living there. Tell them about the friendship between me and Pandu and that nothing will give me greater pleasure than ceremonially wedding my daughter to Arjuna."

Yudhishthira asked Bheema to welcome the brahmin befitting his status. Bheema washed his feet. To the queries of the priest, Yudhishthira curtly replied, "The king of Panchala chose the winner groom for his daughter. As such he has lost his right to demand the suitor's lineage or race. Anyway, you can inform him that he has got what he desired."

A messenger from the king arrived before the priest could leave. "King Drupada has invited the family of the groom for a feast," he informed. The Pandavas did not refuse. They sat with Kunti and Draupadi in the chariot waiting outside, and went to the palace.

Drupada had made an elaborate arrangement to receive the guests. He observed his great hall and was satisfied that his instructions had been carried out to the last details. There were three categories each of seats and plates. There were seats that were richly inlaid thrones for kings, less ornate couches for the vaishyas and the simple wooden one for the shudras. There were plates of gold, copper and tin. Similarly, some walls were decorated with weapons, while sacred texts were placed against the others.

Soon, the Pandavas arrived and were received by King Drupada. He escorted them to the hall, keenly watching their manner and response. He noticed with concealed pleasure that the poor brahmins were completely at ease in the royal surroundings. Their manner was pleasant and charming. They didn't appear confused or surprised, nor did they behave like poor mendicants. They seated themselves on the ornate high seats reserved for the princes. When offered food, they chose gold plates without a thought.

No more proof was needed now. King Drupada was convinced that the five poor brahmins in disguise were, in fact, royal blooded scions. Drupada was fully confident of his guess when he noticed that their eyes lingered on weapons rather than the sacred texts.

Drupada asked the Pandavas, diplomatically, "Do I consider you as brahmins or kshatriyas? I mean the wedding rites! Are they to be of brahmins or kshatriyas?"

Yudhishthira instantly understood that it was no use keeping their secrecy with the wise king. "King of Panchala, you have got what you desired," he said. "We are kshatriyas, sons of Pandu."

"If you are indeed Pandu's sons, let me know how you escaped from Varnavata," Drupada insisted. Yudhishthira briefly narrated the events leading to their escape. Drupada was fully sympathetic to the Pandavas. He had only harsh words for Dhritarashtra, "What can you expect from a weak and vacillating king? I will help you regain your kingdom. Till then you will stay with us as our guests."

Drupada enquired about the time when Arjuna could be married to Draupadi. Yudhishthira interrupted, "I am getting married to her." Drupada didn't follow what exactly Yudhishthira meant. "It doesn't make any difference to me, whether you or Arjuna marries her. Both of you are equally dear to me," he said.

Yudhishthira appeared expressionless. "Your daughter will be wedded to all of us. That's the command of our mother."

Drupada cringed in distaste, "How can that be! Society never condones polyandry." Yuddhishthira tried to assuage the feelings of Drupada. He explained to him the extraordinary circumstances that led to it. Mother Kunti's words could never be falsified.

Drupada was not prepared to be convinced by any argument. "It is sinful. The Vedas and Shastras forbid it as it is against morality."

"The issue of morality goes much deeper. In obeying my mother, I'm following the age-old tradition. Nothing is greater virtue than obeying one's parents," Yudhishthira said.

Drupada gave up. He had no intention to enter into an argument over morality with an authority on the subject. He left the issue to be resolved by his son and the Pandavas' mother Kunti.

Even before Drupada could abruptly leave the court in a huff, Sage Vyasa entered. Everyone stood up to touch his feet. The sage blessed them and took his seat.

Drupada could not resist the inner turmoil he was going through. Promptly, he posed his question. "I have been informed that Draupadi will be wedded to all the five Pandava brothers. Is it not immoral?"

Vyasa, the learned sage, acknowledged that such a custom was no longer approved. Vedas do not approve of it. Before offering his own opinion, he wanted to know the opinion of Drupada and his son on the subject. Drupada made clear that he considered such a practice highly abominable. Dhrishtadyumna too concurred with the opinion of his father.

Yudhishthira interrupted softly. "Jatila, renowned for her virtue and piety, married the Saptarishis," said he, quoting the Puranas, "Varkshi, Rishi Kunti's daughter, married the ten Prachetesas. Varkshi was Daksha's mother and Lord Shiva married her granddaughter. Experts in the subject of morality hold obedience to one's elders as the highest virtue. We cannot be considered to sin in obeying the command of our mother."

Drupada conceded the arguments of Yudhishthira but he still could not reconcile to the fact of his daughter entering into a polyandrous relationship.

Sage Vyasa took the Panchala king aside and told him the story of Draupadi's previous birth. Shiva had granted her a boon of having five husbands in her next life. Draupadi was a sage daughter. She prayed to Lord Shiva to give her a husband. Lord Shiva appeared and she in her fervour, repeated five times her demand. Lord Shiva granted her wish to the letter.

King Drupada grudgingly accepted what had been ordained by Lord Shiva. The Pandavas married Draupadi. Sage Vyasa officiated the ceremony. Dhaumya lit the sacred fire, chanted the sacred mantras and the five Pandavas sat in the *mandap* with Draupadi.

The news of Draupadi's marriage to the Pandavas travelled far and wide. Drupada was happy by now, having set aside his initial repugnance. He was reassured that Drona would not think of harming him. Lord Krishna, on hearing the news of their wedding, sent them rich gifts. Many princes were happy to learn that the Pandavas had not perished in the fire.

But there were many others like Duryodhana who were not happy to learn about Pandavas' survival. Duryodhana brooded over the events to discover the mistake they had made in their plan. "Had Purochana been alive, I would have hanged him for his bungling," thought Duryodhana in his impotent rage.

The Clouds of Conspiracy Gather Again

Since it was now open news that the Pandavas were alive, Vidura thought it best to inform Dhritarashtra. "The Kurus are fortunate, your Majesty! News has come from Panchala that the Pandavas are alive. You will be even more happy to learn that the young man who won the Swayamvara at Panchala is none other than your nephew, Arjuna," informed Vidura. He also informed Dhritarashtra the circumstances under which the five Pandavas were married to Draupadi.

Dhritarashtra hid his feelings well. The news he got was no music to his ears. But feigning joy, he asked Vidura to dispatch precious gifts to Draupadi and the Pandavas. "Pandu's sons are as dear to me as my own and I am extremely happy to learn about them." He also instructed Vidura to take Duryodhana along and escort the Pandavas along with Draupadi and Kunti, to Hastinapur.

Vidura knew his brother well. "Let us hope your sentiments do not change in the coming days," he said politely before leaving.

Soon Duryodhana and Karna came in. Dhritarashtra was alone in his chamber. Having overheard the conversation between Vidura and Dhritarashtra, they were wild with fury. "I was waiting for Vidura to leave. What I have to say is not for his ears," whispered Duryodhana furiously. "I can't understand how you could express happiness at the news of the survival of the Pandavas. Your enemy's good fortune should not fill you with joy. You must do something before Kauravas are wiped out by them. Strip the Pandavas of all power. That done, they will never be a threat to us."

Dhritarashtra shared the sentiments of his son. But he did not want to reveal his true feelings in front of Vidura. Now finding himself in presence of Duryodhana and Karna alone, he could express himself. He asked them to come out with their plans.

Duryodhana proposed a number of ways through which the Pandavas could be weakened. "We can engineer dissension amongst them. We can split the sons of Kunti and Madri. Or we can lavish Drupada with gifts to wean him away from the Pandavas.

Besides this, we can use Draupadi, the common wife, to set one against the other. We can spread the rumour of Draupadi's preference for one brother against the others. If nothing works, we can kill Bheema, the pillar of their strength. With Bheema gone, Arjuna could be defenceless," Duryodhana spoke out his heart enthusiastically and looked towards Karna for approval.

Karna was mature enough in his judgment. His dislike for the Pandavas did not overshadow his reasoning. "You are being too presumptuous," Karna said boldly, "and your reasoning sounds hollow. None of your suggestions seems practical. You couldn't harm the Pandavas when they were young boys, what makes you think, you would be able to do so now when they are grown up and strong? Draupadi would be the last person to fall in your trap. Remember, she chose them when she thought they were poor brahmins. Do you think she would abandon them now when she knows they are princes? A common wife unites them, not the other way round. Drupada is neither greedy nor would he ever even imagine snapping off relations with his sons-in-law. None of your ploys will really work."

"There's no way, but one to overcome them. Defeat them in a straight war. For a kshatriya, virtue lies in war. Might and valour are the strategic pillars of defeating the enemy in a war. But you must strike now, before Lord Krishna's helping hand reaches them. Drupada, who will rush to aid the Pandavas, is no match for us. Defeat them once and for all and they would never be able to stand straight before you. But that must be done now, when we have a fair chance of defeating them. Not only will they be deprived of the throne of Hastinapur forever, we will, in addition, force the king of Panchala to accept the overlordship of Hastinapur."

Dhritarashtra was not blind to Karna's logic. He praised the wisdom of Karna, but withheld his decision till he consulted Bhishma, Dronacharya, Vidura and Kripacharya. So he sent for Vidura and directed him to convene a meeting of the royal council.

A meeting of the council was presided over by Bhishma, who spoke coolly but firmly, "I can never approve of war between the cousins. The Pandavas and Kauravas are equally dear to me. I must advise you to give the Pandavas their half of the kingdom. It is as much their heritage as Duryodhana's. Therefore, they are rightfully entitled to it. You must act honourably, Dhritarashtra. Strength lies in honour. Life without honour is death. You have already tarnished the image of Kurus. Everyone holds you morally responsible for the Varnavata episode, although it is well known that Duryodhana was directly responsible for it. As for the plan of invading Panchala, banish the thought. Do not consider King Drupada and his son weaker than you."

Drona and Kripacharya too shared the same sentiments. But Karna did not give up easily, "Bhishma and Drona being elder patriarchs have gone soft. You are unlikely to get your due if you follow their advice. Sovereignty is directly linked to your destiny. If you're destined to be a king, you would be, no matter what hurdles come in your way."

Drona was full of contempt for Karna. "You are never happy in the prosperity of the Pandavas. But not heeding our advice is a sure path to ensure the end of Kauravas."

Vidura, turning to Dhritarashtra, offered him a measured opinion. "Bhishma and Drona love you and have your welfare in their mind. Go according to their advice and you will be happy. Those wishing to harm the Pandavas are not doing you a favour. A war with them will have disastrous consequences for you."

Dhritarashtra thought over the advice offered by Bhishma and Drona. He decided to follow it and redeem his tarnished reputation.

"We will welcome Pandu's sons with all due ceremony," he offered his reasoned decision. "They are entitled to their share in the kingdom." Dhritarashtra then summoned Vidura and asked him to proceed to Panchala with valuable presents for the Pandavas, Draupadi and Kunti. They were to be escorted back to Hastinapur with full royal honours.

When the Pandavas heard of Vidura's arrival, they rushed out to greet him. Lord Krishna, who was also there at the time, also welcomed Vidura with all due humility.

Vidura informed the Pandavas that the king of Hastinapur was overjoyed to know that they were alive. "So are Bhishma and Drona. Dhritarashtra wants you to return to Hastinapur as soon as you can, so that your due share in the kingdom can be given back to you. We can proceed immediately if Krishna and Drupada have no objection." They had none. As they were about to proceed to Hastinapur, Krishna too decided to accompany them, much to the relief of the Pandavas.

The Kuru elders and all the Bharata ladies came out to receive the Pandavas, Kunti and Draupadi. Dhritarashtra expressed his desire to meet them as soon as they bathed, changed and felt relaxed.

When they finally met, Dhritarashtra showed his happiness by receiving them with royal honours and then, without further ado, he ordered, "Go to Khandavaprastha. The land beyond is yours. I do not want any further bitterness between you and your cousins."

Khandavaprastha Becomes Indraprastha

The Pandavas, along with Kunti, Draupadi and Krishna, immediately set out for Khandavaprastha. The place had indeed been the ancient capital of the Kurus, but it had long been replaced by a jungle since the capital had shifted to Hastinapur. The Pandavas decided to build their capital there. Krishna commanded Vishwakarma, the architect of the Gods, to build a great city at this place. The order was to build a city to rival Amaravati, the capital of Indra. According to the Lord's will, Vishwakarma constructed a stunning city, a worthy capital for the Pandavas, complete with a grand palace, wide streets, a great fort, gardens, streams and every other landmark that a great city should possess. Since the capital city rivalled that of Indra, it was given the name of Indraprastha. After blessing the Pandavas, Krishna went back to Dwaraka.

Once the Pandavas settled in their new capital, a good portion of the people of Hastinapur also followed them, for the princes had been very much loved by their subjects.

Not long after the Pandavas had settled in, Narada, the celestial rishi, visited them. The Pandavas washed his feet, as was the welcome ritual. The rishi stated his purpose of the visit, "I'm here to offer you a piece of advice. You have a common wife in Draupadi. Such a situation calls for caution. You must chart out a set of rules and regulations to guard each individual's right, otherwise you will end up like Sund and his brother Sunda. The two were devoted to each other, but they fell apart over their common wife Tillotama and ended up killing each other."

The Pandavas, impressed by Narada's wisdom, made a rule that assigned separate timings with Draupadi, for each of the five brothers. Anyone encroaching upon the other's time would have to to go into a voluntary exile for a year.

One day a brahmin come to the palace in a distraught state. "Thieves have stolen my cows and cows are the wealth of a brahmin," he complained. "You must get them back for me," he humbly requested.

"You will get your cows back," Arjuna reassured the poor brahmin. As he turned back to collect his weapons, he suddenly realised that Yudhishthira was in the chamber with Draupadi. For a moment, Arjuna was in a quandary. He didn't know what to do. He, however, had to perform his duty. So, he entered the chamber, greeted Yudhishthira, collected his bow and arrow and left.

Arjuna in Exile

Arjuna killed the villain and restored the cows to the grateful brahmin. Having done that, he went straight to confront Yudhishthira. He volunteered to go into exile, having admittedly broken the rule. But Yudhishthira was considerate and forgiving. "There's no reason for you to go into exile," he said. "You had a valid reason. It was your foremost duty to defend the poor brahmin. Moreover, the rule applies only to the elder brother, not the younger brother." But none of these words had any effect on Arjuna. He was determined to undergo the punishment that he thought he deserved.

Arjuna wandered from place to place, having left Indraprastha. He never stayed at a place for long. One day while bathing in the river Ganga he felt some underwater creature tugging at his leg and drawing him deep into the water. Before he could say anything, he found himself in a beautiful underwater palace.

Soon, a beautiful maiden appeared in front of him. "Who are you and where am I?" asked Arjuna.

"I am Ulupi, the Naga king Kaurauya's daughter. I want you to marry me. If you refuse, I will kill myself!" she answered. Arjuna expressed his helplessness as he was undergoing the vow of celibacy.

"I know everything," replied Ulipi. "I know why you are here. I know the agreement between the five of you over your common wife. But the vow of celibacy applies only to her. You won't be breaking any vow by marrying me," Ulupi explained.

Arjuna married her and stayed the night with her. Next day, he expressed his desire to leave. Ulupi helped Arjuna come to the bank and parted with tears in her eyes. As Arjuna was finally leaving, Ulupi gave him a boon, "No underwater creature will ever harm you," she said.

Arjuna went eastwards to Naimisha forest. From there he went to Kalinga and on the sea-shore nearby he offered prayers to the Gods. Finally he turned towards Manipura, famed for its enchanting beauty.

Manipura truly enchanted Arjuna, and Chitrangada, whom he spotted in the palace garden, enchanted him more. He presented himself to the king and offered to marry his daughter Chitrangada after introducing himself as Arjuna, the third son of Pandu of the Puru dynasty.

"You can marry my daughter on the condition that my daughter and her child will stay in Manipura," proposed the king. "I have only one daughter and she is as good as a son to me. Our family has only one child in every generation. My daughter will perpetuate my race and her child will succeed me," explained the king. "I accept," Arjuna responded.

He married and enjoyed the hospitality at the royal palace till a son was born to the married couple. Thereafter, he travelled southwards along the sea-coast, which was teeming with the hermitages of holy men. Arjuna spent time in their company. While spending his time there, he came to know of the five pools of the backwaters of the sea. These pools once used to be holy, where people bathed with devotion. But now these pools were feared by even the saints. All the five pools were now the abodes of ferocious crocodiles. Anyone venturing in any such pool did not come out alive.

Arjuna went inside one such pool fearlessly. Ulupi's boon was with him. He caught the attacking crocodile by its tail and flung it down on the ground. The crocodile got transformed into a heavenly nymph. She introduced herself as Varga who lived in Lord Kubera's court. She lived in the Nandanavana there. She had four other friends, who were also crocodiles like her. They were Saurabba, Samichi, Lata and Budbuda.

The nymph then explained how she and her friends turned into crocodiles. One day they were going from their garden to Lord Kubera's palace. They met a brahmin on the way. He was handsome and of scholarly disposition, and was busy in meditation. The nymph and her friends, out of mischief, disturbed the brahmin. But they learned that the brahmin had control over his senses. He did not fall into the trap laid by the beautiful nymphs. He got angry and uttered a curse on them that they would come down to the earth as crocodiles for one hundred years.

They felt sorry for their mistake and begged the brahmin for his forgiveness. Taking pity on them, the brahmin offered them a respite, "You will regain your original form when a valiant warrior will drag you out of water and fling you on the ground one by one."

The nymph now requested Arjuna to rescue her friends as well, which he happily did. All the five nymphs thanked Arjuna and departed to Nandanavana.

Bheema Kills Wicked Jarasandha

Arjuna continued journeying on the west coast. He reached Gokarus in Malabar. The place is believed to be associated with Lord Shiva. Thereafter, Arjuna continued his journey northwards along the sea coast and came to Prabhasa near Dwaraka, which lay at the edge of the Western Ocean.

When Krishna heard that Arjuna was in the vicinity, he rushed to the forest to meet him. The two friends embraced each other warmly.

Arjuna, who was very happy to meet his friend Krishna, told him about his travels and all the strange and wondrous sights he had seen.

Krishna gazed meaningfully at Arjuna and said, "You have travelled, learned and experienced a lot. Now you need some feasting and relaxation."

Krishna brought him to the Raivataka mountains and sent for musicians, dancers and cooks to entertain and delight his friend. Finally they returned to Dwaraka when the great festival of the Vrishnis drew near.

The Vrishnis celebrated everything with gay abandon. Dancers, musicians and acrobats entertained the crowds that thronged the market place. Arjuna joined the revelry and noticed a girl walking with her maids. Her beauty mesmerised Arjuna. He was transfixed.

Lord Krishna sensed that his friend was besotted. "That's my sister, Bhadra," Krishna smiled. "Subhadra is her other name. She is my father's favourite daughter. I'll put in a word in your favour, if you want," said Krishna, in a mischievous tone.

Arjuna, now looked pleadingly towards Krishna, "What shall I do to make her my wife?"

Krishna replied, "Kshatriya maidens choose their husbands through Swayamvara. Who knows a maiden's moods? There is another way to have Subhadra. The brave kshatriyas abduct their wives. That's the done thing, acceptable and honourable. Do that Arjuna, but before you do that, inform Yudhishthira of the same."

A messenger was dispatched to Indraprastha, who returned with Yudhishthira's consent for the marriage. Meanwhile Krishna too spoke of the plan to his father Vasudeva. Vasudeva raised no objection and Krishna hinted Arjuna to go ahead with his plan.

Lord Krishna gave Arjuna a chariot equipped with all weapons and advised him to carry away Subhadra, while she was on her way to the temple in Raivataka mountains. Arjuna drove his chariot towards the Raivataka mountains.

As soon as Subhadra came out of the temple, Arjuna leapt, grabbed her, and took her to the chariot and raced away even before the maids and attendants could utter a cry. The frightened attendants and maids ran back to Dwaraka crying and sobbing, with the news of her abduction.

The enraged Vrishnis, led by Balarama, instantly armed themselves and rushed to salvage the honour of their sister. Balarama was further enraged when he noticed Krishna sitting calm and unbothered.

"Why are you lounging around? How dare Arjuna do this? We honoured and welcomed him because of you. We just cannot suffer this humiliation lying low. Pandavas are now as good as wiped off the earth," exploded Balarama.

Lord Krishna decided to pacify Balarama. He said, "Dear brother, give a thought to the entire matter. Arjuna has insulted neither our family, nor our hospitality. He didn't want a bride bestowed to him like a gift. A Swayamvara was no guarantee that he would turn out to be the chosen one. So he abducted Subhadra, which is acceptable amongst the kshatriyas. If Subhadra is a princess, he too is a Bharata prince and his lineage is as honourable as hers."

Lord Krishna's words pacified Balarama. His rage melted away as he nodded in agreement to every word that Lord Krishna uttered. The Vrishnis, led by Balarama, went to Arjuna and brought him back honourably along with Subhadra. Their marriage was performed according to the prescribed rites. Arjuna spent the last days of his exile with the Vrishnis. When the exile was over, Arjuna went to Indraprastha along with Subhadra. The Pandavas and their mother Kunti gave Arjuna and Subhadra a warm welcome.

Subhadra went inside the palace and touched the feet of her mother-in-law Kunti, who kissed her forehead and hugged her. Next, Subhadra approached Draupadi and touched her feet. Subhadra humbly requested, "Dear sister, consider me your maid." Draupadi was highly impressed by the modesty that Arjuna's newlywed wife demonstrated, despite being exquisitely beautiful. She blessed Subhadra, "May your husband be ever victorious!"

Balarama and Krishna, along with several Vrishni chieftains, followed Arjuna and Subhadra to Indraprastha. They brought with them valuable gifts for Arjuna, his brothers, Subhadra, Draupadi, Kunti and for all other relatives.

Yudhishthira held a grand feast on the occasion of Arjuna's marriage with Subhadra. The Pandavas too lavished the Vrishnis with valuable gifts to cement the relationship between two strong allies. Soon thereafter, all the Vrishnis except Krishna left for Dwaraka.

As time rolled by, Subhadra gave birth to a lovely son, Abhimanyu. He turned into a handsome, brave and virtuous warrior as he grew up. Everyone doted on the young boy, but he was specially dear to his maternal uncle, Krishna. He was indeed the pride of the entire Pandava clan.

Draupadi bore five sons, one from each Pandava brother. They were Prativindhya, Sutasoma, Shrutakarma, Shataneeka and Shrutasena. The Pandavas were now a happy lot with the young princes growing into brave warriors.

Khandava Forest Turned Into Ashes

Once, on a warm day, the Pandavas proposed to Lord Krishna to go on a picnic on the banks of the Yamuna. Krishna and Arjuna strolled into the nearby grove and sat under a tree, chatting leisurely, when they noticed a poor brahmin approaching them. The brahmin told them that he was very hungry and urged them to feed him. They asked what food he would prefer to have. The brahmin said that he didn't eat the food of men but ate whatever the fire ate, and also warned them that he had a voracious appetite.

Seeing the two unaffected by his challenge, the brahmin said, "I am Agni Deva. I want to burn the entire Khandava forest. However, every time I do it, Lord Indra, the Rain God, extinguishes my fury even before my hunger is satiated."

"But why does he do it?" asked Arjuna and Krishna. "The reason is quite simple," Agni Deva said, "Takshaka, the king of serpents, is his friend. But I want you to help me and defend me till my hunger is satisfied."

"All right," they said, "but we do not have the right weapons to face the fury of Indra and defend you."

"You shall have them," Agni said, and vanished.

Agni Deva went to Varuna, the Lord of Water, and said, "I want Soma's chariot, the bow called Gandiva and the Sudarshan Chakra. Arjuna and Krishna need them so that I can have Khandava."

Varuna gave Agni a chariot drawn by horses that ran swifter than thought, the long, jewelled great bow called Gandiva, two inexhaustible quivers in which arrows would never finish, and Sudarshan Chakra, the shining disc whose sharp blade never failed in its task and came back spinning after slashing the head of its enemy.

Having procured the best of chariots and weapons, the Fire God dutifully delivered them to Arjuna and Krishna. Agni told them, "The Gandiva and the Sudarshan Chakra are capable of destroying men, but not Nagas, Daityas, Rakshasas and Gandharvas. Nothing can withstand their fury."

"Khandava is now all yours to devour," Arjuna said. The next instant, the Fire God was in all his fury. Great and mighty flames leapt across the forest. The trees and bushes got reduced to ashes in no time. Agni did not spare anyone — men, animals or trees. Cries of pain and terror mingled with the mighty roar of leaping flames. The ponds and water bodies dried up, and the fishes perished. The birds that tried to flee were shot down by Arjuna, to be devoured in the inferno.

Seeing this, the Rain God turned his attention towards the Khandava forest. Dark clouds of rain suddenly enveloped the forest sky and sheets of torrential downpour began. However, before rain could play spoilsport for Agni, Arjuna shot a volley of arrows to provide a canopy to the raging inferno. Thunderclaps following the bright lightning sounded impotent before the might of the two warriors. While Arjuna took on Indra, Krishna fulfilled the second demand of the brahmin that no creature escaped out alive. His Sudarshan Chakra mercilessly slashed wild boars, elephants and tigers alike.

They noticed Agni leaping behind a terrified danava, who ran to Arjuna pleading mercy. "Save me from the fury of Agni," he prayed.

"Fire will not touch you!" Arjuna reassured him.

The inferno raged for ten days, which was sufficient to reduce the Khandava forest and all its creatures to ashes, with the exception of six. These six were Maya, the danava whom Arjuna protected, four saranga birds and Ashvasena, a Naga. The two exhausted warriors sat wearily in the chariot after the ordeal, when the grateful danava approached them with folded palms.

He introduced himself as Mayasura, the chief architect of the danvas, and thanked Arjuna for saving his life. "I am really obliged to you. Tell me what can I do for you?" he asked.

"Your kind offer is reward enough," Arjuna responded tiredly, "you are free to go anywhere now." But Mayasura insisted on granting a boon. He said, "I am the architect to the gods and the asuras alike. There must surely be something that I can do for you."

"Build Yudishthira a sabha, the like of which has never been seen before, nor will be seen ever after,"Arjuna demanded.

"That will be done. I am here to obey you sir," said Maya. He set about the task of constructing an auditorium for which Yudhishthira allotted a huge stretch of land. Maya was not satisfied with the locally available building material, and rushed to Mount Kailash where he remembered having left rare and priceless jewels. He also remembered having left a mace there, which he thought would be ideal for Bheema.

Maya returned from Kailash with more than what he had expected. Besides the large mace for Bheema, he also brought the great conch, Devdutta, as a gift for Arjuna.

The sabha was indisputably unparalleled in glory and splendour. The gold pillars and the precious stone-studded archways rivalled Indra's palace. The auditorium, built around a beautiful pool of water, had marble floor studded with precious pearls shaped like various water animals — fishes, frogs, crabs, etc. It was such an artistic endeavour that it looked like a live pool. Inside, there were enormous halls interspersed with cool gardens and lotus ponds. In some places, doors appeared like walls. The sabha was completed in a record time of fourteen moon cycles.

Narada Proposes Rajasuya Yajna

The wondrous building left the Pandavas awestruck. Messengers were sent far and wide. Sages, ascetics and monarchs, with their retinue, arrived in droves, to take a look at the magnificent building.

Narada, who was amongst the last to enter the auditorium, praised it whole heartedly, but quickly switched on to the topic of Rajasuya Yajna. He inspired the Pandavas to undertake this Yajna to proclaim their suzerainty. The idea appealed to all except Yudhishthira, who said that he needed to consult Lord Krishna before arriving at a decision. The Rajasuya Yajna meant subjugating every monarch on land, which was not a trivial feat.

Yudhishthira thought it to be an overtly ambitious idea, though he did not doubt his success. Messengers were sent to Dwaraka requesting Lord Krishna's immediate presence in Indraprastha.

Lord Krishna arrived and found himself in the august company of Sage Dhaumya, Sage Vyasa, King Drupada and King Virata. Addressing Lord Krishna, Yudhishthira said, "Keshava! Narada wants me to perform Rajasuya. But I feel it's no child's game. What do you say?"

"You can certainly perform the Yajna. You have the manpower and the resources," Lord Krishna said thoughtfully, "but there is a big thorn in your way."

"What is that thorn?" asked Yudhishthira.

The Thorn in The Way

Lord Krishna answered, "To perform Rajasuya Yajna, you must defeat every king on land, which you will find difficult as long as Jarasandha is alive. This ruler of Magadh has powerful allies. Shishupala of Chedi (Bundelkhand) is his friend, and Vaka of the Karushas is his disciple. Two powerful warriors, Hansa and Dimbhaka, along with Shishupala, are his three powerful generals. Bhagdatta of the Pragjyotishas was your father's friend, but he owes allegiance to Jarasandha. The Bhojas, the southern Panchalas, the Kulinds and many others have either fled or surrendered to Jarasandha."

"He is not to be dismissed lightly. He ransacked Mathura, and forced us to flee across to Dwaraka. We had heroes like Satyaki, Balarama and Pradyumna but Mathura still could not bear the brunt of Jarasandha. He has several monarchs imprisoned whom he has vowed to sacrifice to Shiva. Before performing the Rajasuya, you must kill Jarasandha and rescue the kings," added Lord Krishna.

Yudhishthira found the task difficult, but Bheema was quite excited at the prospect of defeating Jarasandha.

"Jarasandha, the mighty warrior, has got eighty-six kings in his prison. The day fourteen more kings are jailed, he would perform the sacrifice. Whosoever rescues those imprisoned kings, would win the confidence of the kshatriyas," Lord Krishna declared to Yudhishthira.

The big question was, how the powerful king Jarasandha should be eliminated. Yudhishthira was in two minds about challenging the might of Jarasandha. Bheema and Arjuna, showing excessive enthusiasm, had volunteered to kill Jarasandha in a one-on-one combat. Lord Krishna tried his best to allay the fears of Yudhishthira.

"Leave everything to me, O king. Just send Bheema and Arjuna with me. Once Jarasandha is eliminated, all the other kings will accept your suzerainty," said Lord Krishna.

Lord Krishna found Yudhishthira still unconvinced. He said to him, "It is futile to worry, dear brother. Whatever has to happen, will happen. Everyone must reap the fruits of one's karma. Jarasandha's end is destined. His sins have crossed all limits. I have a plan to defeat him and free the imprisoned kings. Bheema, Arjuna and I will go as brahmins, gain access into his inner chamber, free the kings and challenge him to a duel, in which Bheema will tear apart his body."

Yudhishthira, feeling somewhat reassured now, wanted to know more about Jarasandha. Lord Krishna said, "King Brihadratha, Jarasandha's father, ruled over Magadh. He was married to the twin princesses of Kashi. Unfortunately, the king did not have a child which was a matter of great concern, for he was growing old."

"Once, saint Chandra Kaushika came to Magadh. He sat down

under a mango tree to rest for a while. When King Brihadratha heard about the presence of the great sage, he rushed to get the blessings of the Sage Chandra Kaushika. The king touched his feet and told the sage about his misfortune. The sage closed his eyes and meditated for a while. A mango fell from the tree. The sage picked it up and asked the king to offer it to one of his queens. The king gave the mango to the queens. The mango should have been eaten by only one queen but both the queens divided the mango into two halves and ate one half each. In due course, both the queens gave birth to half a baby each. It was a grotesque experience for them, as a consequence of which they decided to abandon the babies. A maid was instructed to throw away the half-babies on the lonely outskirts of the city."

"A rakshasi named Jara, who was passing by, noticed the half-babies and picked them up for her food. While wrapping the two in a rag, she placed them together. Just then, a miracle took place that surprised the demoness. The parts combined into a whole like the drops of mercury and there was a baby, kicking and crying for attention."

"The news spread in the town like a wild fire and the demoness rushed to the court to testify what she had witnessed. The queens present in the court heard the story as narrated by the demoness in breathless anticipation. Both of them threw furtive glances at each other and admitted to their deeds with a mixed emotion of guilt and happiness. The king was the happiest person when he came to know that the baby was his. The baby was named Jarasandha, after the demoness."

"Sage Chandra Kaushika came to the court and blessed the baby. He told the king that the baby would grow into a handsome man of great prowess, who would defeat a large number of kings. But his own end would be tragic, being torn into two from the middle, just as he was born, on earning the wrath of a mighty king."

After Lord Krishna narrated the strange tale of the origin of Jarasandha, Krishna, Bheema and Arjuna, dressed as brahmins, quietly embarked upon their mission. The capital of Magadh, spread across five hills, was heavily guarded.

The three warriors disguised as brahmins found a rupture in the outer wall of the fortress. It was broad enough for them to enter the city. They walked straight to the palace.

Jarasandha rose up to welcome the three strange brahmins, washed their feet and made the ritual offering. Lord Krishna thanked the powerful monarch for his hospitality and apologised for the silence of his two companions. "They are under a vow of silence and would speak only after midnight," he explained.

Jarasandha escorted the guests to a cosy chamber, leaving them to rest in privacy. At midnight he went into the guest room with the offerings of food, milk and honey. The brahmins blessed Jarasandha but refused his food.

The refusal aroused Jarasandha's suspicion. He questioned the authenticity of their appearance as brahmins. "Brahmins observe severe austerities when under a vow. They do not decorate themselves with flowers and sandal paste. Besides, you have bowstring marks on your shoulders. Tell me your real identity!" commanded Jarasandha sternly. "You have also refused my hospitality. I want to know the reason."

Lord Krishna was quick to reply, "We are snataka brahmins. Anyone can choose to be a snataka brahmin. A kshatriya under this vow considers it proper to have flowers on his arms, for their arms are their words. They do not speak but use their arms. The wise ones have said, one should never enter an enemy's house through the front door, nor should one accept his food and other offerings."

Lord Krishna provoked Jarasandha, but Jarasandha remained puzzled. "I don't know who you are. Nor do I understand how I could be your enemy when I don't even know you," Jarasandha sounded surprised.

"You have imprisoned a large number of kshatriya kings with the intention of sacrificing them to Rudra. That makes you our enemy," Krishna spoke in his sweet and soft tone. "You are an abomination to all kshatriyas. You persist in the savage practice of human sacrifice, which is obsolete. You have reduced the kings to the level of sacrificial beasts. To kill a depraved, cruel man is no sin. In fact, it is recommended. Who knows when you may attack us to increase your tally of imprisoned kings. So as a matter of precaution, we are here to challenge you and release the imprisoned kings," Lord Krishna explained everything to satisfy the query of Jarasandha.

"Which kingdom are you from? And who are these two companions of yours?" questioned Jarasandha.

"I am Krishna, the king of Dwaraka, your old enemy who killed your son-in-law and these brahmins are Pandu's sons, Arjuna and Bheema," Lord Krishna replied.

Jarasandha's face contorted in distaste as he heard the name of Krishna. "I have followed the rules of the game and defeated the kings squarely as I defeated you. Wait a while till I have crowned my son Sahadeva, and then be ready to face my wrath."

In a brief ceremony, Jarasandha hastily crowned his son Sahadeva.

The Duel Begins

Knowing very well that Jarasandha would choose either him or Bheema in a wrestling duel, Lord Krishna bluntly asked, "Who amongst us do you want to fight with?"

Jarasandha took the crown off his head, bound his hair and looking disdainfully at Krishna, said, "I will not stoop so low as to fight a cowherd," deliberately insulting him. "I would rather be defeated at the hands of a true warrior than defeat a cowherd. I choose Bheema for the combat," Jarasandha made his choice clear.

The two bare bodied combatants entered the wrestling arena, each determined to beat the other. Word about the combat soon spread across Magadh and spectators poured in hordes to witness the wrestling bout.

The wrestling bout was long and blood curdling. The two combatants were fighting to kill. It was a well-matched combat. It began on the first day of the Kartika moon and went on till it grew to fullness. The combatants neither ate, nor drank, nor slept and with each passing day, the combat was getting vicious and cruel, destined to end in the death of one of them.

The ferocious wrestling went on for thirteen days but neither of them showed any sign of fatigue. On the fourteenth day, Krishna spoke to Bheema, diplomatically aiming at demoralising Jarasandha. "Your opponent looks very tired, O, Bheema," Lord Krishna taunted, "don't attack him fatally otherwise he will be killed. Don't use your divine power that you have got from the Wind God."

Jarasandha Meets His End

This was indication enough for Bheema, for every word that Lord Krishna spoke had some hidden meaning in it. Lord Krishna wanted Bheema to go in for the final attack. Taking cue, Bheema rushed at his opponent, head on with a mighty force, held him high up in his hands, rotated him across and flung him down with a loud thud.

Lord Krishna, who had been watching the show with delight, deftly winked at Bheema showing him a leaf that he was tearing through the middle. Bheema took the message, and tore apart Jarasandha's body along the mid-rib and hurled the two sides away.

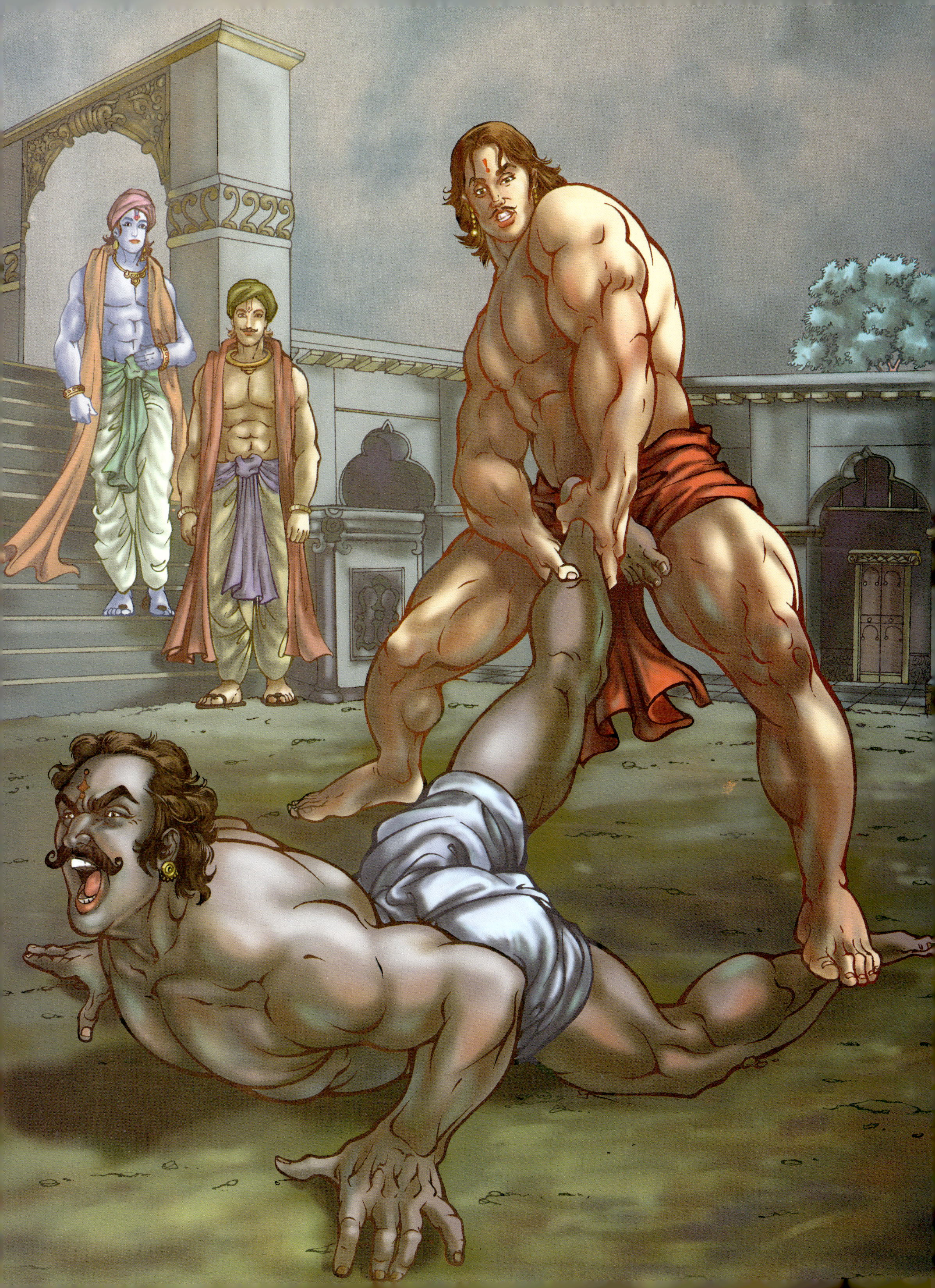

Bheema was too worked up to display happiness. But even before a jubilant Bheema could relish the taste of victory, Jarasandha stood there again, ready to face him. Bheema was shocked, and looked towards Krishna expecting further guidance. Lord Krishna indicated again with a leaf, to tear apart Jarasandha's body and throw each part away in the opposite direction. Bheema followed the instruction to the letter this time. He not only tore apart Jarasandha's body, but ensured that the two parts were flung in opposite directions. The dead body did not stir this time.

The crowd stood speechless as the cry of victory from Bheema boomed. Bheema, Arjuna and Krishna walked past the spectators while they split in a neat serpentine manner to make way for them. Walking down the palace dungeons, the first thing they did was to release the hapless kings.

The grateful kings, whose eyes dazzled in the bright light, were too keen and willing to be of any help they could be to the men who had rescued them. "How can we repay you?" they asked.

"By showing your allegiance to Yudhishthira," Krishna replied. "King Yudhishthira is going to perform Rajasuya Yajna. Offer no resistance when his army marches across, and consider yourself as having paid your debt."

Lord Krishna then formally crowned Sahadeva, son of Jarasandha, as king of Magadh. The young king lavished rich gifts upon the warriors as they were leaving for Indraprastha.

On reaching Indraprastha, Yudhishthira was informed about the success of their mission. Yudhishthira could now carry on the Rajasuya Yajna without the fear of resistance coming in his way.

Lord Krishna returned to Dwaraka, taking leave of Yudhishthira, who presented a beautiful chariot to Lord Krishna.

Conquering All Corners

A few precautions needed to be taken before the Yajna began. Some headstrong rulers, who could be a source of trouble, needed to be vanquished. A lot of funds were required to perform the Yajna. That needed to be taken care of as well. Sage Vyasa was chosen to preside over the affairs of the Yajna.

Arjuna was sent to conquer the northern rulers, Bheema to the east, Sahadeva to the south and Nakula to the west. Thus Yudhishthira's brothers, who rode out in all four directions, brought all kingdoms under their suzerainty. While many kings surrendered without a fight, a few succumbed after a fight.

The four brothers returned to Indraprastha, laden with tributes and promises of allegiance. The royal coffers overflowed and the kingdom grew strong. Cities prospered, herds multiplied, agriculture and trade flourished. There were no droughts, no crop failure, no plagues, no evil-doing. Indraprastha became a prosperous land of the virtuous people.

Friends and counsellors impressed upon Yudhishthira to begin the auspicious Rajasuya Yajna. At about the same time, Lord Krishna too reached Indraprastha, which enthused the Pandavas. Lord Krishna too favoured an imperial Yajna without delay.

Everyone set about the task of making preparations for the Yajna. Sahadeva was entrusted the task of extending invitations to learned brahmins and saints. Nakula was sent to Hastinapur to personally invite the Kuru elders and his cousins.

Kings and princes began pouring in. They brought rich gifts with them. The Kurus arrived in full strength. Yudhishthira entrusted his uncles and cousins with various tasks. Dushasana was put in charge of the banquet. Ashvathama was to wait on the brahmins. Vidura distributed gifts to the guests. Kripacharya was to see the performance of all the religious and sacred rituals.

Duryodhana was assigned the task of receiving the guests. Lord Krishna chose the humblest of all jobs — washing the feet of brahmins and saints. Karna was entrusted with the responsibility of making charities. Sage Dhaumya was given the seat of the chief priest at the Yajna.

The Sabha was full, lively and thriving. All arrangements having been completed, Yudhishthira inaugurated the Yajna amidst chanting of the sacred mantras and oblations of sacrificial butter into the fire. The Yajna was completed when Yudhishthira was anointed with holy water. The sacred chanting echoed till the final conclusion of the Yajna.

The kings, princes and the other participants were to be seen off with valuable gifts. Also, according to the ritual of the Yajna, *arghya* was to be offered to the participants.

Bhishma rose to address the newly anointed emperor. "Bharata, you must now offer *arghya* to all the guests here. Begin with the most deserving one."

Yudhishthira took a hurried glance at all the kings and monarchs, but stood indecisively. Sahadeva, the king of Magadh, stood up to propose the name of Lord Krishna as the most deserving one amongst a galaxy of luminaries. Bhishma and Dronacharya seconded the proposal in unison. A large number of other kings also followed suit.

Yudhishthira solemnly walked up to Krishna with all due humility and grace. Suddenly, someone laughed in the crowd and distracted the members of the Sabha. It was Shishupala, the king of Chedi and Lord Krishna's cousin. He was very jealous of Krishna's popularity. He could not tolerate the highest honour being bestowed upon Lord Krishna.

"Son of Pandu!" thundered Shishupala, "You may be unwise with the code of conduct, but Bhishma is not, and yet I wonder, what made him advise you to offer *arghya* to this cowherd. There are seniors and elders around. There are Kuru elders. Krishna's father Vasudeva is present here. Vyasa, Drupada, Bhishma himself are all far more deserving, and yet Krishna was offered the *arghya* first. What is the merit of this cowherd? He is bereft of both virtue and nobility. He had Jarasandha slain by treachery. Yudhishthira! We brought the tributes not because we fear you, but because we respect you as a gentleman."

Shishupala stood up and began stepping out of the Sabha, when Arjuna rushed and begged Shishupala not to leave in the manner he was doing.

"King of Chedi, it was Bhishma himself who thought Lord Krishna was the right candidate. Who are we to question his wisdom? Moreover, others also seconded his name. Even you wouldn't have objected to his name had you known him a little more intimately." Yudhishthira tried to appease the infuriated king.

Bhishma could not take the insult any longer. "Don't waste your time in appeasing a person who doesn't regard Krishna as virtuous and honourable. Nobody can deny that among the brahmins, the most learned person is worthy of being worshipped and among the kshatriyas, the most valiant one. On both these scales, Krishna surpasses everyone. He is not only a courageous man, but also the most learned one in the scriptures," explained Bhishma and went on to chastise Shishupala. "The decision to honour Krishna was not arrived at out of fancy. You are immature and capricious; you lack the grace or wisdom to cover your animosity. Leave the Sabha, if that suits you."

Shishupala was sufficiently enraged to cross all the bounds of civility and decency. He turned his ire towards Bhishma. "You are old, infirm, withered, soulless and impotent. Arrogance doesn't suit you. Why would you choose an undeserving cowherd for such an honour? So what if he killed a monstrous vulture and demoness Putana in his infancy and lifted mount Govardhana on his little finger? He is still a cowherd after all. As for you, you are witless, sick and imbecile! You remain celibate, not for nothing. Either you are stupid or impotent! It was Krishna who made Bheema and Arjuna refuse Jarasandha's hospitality and kill him by deception. You are unfit to offer any counsel!"

Bheema, the short tempered amongst the Pandavas, could hardly tolerate the rude monarch vilifying his grandfather. He rose to challenge Shishupala, but Krishna held him back. Shishupala was as oblivious to his fate as a moth is to a flame. Arrogance and stupidity clouded his reasoning. "Let him come!" he shouted, looking disdainfully at Bheema.

Bhishma's voice rose above the din, "Perhaps you do not know why you are still not dead! It's because Krishna's magnanimity compels him to forgive your faults. You were a deformed infant with an extra pair of arms. It was foretold that you would be killed by the same person who could make your extra arms drop off. They fell off when you went into your cousin Krishna's lap. Knowing him to be your annihilator, your mother asked him for a boon of one hundred pardons for you. No one has ever behaved with me the way you have done and lived to see the next day. Don't be rash, my child."

Reason had completely forsaken Shishupala. "If your hobby is to sing panegyrics, then you have incomparable warriors like Ashvathama, Drona and Jaidratha to praise. Why choose a vain cowherd?" He went on to challenge Krishna, "Come, Krishna! Come on, face me! The Pandavas are meek and naive. They do not know your real character — low-down, conniving, unscrupulous scoundrel!"

Krishna was a silent witness throughout the ugly quibbling. He rose up quiet and expressionless. "I never harmed Shishupala, but he lost no opportunity to harm me. I forgave him because he is my aunt's son. He went to the extent of burning down Dwaraka. I forgave that. He coveted my wife Rukmini. I overlooked that too. But today he has gone too far. I cannot pardon his mud-slinging," Krishna said.

Haughty Shishupala uttered an uproarious laugh. "You are shameless enough to admit I desired your wife. I don't need your pardon. Come on, let's see what you can do anyway."

Krishna meditated on his divine weapon, the discus, Sudarshan Chakra. In an instant, it appeared in his hand. He said, "Listen O kings, I had promised my aunt that I shall pardon a hundred sins of this wretch. That number is now up. I will now slay him in your presence!" With these words, he launched the discus and cut off the head of Shishupala in one stroke. From the slain body of the king of Chedi, a divine light rose and merged with Krishna.

[Shishupala was originally Vijaya, the gatekeeper at Vaikuntha, the abode of Lord Vishnu. As a result of the curse of some sages, he and his twin Jaya had to be born many times as mortals. They were offered the choice of having nine virtuous births or three sinful ones. Both chose the sinful births in order to be reunited faster with Lord Vishnu.]

Yudhishthira then commanded his brothers to perform the funeral rites of King Shishupala; his son was crowned the ruler of Chedi. The rest of the Vedic ritual went off without any problem. All the monarchs returned to their kingdoms, pleased at having witnessed the grand spectacle of the Yajna. After staying a while longer, Krishna also returned to his city of Dwaraka.

The Ill-fated Game of Dice

After the Rajasuya Yajna was completed, and honours bestowed on the visiting kings and queens, the guests left. However, Duryodhana chose to stay. Mesmerised by the wonderfully fascinating Sabha, he wandered around. Jealousy overcame wonder, and he bemoaned that Hastinapur didn't compare to the grandeur of Indraprastha.

Along with his maternal uncle Shakuni, he stayed in Indraprastha for quite some time. One day the duo was caught in a peculiar circumstance. Duryodhana, followed by Shakuni, came across a crystalline pool covered with the most exquisite lotuses. Drawing his garments fastidiously about his ankles, he carefully stepped into the pool only to realise it was but a plain and solid surface. He felt humiliated when the Pandavas laughed merrily at his confusion.

He found himself an object of jest once again few days later. Coming across a lake with fragrant lotuses, he eyed it suspiciously. He was not going to be fooled again. He stepped in confidently but fell in the water. This time again, Draupadi and the Pandavas giggled with amusement. Duryodhana's face contorted with rage.

One day he banged straight into a crystal door thinking it was a space in the wall. Draupadi, standing across a window, couldn't help remarking in amusement, "A blind son of a blind father." The pain of insult surged deeper in Duryodhana than the pain in his head. Yet another time he passed along a door, thinking it to be a wall, only to be led back to it by the amused Pandavas.

Duryodhana's self-esteem lay shattered. The more he pondered over the popularity, prosperity and success of the Pandavas, the more restless he became. The incidents at Indraprastha had only added to his ire. On returning to Hastinapur, he lost interest in everything else. He directed himself to the single most important purpose of his life — to cut the Pandavas to size.

His uncle Shakuni was his sole relative, with whom he could share his evil designs and venomous thoughts. Shakuni asked what was the matter with him, why he had lost interest in the beautiful things that life had to offer, and what made him worry. Duryodhana came out with a candid reply, "I cannot bear to see the prosperity of the Pandavas. They have been bestowed with celestial weapons and chariots. Their capital Indraprastha surpasses every other city in grandeur. When Shishupala was killed, not a king present in the assembly resisted them. But what rankles the most in my heart is their sarcastic laughter when I fell in the pool and banged my head against the wall. Kunti's sons have all the glory while Dhritarashtra's sons languish in oblivion. Is there any wonder that I have lost the zeal for life?"

"You have nothing to worry," reassured Shakuni, "Pandavas have got what they deserved. It is true that they won Draupadi. King Drupada and Krishna are their friends. But you have Drona, Karna, Kripa and me, and if you wish, you can conquer the earth. Fortune is on their side today, but who knows tomorrow it may turn on to your side!"

"I will have no rivals, if I defeat the Pandavas in a war," Duryodhana expressed his thought. "But that will never happen," he sulked.

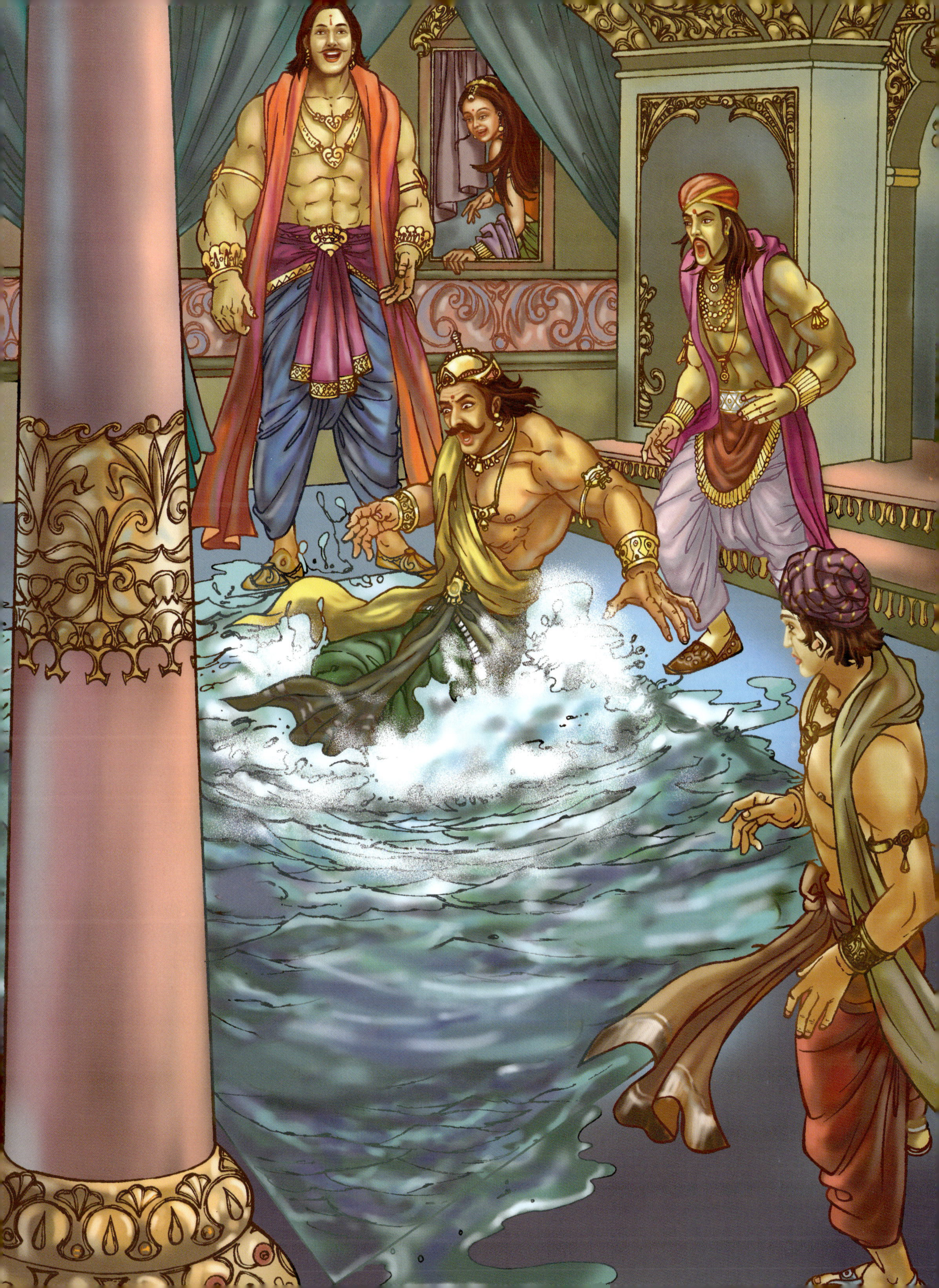

"Not perhaps in war, as they are mighty warriors," Shakuni's crafty mind was busy making dirty plots. "There are other ways to draw venom out of a snake. Yudhishthira is a compulsive gambler but a rotten player, while I am a master gambler. Invite him to the game of dice and he being a kshatriya won't be able to refuse the challenge. Once he agrees to the game, consider him having lost everything — kingdom, prosperity and peace. Invite him to the game on some ruse and the victory is yours, dear nephew."

"You take the king's permission, I don't have the courage," Duryodhana requested his maternal uncle.

Shakuni, finding an opportune moment when the king was alone, approached Dhritarashtra, "King of Bharata, how can you be so ignorant of the condition of your dear son, who is languishing? He neither eats, nor drinks, nor sleeps. Why don't you find out what's bothering him?"

As a concerned father, Dhritarashtra immediately rushed to Duryodhana's chamber. "What is this that I hear, dear son? What are you grieving for? What is bothering you? You have the best comforts of life. Anything you desire comes to you on a platter. Everyone loves you and your brothers obey your slightest command. Then what is it that is bothering you, my son?" asked Dhritarashtra.

"How can a man watch growing fortunes of his enemies helplessly?" Duryodhana spoke out his heart, "Kunti's sons have everything — fame, power, sovereignty, while I am languishing as an ordinary prince. The success of their Yajna made them the monarchs. The mightiest of kings and princes and the most learned brahmins and sages paid them their tribute in the costliest jewels and gold."

Shakuni bent over Duryodhana and spoke in a voice loud enough for Dhritarashtra to hear and low enough to ensure the secrecy of his game plan. "I can win everything from Kunti's sons for you. I can win their kingdom for you. I am the dice champion and know every little trick in the game that is there is to know. Yudhishthira loves this game but is a weak player. Invite him to the game and I'll lay all his possessions at your feet," boasted Shakuni meaningfully.

"Exactly, dear father. Invite Yudhishthira to the game of dice, if you want to see me happy and the Pandavas humbled. Everything they have will be ours," Duryodhana said with gusto.

Dhritarashtra vacillated. "I will have to consult Vidura first," he said as an afterthought.

"You will spoil all our plans, dear father. Vidura can never consent to it because he is not our well wisher. I'll kill myself before letting the Pandavas lord over me. You and they can very well enjoy your kingdom with Vidura over my dead body," protested Duryodhana.

"No my son, you will have your wish fulfilled," Dhritarashtra said, "I will have a magnificent Sabha constructed in Hastinapur, where I will invite Yudhishthira and his brothers for a game of dice."

However, Vidura came to know about the proposed game of dice. He met his brother and warned him against such a thoughtless adventure. "King of the Kurus, this decision of yours is neither wise nor in the interest of your son. It is bound to bring sorrow and misery," he said.

Dhritarashtra had a weakness for his son which clouded his vision. He proffered the flimsy, but ultimate argument, "It's all in God's hands. It's not in our power to change what is destined. There will be no violence if Gods don't will it. Bhishma, you, Drona and I will be present during the game and ensure that no ugly scene takes place there. Go to Indraprastha and convey to Yudhishthira my message that I have invited him and his brothers to Hastinapur."

Vidura thought over the matter painfully, knowing well that Dhritarashtra was too blind to reason. He made no further attempt to convince him.

As soon as Vidura left, Dhritarashtra sent for Duryodhana to try, one last time, to persuade him against the tactless endeavour he was bent upon. "Stay away from dice my son," he said, "it brings nothing but ultimate ruin. Vidura, the greatest authority on science of politics and ethics, foresees nothing but disaster at the end of it. You have everything. Why do you then envy Pandava's wealth?" Dhritarashtra asked.

Duryodhana was not prepared to listen to any reasoning. "I have nothing in comparison to the sons of Kunti. I know what I have and how much they have in their coffer. I saw the tributes brought by the kings. The Sabha built for them by Maya can rival Indra's palace. It's magnificent, full of wonders and illusions, floors that look like lakes, doors that look like walls, and walls that look like doors. I kept bumping here and there taken in by the illusion, and they kept laughing and mocking at me. I can still hear their laughter. I can never forget it. And you want me to suffer in silence and not even make an attempt to redeem my honour. I cannot rest in peace till I have taken away everything they have."

Dhritarashtra was shocked by the hatred and malice that his son exhibited towards the Pandavas. "Do not covet your cousin's prosperity, my son. You have as much wealth as Yudhishthira has. He doesn't covet what you have. If you persist in your ways, you will meet with nothing but disaster," Dhritarashtra tried to reason.

But reason had no impact on Duryodhana; his hatred ran too deep. "Discontent is the root of all progress and prosperity, therefore, I choose to be discontented," replied Duryodhana, "but more than anything else, you and I are tied to each other as father and son, and if you want to see me happy, you must go according to my wishes."

Dhritarashtra ultimately had to succumb to the demands of his son for a game of dice with the Pandavas. Vidura had been sent to Indraprastha to escort the Pandavas honourably to Hastinapur. Before leaving, Vidura made the last effort to dissuade the king from approving this game.

"Don't permit it," Vidura urged. But Dhritarashtra surrendered to the fate. "There will be no quarrel if fate doesn't will it. Leave everything to the will of God."

Vidura Reaches Indraprastha

Yudhishthira noticed the sullen face of Vidura. "What's the matter? Is everything all right in Hastinapur?" he asked.

"Yes, everything is well. The king has built a Sabha and has invited you to visit it. He has also invited you to a friendly game of dice," Vidura informed.

Yudhishthira immediately sensed trouble. "Game of dice always leads to conflict," he murmured, "but I will accept it, if the king has invited us."

"Gambling leads to nothing but misery my child. I tried to dissuade the king but he didn't listen to me.

"Who are the players, apart form Duryodhana?," asked Yudhishthira.

"Shakuni, Chitrasena and Jaya are some," Vidura replied.

"I sense trouble. All of them are seasoned players. I don't expect Shakuni to play a fair game. But I accept the challenge, if the king himself has demanded my presence," Yudhishthira spoke thoughtfully.

Vidura escorted the Pandavas, Kunti and Draupadi to Hastinapur. Pandu's sons greeted the king and the queen. They were led to the Sabha where the arrangements for the game had been made. The Kuru elders and the other kings seated themselves around the players. Yudhishthira and Shakuni sat facting each other while Shakuni held the dice.

"Shall we begin?" asked Shakuni, "Fix the stakes." Yudhishthira, who knew Shakuni well, remarked, "We are going to play a fair game, which excludes cheating and fraud."

"It's the dice that decides the game. A skilful player plays well — fair or unfair. All games are fair so long as unfairness is not detected. Don't digress. Fix the stakes."

Yudhishthira made a fruitless effort to control Shakuni's duplicity. "A sport is a sport only if evenly matched. That goes for gambling too. Even sworn enemies should not be duped or swindled, there's no honour in it. No one considers victory a victory, if achieved unfairly. You are welcome to defeat me Shakuni, but take care not to adopt unfair means."

Shakuni was the last person to pay heed to ethics and morality. "It is the end that decides the means. A game is played to be won and a more skilful player will always win," said Shakuni, adding, "you can quit if you don't want to play." Shakuni knew well that Yudhishthira wouldn't. In fact no kshatriya would, when it was the question of honour.

"I have never retreated in the face of a challenge," Yudhishthira declared, "I stake my treasury. What will you match that with?"

Duryodhana replied, "I have gold enough to match your treasury, but my Shakuni uncle will play for me."

Yudhishthira was alarmed, "Since when has the game of dice begun to be played by proxy? But if that's your wish, so be it."

Bhishma and Vidura got tensed up as they foresaw nothing but disaster awaiting the Kurus. Yudhishthira, wise enough to evaluate the consequences, had no option but to accept the challenge.

The Game Begins

Shakuni went on to win every throw as Yudhishthira went on losing everything he had —horses, chariots, elephants, palaces, villages, forests, cities, precious jewellery etc. Each time Shakuni won, Duryodhana let out a jubilant cry, "I have won."

Vidura, who was thoroughly alarmed, turned to Dhritarashtra, "Listen O king, it's my duty to remind you again. What Duryodhana is doing doesn't augur well for the Kuru clan. Unfortunately, you refuse to see the danger even though you are well aware of it. Chastise Duryodhana and win the Pandavas over. The wise condone the sacrifice of one to save a race. Why keep a crow when you have peacocks? I warn you, should there be a war, the Pandavas will win, and a war will definitely take place should this game of dice continue any further. And it will be no ordinary war."

Duryodhana, who overheard the conversation, fumed in anger, "You have always been partial to the Pandavas. You hate me. Kindly do what your duty expects you to do; which is, taking orders from your elders. Don't interfere in the affairs that do not concern you."

Vidura's advice had no impact on the Kauravas. Shakuni won everything that Yudhishthira put at stake. Having lost every material possession, the miserable, helpless Yudhishthira put Nakula, Sahadeva, Arjuna, Bheema and himself at stake. And he lost all of them, including himself.

"You are still not completely bankrupt," said Shakuni with a mischievous gleam in his eyes, "Stake the princess of Panchala, Draupadi, and who knows she might restore your luck back to you."

There was grim silence in the pavillion. Staking a wife was unknown and unheard of before. The Kuru elders watched it helplessly.

"I stake Draupadi," Yudhishthira said meekly. A murmur of protest rose, weak enough to subside as the Kuru elders Bhishma, Drona, and Kripa bowed their heads

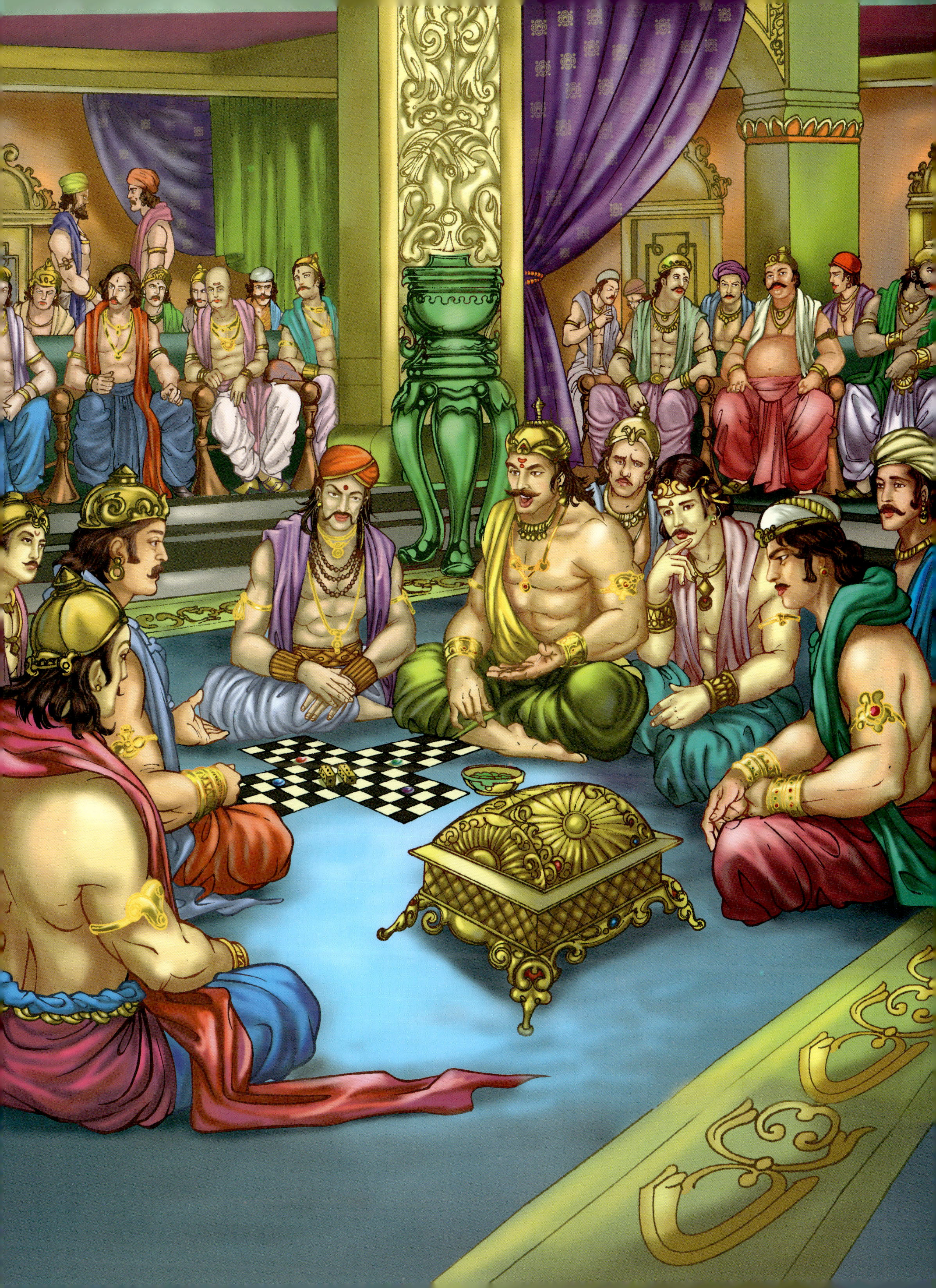

low in shame. Vidura was aghast and held his head low in his open palms. Karna and Dushasana laughed loudly.

"I have won Draupadi," announced Shakuni with malicious cheer. Karna, Duryodhana and Dushasana celebrated the announcement with a thunderous cheer.

"Bring the Pandavas' wife here. We have won her and she is our slave now," shouted Duryodhana to Vidura, who could visualise the impending doom and destruction awaiting the Kuru clan.

"Don't test the patience of the Pandavas. Draupadi can never be your slave. Yudhishthira lost himself first, before losing Draupadi. How can he lose Draupadi, when he was himself no longer his own master? Kunti's sons have always extended their hands of friendship to you. Take care not to invite their wrath. They are capable of defeating Indra and Varuna. This game wasn't played fairly. But why am I wasting words on you? It's futile," Vidura fumed.

Turning contemptuously, Duryodhana commanded a servant to fetch Draupadi. "And don't fear the Pandavas. They are as good as chained," thundered Duryodhana as he found him scared of the Pandavas.

The guard approached Draupadi in her chamber timidly and said, "I am here to take you to Duryodhana. Yudhishthira has lost you in the game of dice."

Draupadi flared in anger, "Go and ask that wretched man who lost his wife in dice, what right he had to stake his wife? Did he lose me or himself first?"

The servant came back shocked and scared. He timidly put the question, the answer to which was known to all. "Tell her to come here at once and ask whatever she has to," thundered Duryodhana, "Dushasana, go and get Draupadi here."

Dushasana swaggered boldly to Draupadi's chamber and commanded, "Come! You are lost to Pandavas. You are at our mercy and service now."

Draupadi was truly scared and ran towards Gandhari's chamber. Even before she could reach Gandhari and pray to her, Dushasana caught her by her hair and dragged her to Duryodhana. Draupadi begged and cried, but the heartless Dushasana remained unmoved, cursing her even as horrified Kaurava elders watched the spectacle in silence.

Draupadi looked around helplessly but the Pandavas and elders didn't have the courage to meet her eyes. "Has virtue left this land? Why is everyone silent?" she wailed, "Why are my husbands silent? How can Bhishma and Drona permit this sacrilege?"

Bheema restrained himself but cruel images of her tormentors — Dushasana, who called her a slave and dragged her by hair, Karna, who laughed aloud, and Duryodhana who looked on with malicious glee — remained vividly stamped in his memory.

Draupadi repeated her question. "O, great Kuru elders, answer me, what right did my husband have to stake me when he lost himself in the game of dice?"

No one answered. Bhishma dithered in reply, "I cannot really decide whether Draupadi has been won or not. If Yudhishthira, who is an incarnation of morality, has staked Draupadi in the game, what can the others say?"

Bheema could barely control his anger. "Staking one's wife is unheard of even amongst most hardened gamblers. Draupadi has been vilified and abused only because she has the misfortune to be our wife. I'll torch the hands that rolled the dice," Bheema thundered.

Arjuna restrained Bheema, "This is not the time to fret and fume, brother. Restrain yourself and be calm. Don't allow them to cause dissent amongst us. This is what they want. No kshatriya can refuse to play when invited and challenged."

Vikarna, one of Dhritarashtra's sons, had no bitterness towards the Pandavas. He protested. "Answer Draupadi's question," he addressed the Kuru elders who kept silent. "Listen then, to what I have to say. Not only Yudhishthira lost her after having lost himself but he had no right to stake her in the first place. She is not the exclusive wife of Yudhishthira, but the common wife of all the Pandavas. Therefore, the question of her being lost to Duryodhana is null and void." Vikarna's arguments fell on deaf ears.

Karna countered Vikarna saying Draupadi deserved no mercy since she had wedded five husbands which was against moral norms. She was not to be treated fairly and honourably for the very same reason. Turning to Dushasana, Karna commanded, "Strip the Pandavas and Draupadi of all royal garments."

Pandavas meekly took off their royal gear and ornaments. Dushasana held one end of Draupadi's garment and began pulling it. Draupadi cried out in helplessness, "O, Krishna where are you? Save me, can't you see how miserable I am?"

Dushasana who tugged her raiment brusquely, found himself pulling off Draupadi's garment endlessly even as a big pile had collected at the other end. He sweated but Draupadi was fully clothed as before. Dushasana sat down tired, while the amazing spectacle stupefied the Kauravas.

Nature expressed its fury. Thunder and lightning, howling jackals and screaming vultures broke the silence. A disembodied heavenly voice rumbled, "History will remember the gravest of sins committed in Hastinapur today. The Kaurava clan will regret its misdeeds. Get your hands off Draupadi or lightning will strike you."

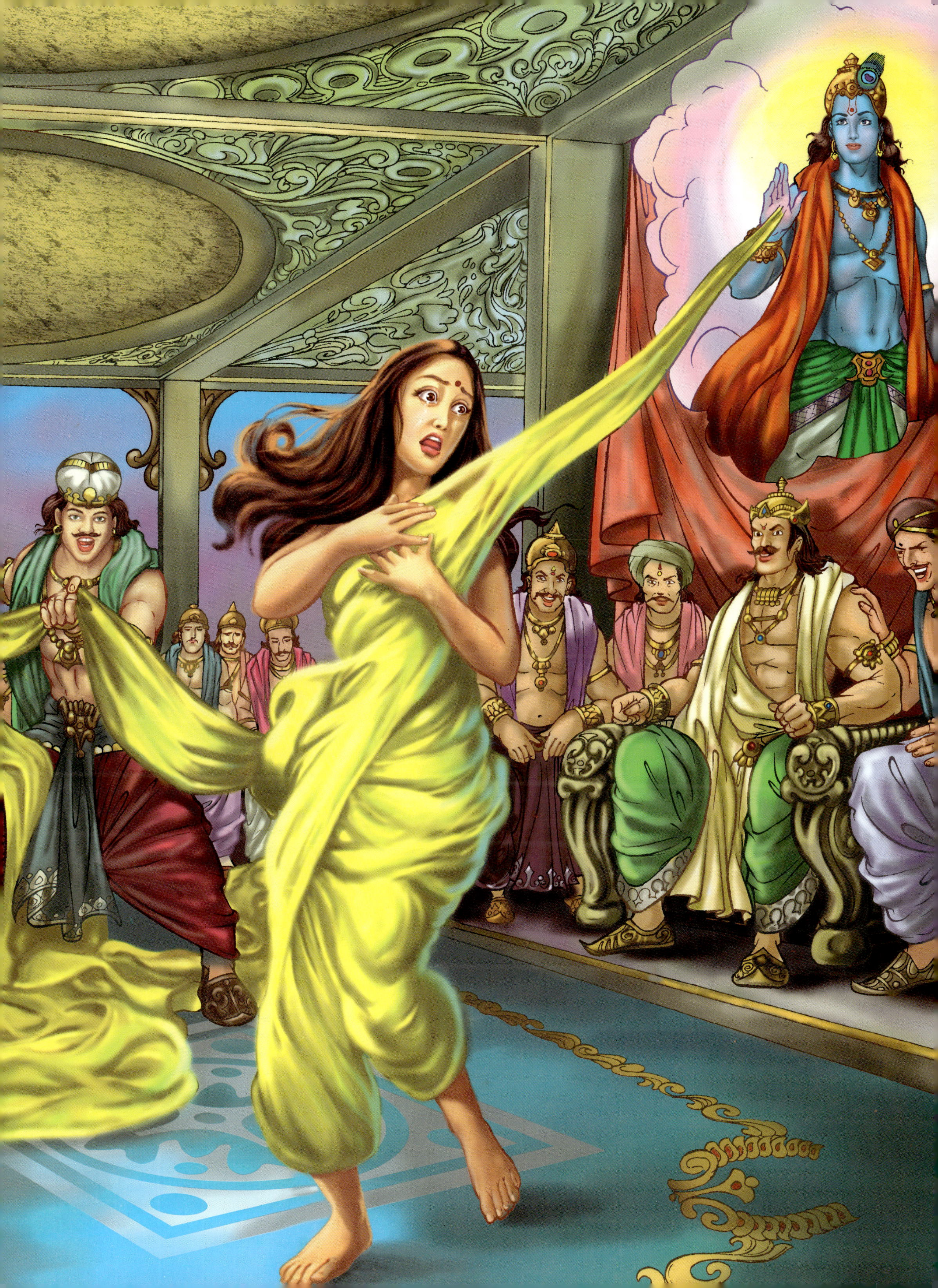

Dushasana, like a scared rat, scurried away to a corner. An incorrigible Duryodhana, looking lasciviously at Draupadi, jeered, "Come, sit here," pointing at his left thigh.

The lewd gesture was enough to enrage Bheema, who stood up and declared, "I, Bheema, son of Pandu, vow today in this assembly that I will know no peace till I break this thigh of yours with my mace. May I be bereft of heaven, if I fail to tear Dushasana's chest and wash Panchali's hair with his blood."

Bheema's vow stunned everyone present, for Bheema was known for keeping his vows. Gandhari too reached the assembly. She understood the grave calamity the Kurus had invited upon themselves. "Today's deeds will lead to havoc," she said to Dhritarashtra.

Draupadi Gets Her Husbands Freed

The blind king finally interceded, "What you are doing Duryodhana, is not fair. Panchali is innocent and pure. You will regret it." Then he said, addressing Draupadi, "Panchali, what has happened today should not have happened. Ask for a boon."

"Free Yudhishthira, the best of men, who has always been devoted to you," replied Draupadi.

"Ask for another boon," Dhritarashtra said, perhaps with the intent to undo the horrendous deed committed by his son.

"Free the other Pandavas," Draupadi replied.

"It will be as you wish," Dhritarashtra replied.

"Ask for the third one," Dhritarashtra was magnanimous.

"No, thank you, the best of kings. My husbands, who are free, will take care of all my needs," Draupadi said.

Karna jibed, "What brave kshatriyas! Owing their freedom to a woman!" These words were enough to rouse Bheema, who stood up bracing his muscles but Arjuna held him saying it was not the right time for action.

Then Yudhishthira stood, and slowly bowing to the king and the other elders said, "Let us know your command for us. Tell us and we shall obey."

"Go son, and rule peacefully. Forget whatever has happened today. You are wise and virtuous. The wise do not harbour animosity even against their foes. Be kind to elders. Duryodhana, as you know, is difficult to deal with. He is hardened and I do not expect him to change his ways," Dhritarashtra said.

The Pandavas headed for Indraprastha and were barely out of sight when the sons of Dhritarashtra demanded an audience with the king. "What have you done father?" They complained. "The wise men say enemies should never be pardoned, otherwise they emerge stronger and more vindictive. I saw Arjuna holding his Gandiva tight, and Bheema held his mace with grim determination. Do you think the sons of Pandu will not retaliate? They will be vindictive and will look for the slightest opportunity to avenge us." "Let us invite the sons of Pandu once more to the game of dice. This time, we shall put the condition that the loser will have to live in the forest for 12 years and another one-year incognito amongst people. If they are discovered in their 13th year, they will have to live another 12 years in the forest," Duryodhana proposed. Dushasana and he appeared to be really scared of the Pandavas. They were determined to get rid of them by any means.

"If they manage to complete their term in exile successfully, we will be in a position to not only face them but also defeat them. We will have sufficient time to strengthen our forces and forge stronger alliances," suggested Duryodhana to his father.

The logic appealed to Dhritarashtra. He summoned a messenger to bring back the Pandavas for a replay of the game of dice.

The king's decision met with a strong protest. Bhishma, Drona, Ashvathama, Vidura and the others strongly advised Dhritarashtra against his thoughtless decision. Even the queen reminded the king of the prophecy of doom to be brought by the action of their son Duryodhana. But Dhritarashtra remained undeterred. Like his son Duryodhana, he too was mortally afraid of the sons of Pandu, as also jealous of their prosperity. Therefore, the wise words of Gandhari had little impact on the baser instincts of Dhritarashtra. "If the doom of Kuru clan is foretold, there's little I can do about it," he said adamantly.

The Game is Played Again

When the approaching messenger stopped Yudhishthira to convey Dhritarashtra's message, the wise Yudhishthira smiled. He knew there was little he could do to alter the fate. The kshatriya code of not refusing an invitation or challenge, closed all options for him. He had no option but to play the game once again.

"Dhritarashtra gave you back everything you lost. But the stakes will be different this time. The loser will go into an exile in the forest for 12 years and will remain incognito in an inhabited territory in his 13th year. If spotted in the 13th year, he will have to go to the forest once again for 12 years. Otherwise, at the end of the 13th year, the victor returns the loser's kingdom. If you want, you can decline to play even now," Shakuni smiled mischievously.

"No, I won't. I am a kshatriya," Yudhishthira said.

The outcome of the game was as expected. Yudhishthira lost to the clever tricks of Shakuni. The Pandavas were divested of their royal robes and honour. They were ready to embark now for the exile.

"Duryodhana is the sovereign king now. The sons of Pandu laughed at us in Indraprastha. It's our turn to laugh now," said Dushasana caustically and turning to Draupadi, passed a lewd remark, "Leave these mendicant husbands of yours and choose one amongst us. You'll be happier."

The remark didn't go unnoticed to Bheema, who roared, "Say what you want now. The score of the rigged game will be evened when I rip apart your chest and kill all of Dhritarashtra's sons." Then turning to Duryodhana, who was parodying his walk as he exited, Bheema spoke sternly, "The day is not far when Arjuna will kill Karna, Sahadeva will kill Shakuni and, I will break your left thigh before crushing your head. Dushasana too will not meet a better fate, when I will tear apart his chest to wash Panchali's hair with his blood."

Pandavas Are Off For a Thirteen-year Exile

The Pandavas were ready to depart to the forest, having surrendered their throne and royal robes. Panchali let her hair loose, vowing not to tie it till she washed it with Dushasana's blood. She followed the Pandavas to the forest.

Vidura had requested that Kunti be permitted to stay with him. So, she stayed back at Vidura's house, while Subhadra, Abhimanyu and the five sons of Draupadi went to Dwaraka to stay with Krishna.

People ran in the streets weeping that their protectors were leaving. They blamed Dhritarashtra and his greedy sons for their misfortune.

Soon after the Pandavas left, sage Narada appeared in Dhritarashtra's chamber and said, "Listen O, king. I am here to pronounce your doom. Fourteen years from now, the Kauravas will perish at the hands of Pandavas." The sage vanished soon after declaring the prophecy.

Duryodhana, Shakuni and Karna were really afraid of the consequences that might befall them, and rushed to the protection of Dronacharya, and sought an assurance that should a calamity come, guru Drona must stand as an armour for them. Drona consented to their request, only because he was employed in their court, otherwise he said he had no inclination to stand in their favour.

As Pandavas left Hastinapur, hordes of wailing citizens followed them, refusing to let them go to exile alone.

Most of the citizens returned, but a group of brahmins and ascetics insisted on being with them. They refused to relent and spent their first night under a large banyan tree by the bank of river Ganga along with the five Pandavas. The next day, Yudhishthira spoke out his worry to his family priest Dhaumya. "We have no kingdom nor any resources. Tell me how would I be able to feed these brahmins in the forest, when we ourselves don't know where to get our meals from?"

"Propitiate the Sun God, the bounteous giver of all food and nourisher to everyone. I will teach you the appropriate mantra to invoke the Sun God," said Dhaumya and taught him the mantra.

Yudhishthira did as instructed by Dhaumya and Surya deva, the Sun God, appeared before him. "Take this *akshaya patra*," said the Sun God, holding out a copper vessel to him, "It will feed as many people as are present at a meal and will never exhaust till Draupadi has had her meal."

The most pressing problem having been taken care of, the Pandavas made their way to Kamyaka Vana, a forest thriving with animals and scenic beauty.

While on their way to Kamyaka forest, the Pandavas met with their first resistance in the form of Kirmira, a demon, who was the terror of the forest. "Hold on! Who are you? What are you doing here in my territory?" Kirmira thundered.

"I am Yudhishthira, son of Pandu, and the other four are my younger brothers. The lady here is our wife," Yudhishthira replied calmly.

"I am Kirmira, Vakasura's brother. I will not leave you. I know Bheema had killed Vakasura and also Hidimb, brother of Hidimba."

Bheema braced up his muscles, stopped ahead and challenged Kirmira, "Wait, I will send you to the abode of Yama as I sent your brother and Hidimb."

Soon, the two entangled and began fighting ferociously. Bheema, finding the right opportunity, uprooted a huge trunk and flung it at the demon with all his might. The demon crashed to the ground and even before he could recover, Bheema strangulated Kirmira to death.

The Pandavas' exile was a news that rippled through every corner. The Bhojas, Vrishnis, Panchalas, Chedis and Kekayas all came to Kamyaka in strength to offer their unconditional support to Yudhishthira.

Krishna too came to see him and was roused with anger when Draupadi wept bitterly complaining to him how she had been humiliated in presence of everyone by Dushasana, Duryodhana and Karna. She asked what was the use of her five warrior husbands and of her sons, father and brother when none came to rescue her in her hour of indignity?

Krishna consoled her, "The ones who have insulted you will weep more than you. The earth will drink the blood of Duryodhana, Karna, Dushasana and Shakuni. It all happened because I was away fighting King Shalva. But I assure you, my promise is not hollow. You will regain your rank and honour. Yudhishthira will be the sovereign king."

After the guests departed, Yudhishthira, still worried about a proper place to inhabit in the forest, sought Arjuna's advice on the matter. "Dvaitavana," suggested Arjuna, "is the ideal place, with a fresh water lake and woods around it."

The Pandavas headed for the Dvaitavana. They found it more charming than Arjuna's description. But the humiliation meted out to them by Duryodhana was difficult to forget. Sage Vyasa made a sudden entrance in their cottage and the Pandavas humbly touched his feet.

"I am here to advise you to be patient. You would be victorious in the war that will follow and Arjuna will slay the foes. But before that happens, Arjuna must go to Mount Mahendra and procure the celestial weapons of Shiva, Varuna, Kubera and the other Gods. He will need them in the war that follows," spoke sage Vyasa gently and vanished.

Yudhishthira told Arjuna to do as the sage had advised him, for Bhishma, Drona, Kripa and Karna were great warriors who could not be defeated without celestial weapons.

Arjuna did as he was commanded. He went north, crossed the Himavat and plunged deep into the mountains till he reached Indrakuta. Arjuna had obtained an incantation called Pratismriti from Yudhishthira, who had got it earlier from sage Vyasa. It could help him see what was happening and where.

Arjuna was tired. He sat down to rest when he heard a voice, "Stay where you are. Who are you and why do you come here armed? You are in the retreat of holy sages. What use do you have of the arms? Throw them away!" Arjuna turned and saw an old sage with matted locks commanding him authoritatively.

Arjuna stood still but gripped his Gandiva even more tightly, reluctant to surrender his arms. The sage smiled. "I am Indra, my child. I know why you have come here. Ask me for a boon."

Arjuna bowed low with palms joined and said, "Give me the knowledge of weapons and warfare."

"All right, I will grant you your request, but you will have to first appease Lord Shiva and get a boon from him. Go to mount Kailash, my child, and invoke Maheshwara. See Shiva first and then come to me," Indra said to Arjuna.

Arjuna, as advised by Indra, immersed himself in severest penances. His penance turned out to be so severe as to scorch the earth and shudder the three worlds. The sages and Gods were scared. They ran to the trident bearing, three-eyed God, Lord Shiva and complained, "Lord! Do something. A man has trespassed into our territory and shaken the world. Grant him his wishes or the world will crash."

"Don't worry. I know why he is here," Lord Shiva assured them.

Shiva Comes to Meet Arjuna

One day as Arjuna was lost in deep meditation, he suddenly became aware of a great boar charging at him ferociously. In a split second, he strung his Gandiva and was about to release the arrow when he noticed a hunter at the other end aiming at the same boar.

"The boar is mine," claimed the hunter in a loud voice as he released his arrow. Arjuna paid little heed to the hunter before releasing his own arrow. The two sharp and swift shafts instantly stuck deep into the fleshy boar, wounding it fatally. The beast lay dead.

Taking his eyes off the dead beast, Arjuna noticed a jubilant hunter dancing in joy at his success. "Who are you? What makes you think, you killed the boar. The prey is mine. I killed it. Get out of my way or I will ensure the same fate for you," Arjuna was sharp and bitter.

The hunter was amused. "The boar is mine. My shaft killed it. You should be thankful to me. Had I not intervened in time, the deadly beast might have killed you. It's no ordinary boar. It's the demon, Muka in disguise. But why are you here? It appears you are not accustomed to the harsh life of this place. You say, you will kill me. Try it," the hunter smiled in a mocking tone.

Arjuna shot a volley of arrows at the hunter, who had them split in mid air as if it was a child's play. Arjuna was stupefied. Arrows released from Gandiva had never failed to hit their target. Only Lord Shiva could deflect those powerful arrows. Arjuna was puzzled, yet he shot the powerful volley of arrows which clouded the sky and raised a dust storm. The hunter remained unharmed and smiling. The arrows released from Gandiva could not so much as make a scratch on his body.

An infuriated Arjuna was determined to send the hunter to Yama's court. Reaching out for another arrow, he found his inexhaustible quiver empty. Not ready to give up easily, he rushed to the hunter with a sword in his hand, throwing aside the Gandiva. The sword struck the hunter's head without even a 'thud' sound. Arjuna had expected the hunter's head to split into two. Arjuna flung his sword in disgust and rushed at him for a hand-to-hand combat, only to find himself pinned to the ground.

The smiling hunter taunted, "You appear to be quite tired and defeated. Over-confidence is a vice that fools harbour. Bravery calls for politeness, not haughtiness. You are still a baby in the art of archery. Go and play with your toys."

His utter defeat at the hands of an ordinary hunter had already bruised his ego. The taunts added to his insult. "Wait a while! Let me pray to Lord Shiva and I shall tell you what I can do with my Gandiva!"

Crouching down where he stood, he made a Shiva-linga out of sand and invoked the Lord. He collected some wild flowers, wove them into a garland and put it around the Shiva-linga. Next he joined his palms and closed his eyes in devotion to the Lord. As he opened his eyes, he found the garland not on Shiva-linga but around the hunter's neck.

Arjuna quickly lay down prostrate at the feet of the hunter, who was in fact Lord Shiva himself. Arjuna felt lucky, blessed and remorseful at the same time.

Shiva raised Arjuna and gave him the deadliest of weapons, Pashupata and explained how it was to be used. Before departing, Lord Shiva assured Arjuna of more such divine weapons through various other Gods, including Indra.

Soon after Shiva left, the other Gods, including Varuna, Kubera and Yama, arrived to offer Arjuna their weapons and taught him the appropriate mantras to empower them.

The Years in Exile

When Shiva, in the guise of a hunter, left, Varuna, Kubera along with Yakshas and Yama came to visit Arjuna. Yama, the Death God, blessed Arjuna, "We have our divine weapons and divine sight to offer you. Our boon will successfully see you through the most powerful kshatriya warriors like Bhishma, and other powerful beings as vicious demons," Yama told Arjuna. Then Varuna gave Arjuna the Varunapash, Yama gave him Dandastra, and Kubera offered him Dutardhanastra.

Indra, happy to find his son having fulfilled the condition he had put before him, dispatched his charioteer Malati to invite Arjuna to Amaravati.

"I am here to take you to Amaravati," Malati said to Arjuna.

Arjuna happily sat in the chariot, not forgetting to take all the celestial weapons given to him. As the chariot rose swiftly in the sky, Arjuna noticed with amazement the stars that grew enormous. The sky appeared endlessly black. Arjuna was wonder-struck at the lighted lamp-like huge stars which appeared so small and twinkling from the earth. Streaming past skies, he finally arrived at Indra's heaven.

A large number of gods, demi-gods, nymphs and saints were waiting at the gates of heaven to accord a rousing welcome to Arjuna. He saw Airawata, Indra's elephant. He was also taken for a tour of Indra's palace, and he immersed himself in blissful joy at the sight of charming nymphs strolling in the pleasure garden.

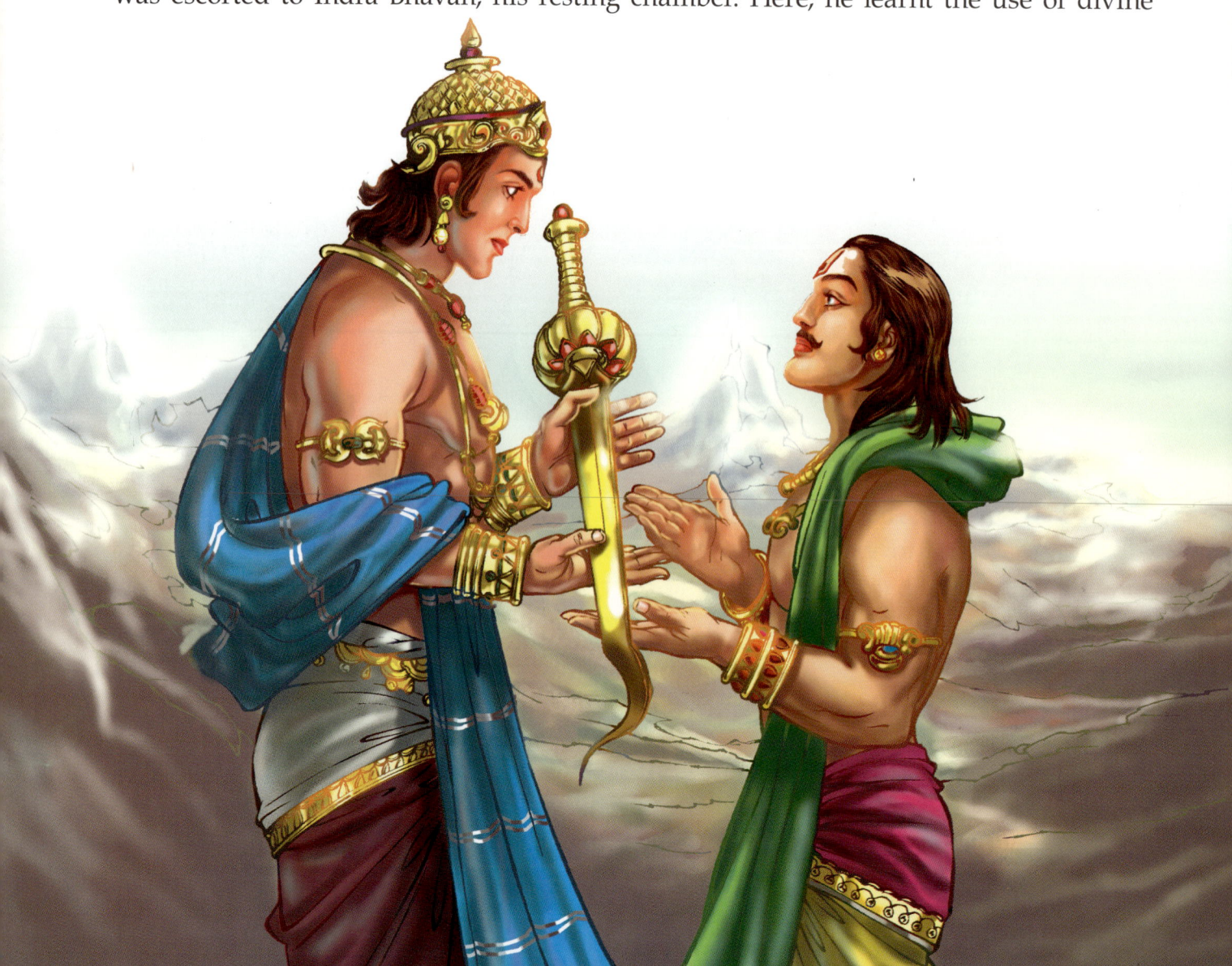

Arjuna was then led to Indra's court, where he was offered a high seat. The Gandharvas played melodious tunes to honour Arjuna, while the nymphs danced. Finally Arjuna was escorted to Indra Bhavan, his resting chamber. Here, he learnt the use of divine weapons obtained from the gods. He was quick to learn the use of Vajrastra, the weapon that produced mighty thunder accompanied by dark, swollen clouds.

When Arjuna expressed his desire to go back, his heavenly father Indra insisted on him spending some more time there and making the best of the heavenly resources. Indra said, "Chitrasena, the Gandharva chief, is here. He will teach you music and dance, which will be useful to you later."

One evening Arjuna was overawed by the beauty of Urvashi, as she danced in Indra's court. He stared at her, wide eyed, mesmerised by her beauty, or so it appeared to Indra, who noticed Arjuna staring at her.

Indra called Chitrasena aside and instructed him to arrange a meeting of his son with Urvashi. To Urvashi he said, "I want my son to taste all joys of heaven. Teach him your art. Go and please him."

Urvashi's Curse

Urvashi was just too happy. She welcomed Indra's instructions with open arms. She anointed her body with the best of scents, braided her hair with fragrant flowers, and draped herself in shining jewellery and best silks. Walking in a measured gait, she entered Arjuna's chamber. He stood up and bowed to her as he would do to an elderly lady.

Urvashi smiled. "Indra has commanded me to be with you for the night."

Arjuna was embarrassed to the core. He bowed once again humbly, palms joined in reverence, "You are like my mother Kunti, Madri or Sachi. I stared because I saw the mother of my ancestors in you. Your sons by Pururva are my ancestors."

"I am an Apsara, unfettered by the laws of worldly men," said Urvashi, "I enjoy an everlasting youth and I choose my men according to my fancy."

Arjuna bowed to Urvashi a third time with utmost honour and dignity reserved for his own mother Kunti. He touched her feet and said, "I am only your humble son. I touch your feet."

Urvashi turned cold, shocked and furious. Her lips trembled in rage. Without a moment's thought she inflicted a terrible curse on Arjuna, son of Indra. "You have spurned me — me who was never spurned before. So you will be robbed of your manhood. You will become an eunuch!" She left Arjuna's chamber instantly after pronouncing her curse.

The curse was unbearable for Arjuna and he panicked. He told Chitrasena all that had happened, with a sad face. Chitrasena reassured Arjuna and brought the incident to the notice of Indra.

Indra rejoiced and informed Arjuna that he was lucky to be cursed. It was a blessing in disguise which would be useful in the thirteenth year of his disguised exile, when no one would expect him to be a eunuch. What better disguise could there be?

"The curse will last for a year, at the end of which, you will regain your manhood," Indra informed Arjuna.

It was five long years since Arjuna had been away in search of divine weapons. There was no news of him, causing much anxiety to Yudhishthira and the other Pandavas. Draupadi too was worried for him.

About the same time, Krishna arrived in Kamyaka, knowing the Pandavas would be worried about Arjuna's long absence. The Pandavas were quite thrilled with the visit of Krishna. Bheema thought it as the best opportunity to convince Yudhishthira to declare war on Kauravas. "The Vedas say that for a man performing a severe penance, a day is more than thirteen years," argued Bheema,"We are kshatriyas. War is our creed, and to deal wickedly with wicked is no crime. Krishna and Drupada will back us any time. It is the right time now to declare war on Kauravas."

Yudhishthira said, "I know you and Arjuna together are capable of sending the Kauravas to the abode of death. But we have to wait for the right time. I have given them my word. Now do you want me to go back on my word?" Yudhishthira tried to pacify Bheema.

Krishna returned to Dwaraka after being convinced that the four Pandavas and Draupadi had settled down well in the Kamyaka forest.

One day Lomash rishi arrived at the Pandava's retreat in Kamyaka. Yudhishthira and his brothers greeted the rishi showing him all courtesy. Lomash rishi disclosed the news of Arjuna's arrival in Amaravati, to the surprise and happiness of Yudhishthira, his brothers and Draupadi.

"I had an opportunity to be in Amaravati, and had the pleasure of seeing Arjuna, sharing his father Indra's throne. He is the fortunate one amongst warriors to have obtained the mightiest of weapons, Pashupatastra, directly from Lord Shiva. Besides, his armoury is brimming with an array of weapons received from the best of Gods as Yama, Kubera, Varuna, and the king of Gods Yama himself. Arms apart, he is mastering the finest skills in music and dance under the tutelage of Chitrasena, the chief amongst the Gandharvas."

The news exhilarated Yudhishthira, the younger siblings, and Draupadi. The air of unease hanging over them disappeared. They decided to go on a holy pilgrimage, accompanied by Sage Lomash.

When they arrived at Prabhasa near Dwaraka, Krishna and his entire Vrishni clan came to welcome them. Krishna, Balarama and Satyaki were touched by their sorry plight. Balarama was moved to remark that virtue was no good as Yudhishthira, the most virtuous amongst men had his hair matted, body wasted and clothes in tatters, while Duryodhana, reputed for his evil ways, enjoyed the pleasures of life as the crown prince of Hastinapur.

Satyaki volunteered to attack Kauravas and do justice to the Pandavas, but Yudhishthira restrained him. The Vrishnis returned, while Yudhishthira promised them to meet in better times.

Yudhishthira and his brothers as well as Draupadi, led by Lomash rishi, reached Badrikashrama. They decided to rest there for some time, before proceeding to the higher mountain ranges leading to Mount Kailash.

One day while at Badrikashrama, Draupadi was lost in the breathtaking panoramic beauty of the mountain vale, enjoying the cool north-westerly wind, when a resplendent lotus flower dropped near her. Draupadi was startled by its beauty and sweet fragrance. She was so bewitched by the divine flower that she could not resist requesting Bheema to get her more such flowers.

Bheema went on and on in search of the flowers. Finally his desperate search brought him to Gandhamadana mountain, whose charms compelled Bheema to wonder in amazement. He searched every nook and cranny of Gandhamadana, but the divine lotus eluded him. Irritation was now getting better of him and he roared furiously. The beasts and birds screeched in panic.

Bheema, who was tired now, jumped into a cool, refreshing lake and bathed to invigorate himself. He began a more determined search, this time along the narrow lanes and serpentine foot trails. He darted along the trail till abruptly stopped by the limpid tail of a frail old monkey in his way.

Bheema stomped his mighty foot to move the old monkey out of his slumber, which went unheeded. An enraged Bheema shouted, "Get out of my way, you fool!" The old monkey responded in a feeble voice, "Being old and ailing, I am worn out of energy to move my tail. Be gracious and move it so as to make your way."

"All right, I'll do as you wish," Bheema said in a huff and briskly attempted to shrug the tail off his way. To his horror and surprise, the tail stood firm, almost rock-like, in its place. Now Bheema used both his hands to move the tail but it refused to budge. Bheema heaved and panted but the tail remained plastered to the ground.

Bheema bowed respectfully to the old monkey with palms joined in reverence, "You are no ordinary monkey! Tell me who are you and be kind to me. Forgive me if I have offended you in any manner," Bheema requested humbly.

"I am Hanumana, devotee of Lord Rama and son of the Wind God. I was here just to relax for a while," the monkey said. Saying so, the son of wind came to his original gigantic form.

Bheema once again bowed in humble reverence to Hanumana even as he looked up in wonder at his mammoth form. He felt happy and thrilled at the experience. "You are my young brother, being the son of Wind God yourself," said Hanumana and embraced Bheema.

Bheema, with his eyes moistened with joy, touched the feet of Lord Hanumana, his elder brother. "I am here to help you in your war against the Kauravas. I will be seated on the top of Arjuna's chariot and bless the Pandava forces guiding them to victory," Hanumana offered his unconditional help.

The offer cheered Bheema. "I could not have asked for anything more. I am delighted and lucky to receive the honour from you. Your assurance makes me confident now, that we shall be victorious over wicked Duryodhana," Bheema spoke respectfully with joined palms and requested Hanumana to direct him to the spot where he could find the flowers he was looking for. Hanumana directed him to Mount Sangandhika, on which stood the verdant, evergreen garden of Lord Kubera, where these flowers could be found in abundance.

Bheema arrived at the garden of Mount Sangandhika as directed, and found it lush with the lotuses as described, in a beautiful lake. As he approached the lake, he was stopped by a horde of Kubera's armed guards. Bheema tried to appease them with his mild manners and words indicating he meant no harm to them, but just needed the flowers.

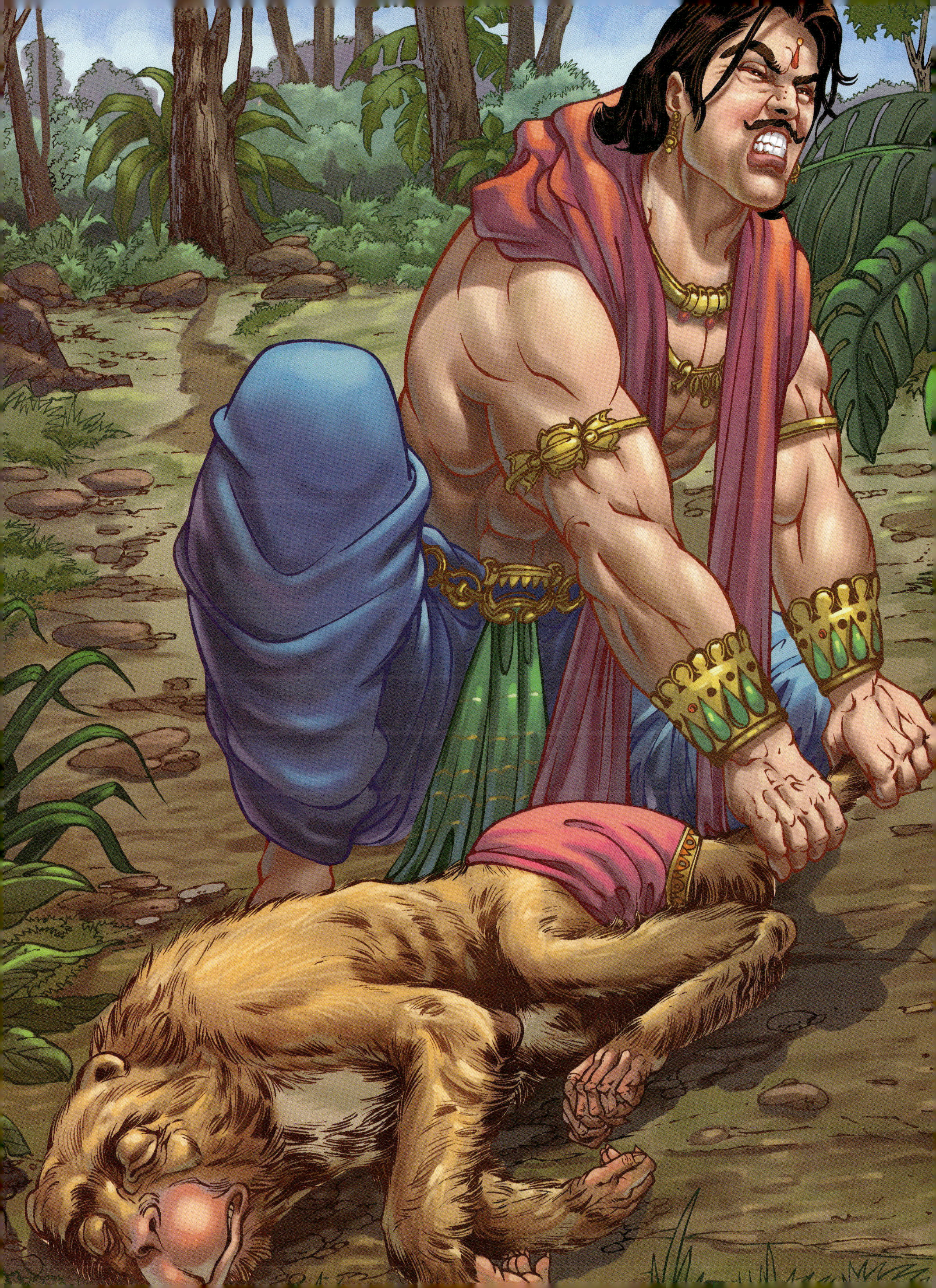

The arrogant army of guards not only rebuked Bheema in harsh words but threatened him with dire consequences. The mighty son of wind, who had restrained himself so long, lost his temper and pounded the armed guards with his mace in retaliation as they attacked him. The guards ran for their life to Kubera, who aware of Bheema's prowess, commanded them to let him have the flowers and also apologise to him.

Bheema came back victorious with a handful of lotus flowers. Draupadi was thrilled to have those flowers. She presented them to the eldest Pandava, Yudhishthira, who felt proud and honoured.

Arjuna's return was imminent. The Pandavas had promised to meet him at Mount Gandhamadana. The trek was difficult. Bheema took upon himself the responsibility to carry Panchali on his shoulders. On their way to the mountain, there was a raging storm. When the storm subsided, they began their journey once again. Barely two miles later, Draupadi collapsed with exhaustion. She quivered and lay unconscious.

Bheema called Ghatotkacha. The mighty son of Bheema offered to carry not just Draupadi but all of them to the mountain peak. In an instant, he flew upwards carrying them all to the mountain top, alighting at the hermitage of Sage Narada and Narayana. He set them down gently. They waited for Arjuna there.

One day the Pandavas were wondering how much more they would have to wait for Arjuna to arrive, when they saw a radiant chariot zoom past in the sky. The glowing chariot driven by a hundred divine horses landed at the mountain top. They discovered to their joy, Arjuna, crowned, jewelled and in princely raiment, alighting from the chariot.

Arjuna touched Dhaumya's feet first, followed by those of his elder brothers. The twins, Nakula and Sahadeva, touched Arjuna's feet. All of them rejoiced his arrival. Arjuna was quite enthusiastic about the celestial weapons he had brought. He showed them to Yudhishthira and was about to demonstrate their use out of excitement when Narada appeared.

He rushed to Arjuna and held his hand. "Stop," the great rishi said, "do not use the weapons unless absolutely necessary. Your one wrong move can destroy the three worlds." After Narada's warning, Arjuna always remained careful in using his weapons.

One day, during the course of their pilgrimage, Bheema entered a mountain cave looking for food. A huge, ferocious python sitting at the mouth of the cave attacked Bheema and held him in its powerful coils. Bheema found himself completely helpless. "Who are you and why have you gripped me in your coils?" Bheema asked and introduced himself, "I am Bheema, son of Pandu of Kuruvansha."

The python said, "I am King Nahusha, one of your great ancestors. I am suffering the curse uttered by Sage Agastya, who changed me into a python, for the blunder of insulting brahmins. And I will swallow you unless you answer my questions correctly."

When Bheema did not come back after a long time, Yudhishthira got worried for him. He went along with Dhaumya looking for him. Finally they arrived at the cave where Bheema was still in the deadly grip of the python. Yudhishthira answered all the questions of the python and got Bheema freed. The python too, was relieved of its curse. It assumed its divine form and proceeded to heaven.

Back in Hastinapur, Dhritarashtra was constantly assailed by the pangs of guilt. He feared the impending doom and the fate of his sons. However, Duryodhana, Shakuni and the Kauravas seemed oblivious of the danger that lay ahead.

Shakuni overheard a group of brahmins complaining to Dhritarashtra about the miserable life the Pandavas were leading in the forest. The king felt sorry for them and tears welled up in his eyes.

But Shakuni rushed to Duryodhana. "I hear the Pandavas are in Dvaitavana. Wouldn't you like to visit them in all your glory and splendour, while they are in rags?" asked Shakuni, smiling at Duryodhana.

Duryodhana liked the suggestion but said, "I doubt I would be given permission to go to Dvaitavana. The king still regrets the decision to permit that game. He constantly rants and raves. He would not like to see any confrontation between us."

Karna, ever devoted to Duryodhana's cause, suggested, "I know how we can get the permission. Our cattle herds are grazing near the lake. Our cattle stations are in frequent need of repair. We shall be given permission to inspect the cattle stations, and for branding the calves."

Karna's suggestion appealed to everyone. A cowherd, incited by Duryodhana, made his entry to the court and said to the king, "The calves have to be branded and head count made of the three-year-olds. The presence of the princes, therefore, is requested. Moreover, in this season the forest abounds in game. The princes will have a nice time."

The king disapproved the plan. "I have heard the Pandavas are in Dvaitavana. I do not want any fracas between cousins. You will have a small armed contingent with you, but the Pandavas are extremely powerful and I fear for your safety."

Shakuni interrupted, "Yudhishthira will never permit his brothers to take to violence. His word is law." Dhritarashtra, very grudgingly permitted his sons to do as they wished.

Duryodhana Rescued by The Pandavas

The Kauravas arrived in Dvaitavana in full royal glory. Chariots, cavalry, cooks, servants and attendants in tow, they were planning to have a really gala time. The evenings saw Kauravas dining, feasting and carousing to the tunes of musical instruments.

One day, Duryodhana walked leisurely to the nearby lake where he had planned a sumptuous feast. The royal ladies and the attendants had gone there ahead of him. He had visions of the miserable Pandavas in contrast to his own glory. On the way, he was stopped by the Gandharva guards.

"You cannot go beyond," the guards said, "King Chitrasena is here with his ladies. No one can enter these precincts."

Duryodhana, not accustomed to taking orders, bluntly told them get out of his way. Chitrasena's men were still polite to him and requested him not to cross the bounds. Duryodhana became aggressive and commanded his attendants to mobilise his forces. "I want these Gandharvas out of this place," he commanded his men.

The Gandharvas were amused by the impotent rage of Duryodhana. "Ask your foolish king to restrain himself. Gandharvas are not his vassals. One wrong step will see him gracing the Yama's court," the Gandharvas warned his men.

The two forces clashed the next instant. Bodies fell as the cries of pain and terror echoed in the woods. The Kauravas' initial attack was swift and heavy. It broke the Gandharvas' rank. But soon Chitrasena himself arrived and rallied his men to action once again with doubled vigour. Chitrasena used Sammohanastra, and made them motionless. Even Karna could not face them and fled away in Vikarna's chariot after his own chariot was destroyed. Duryodhana fought bravely but the Gandharvas overpowered him and took him to Chitrasena. His men made the Kaurava ladies captive.

Some of the Kaurava men, who eluded capture, rushed to the Pandavas for help. War-weary and bleeding with battle wounds, they bowed before Yudhishthira with joined palms, "We are here to seek your help. Duryodhana, along with the royal household ladies has been taken captive by Chitrasena, the Gandharva king."

Yudhishthira was moved by their plight. He asked Bheema to go and help his cousins, but Bheema was delighted at their condition. He laughed loudly, "Duryodhana deserves what he has got. What Chitrasena has done, we should have done long ago. It's good that someone is taking the fight on our behalf. Duryodhana came here to humiliate us. So, what he got in return, serves him well."

Yudhishthira didn't appreciate Bheema's unabashed display of glee. "Bheema, this is not the time to spill out our personal rancour. Duryodhana is one of us. Our personal differences can be sorted out later, but we should not let an outsider put the Kuru honour at stake. Go now and release Duryodhana and Kaurava ladies out of their bondage. Take Arjuna, Nakula and Sahadeva with you."

The four Pandavas armed themselves, to battle for Duryodhana's freedom as well as that of the other Kaurava ladies. The princes attacked the Gandharva army. Arrows from Gandiva mercilessly broke their defence, while Bheema decimated their army with his mace. Though the brave Gandharvas returned their fire, they were no match before Arjuna's newly acquired celestial weapons. Agneya created horror in their ranks.

Chitrasena, with perfect mastery over the art of illusion, attacked Arjuna, while remaining invisible. But Arjuna tore through the illusion and was pleasantly surprised to see his music tutor right in front of him. He bowed to his tutor and commanded his men to drop their arms.

"Why did you imprison Duryodhana and his ladies?" asked Arjuna, bewildered.

"Because your arrogant cousin is rude and haughty. Do you know why he was here? He was here to mock you at the difficult life you and your brothers are passing through. Lord Indra was extremely enraged on the same account. So he instructed me to descend here and teach them a lesson. I came to stay where Duryodhana had planned a feast. He was arrogant enough to misbehave with my men. He challenged me and entered into a combat with my men. We defeated and imprisoned him along with his ladies. However, Karna and Shakuni managed to run away. His behaviour towards you all has never been honourable," Chitrasena said. He ordered one of his men to put Duryodhana and his men in chains and bring them to him.

"Let Duryodhana go. He is my cousin," Arjuna requested politely.

Chitrasena, no doubt, sympathised with Pandavas' fate and therefore found it surprising that Arjuna was still compassionate towards them. "No," Chitrasena countered, "they do not deserve your compassion. I have put him in this position so that he is jeered by his own ladies. By seeking your help, he has already put himself in a humiliating position."

As an afterthought, Chitrasena added, "He has treated Yudhishthira and Draupadi in a very humiliating manner. I cannot release him. I will drag him to Yudhishthira, who will decide his fate."

Chitrasena dragged the chained Duryodhana to Yudhishthira like an ordinary criminal. Duryodhana burned with shame and anger. His plans to meet his cousins in royal pomp and grandeur fell flat on his face. Yudhishthira was happy to see his cousin's life spared. "I am glad you didn't harm him," Yudhishthira said, thanking Chitrasena. "Now do me one more favour," Yudhishthira requested, "set him free."

Chitrasena ordered his men to unfetter him. Feeling ashamed, guilty and humiliated at the same time, Duryodhana rose and bowed humbly to Yudhishthira.

Cursing his fate and chafing at his disgrace in the presence of the royal ladies, Duryodhana bowed once again to the eldest Pandava and left for Hastinapur. There lay a river across the way and Duryodhana camped at its bank for the night. A little later, Karna also came there.

"How lucky of you to have come unscathed. I am sure the Gandharvas have been rooted and sent to the abode of death. No wonder, only you could have achieved that feat!" Karna praised Duryodhana. But Duryodhana's sullen face told a different story altogether.

Duryodhana shamefully admitted that nothing of the sort took place. On the contrary, he was defeated and chained only to be brought before Yudhishthira. It was because of the mercy of the Pandavas that he was alive.

What hurt Duryodhana more was not that he was defeated and dishonoured, but that he was the object of humiliation in presence of the Pandavas. He felt so dishonoured and miserable that he decided to starve himself to death instead of retreating to Hastinapur, defeated and humiliated.

Karna consoled his friend, "Don't disturb yourself with silly thoughts. Great generals do get trapped and are rescued by their men. You will make a fool of yourself by committing suicide. People will laugh and mock at you. Don't worry, I will kill Arjuna when the time comes and defeat the Pandavas. Don't let this trivial incident get the better of you."

Both Shakuni and Karna tried their best to boost the sagging morale of Duryodhana. He felt uplifted and came back to Hastinapur. He felt further elevated on coming to know that he could perform Rajasuya with even greater pomp and splendour than the Pandavas had performed in Indraprastha.

Duryodhana could never forget the insult. It rankled in his heart. He saw his rescue by the Pandavas as an insult, and his public humiliation before them hurt him even more. He thought on endlessly over his predicament and on ways to redeem his honour.

Durvasa and His Hungry Horde

Not much later, opportunity presented itself when Durvasa rishi came to visit them. Durvasa always moved with his ten thousand disciples wherever he went. The rishi was known for cursing people at the slightest pretext. He was irascible and short tempered. Therefore, his hosts were careful enough to attend to his slightest demands and needs without a murmur.

Durvasa informed his reluctant host that he would be staying there awhile. The Kauravas were on their toes, so as not to invite his wrath. His curse was feared, and no one could guess when, how and what curse he might inflict. His ways were eccentric. He came and went anywhere, anytime he pleased, without prior information. He demanded food at odd hours and expected prompt service. He could also whimsically refuse the food brought to him.

Duryodhana found an opportunity in Durvasa's visit. He waited on the ill-tempered rishi day and night with the sole aim of pleasing him to win his favour. His unflinching dedication pleased the rishi. He asked him to ask for any boon. Duryodhana's joy knew no end. He had been waiting exactly for this moment.

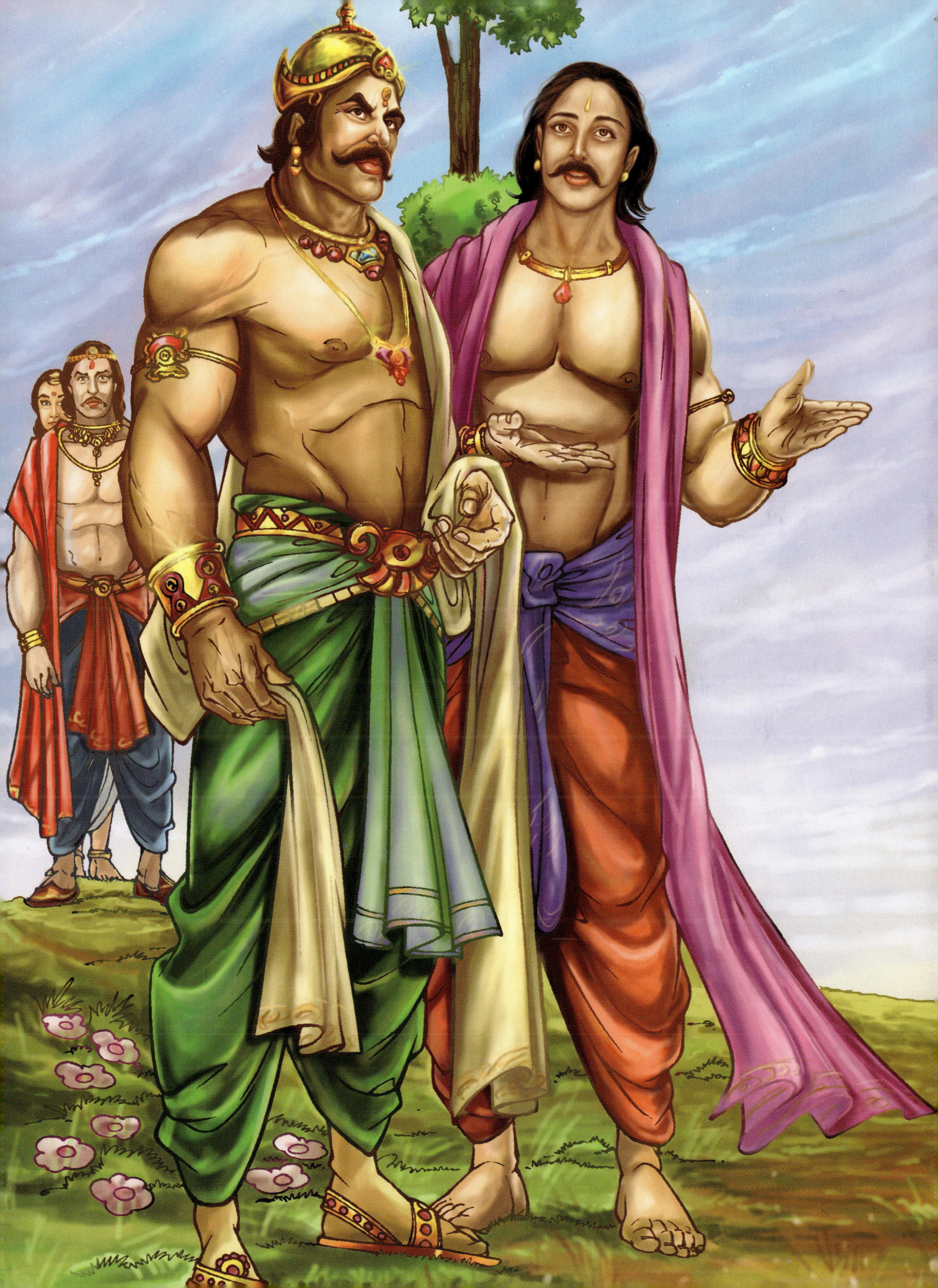

"Pandavas are my cousins. Unfortunately, they are leading a difficult life in the forest. If you visit them with your ten thousand disciples, they would be blessed and they will feel a little unburdened of their hardship. That is the only boon I ask of you. It would be advisable for you to go when Draupadi is free after feeding the brahmins," Duryodhana said.

In his heart, he congratulated himself on his perfect plan. He knew the *akshaya patra* that Draupadi had, lost its efficacy after Draupadi ate out of it. The Pandavas would find it hard to feed the rishi and his ten thousand disciples, who would demand fresh food. Duryodhana thought that Durvasa would definitely curse the Pandavas if they were unable to feed his disciples and him.

"I am surely going to visit the Pandavas," said Durvasa, pleased with the generosity of Duryodhana.

The rishi departed highly satisfied. Duryodhana couldn't stop himself from laughing as soon as Durvasa went out of his sight. He narrated to Karna and Dushasana, how he had planned to use Durvasa to curse the Pandavas. They doubled with laughter imagining the predicament the Pandavas would land in. "Let us see how Pandu's sons save their skin this time," they laughed merrily.

Durvasa and his ten thousand disciples stormed through the forest and arrived at Pandavas' hermitage uninformed. The Pandavas, a little taken aback, touched his feet and asked him to have a seat. The rishi expressed his desire to have hot and refreshing meal for himself and his ten thousand disciples. "We will go for a bath before our meal," declared the rishi and left with his ten thousand disciples for a bath.

The Pandavas were completely unprepared for Durvasa's demand. When they informed Draupadi about the arrival of Durvasa and his demand, she was shocked. "How can I feed him and his disciples when I have already eaten from the *akshaya patra*?" she asked nervously.

Draupadi wondered what she should do to not invite the wrath of the highly short-tempered rishi. She felt completely helpless and out of her wits, when suddenly Lord Krishna walked in. She found a ray of hope in Krishna. "Durvasa rishi is here," she said, "and has demanded food for himself and his ten thousand disciples. There's not a morsel left with us. I have already eaten from that inexhaustible vessel, which means I cannot feed anyone out of it now. What shall I do?" Draupadi desperately asked Lord Krishna's help in her predicament.

"I am hungry. Give me something to eat." Krishna spoke without heeding to Draupadi's plea.

"I told you, there's nothing to eat," Draupadi said in exasperation, "and Durvasa with his men can arrive here any time."

"I am really hungry. This is not the time to joke. Get Surya's *akshaya patra*," Krishna smiled.

Draupadi gave him the empty pot wondering if Krishna was in the right frame of his mind. Krishna peeped inside the pot looking for something. He found a grain of rice stuck inside. Krishna smiled at his discovery, and taking it out neatly, he ate it up with satisfaction. As he ate the single grain of rice, he said, "May Hari, the soul of universe, be fed to satisfaction." Turning to Draupadi with a mischievous twinkle in his eyes, he said to her, "Let the rishi come for the lunch."

Durvasa and his disciples, bathing in the river, felt satiated. They were no longer feeling hungry. They looked at each other in amazement as each one of them felt the same. They had no desire to eat as if they just had a hearty meal. Some of the disciples made their way to Durvasa and said, "We have told Yudhishthira to be ready with hot meal when we come after the river bath. But we have no desire to eat now. Not only are we not hungry but we feel as if we have just eaten more than we could, although we have had nothing to eat."

Strangely, Durvasa himself was feeling no different. "We cannot ask the Pandavas to be ready with meals for all of us and then decline his hospitality. Yudhishthira, the Dharmaraja, will find our manners in bad taste. His ire will reduce us to ashes. Even I don't have the least desire to eat at the moment. The best way for us is to quietly slip away from here."

The rishi and his disciples quickly changed their clothes after the bath and retreated hastily out of there, without the slightest murmur.

The Pandavas kept waiting with bated breath for Durvasa, but he was nowhere in sight. Yudhishthira asked Bheema to go the river and escort the rishi back to the hermitage. Bheema came back disappointed. Durvasa and his disciples were nowhere to be seen.

Yudhishthira got even more worried, being aware of the eccentric ways of the rishi. He thought the rishi and his disciples might land up at an odd hour in night demanding the meal.

"Durvasa will not come," smiled Krishna amusedly, "When Draupadi spoke to me about her predicament, I took the lone rice grain out of Surya's copper pot and ate it up and his hunger died. His disciples too felt full and satisfied."

The Pandavas smiled back.

Days passed by. Many sages and saints reached the dwelling place of Pandavas for talks and discussion on various aspects of the holy scriptures. Topics like duties of householders, aim in life, and spiritual practices were also brought up in the discussions with Yudhishthira.

It was getting obvious to the five brothers and Sri Krishna that Duryodhana and Shakuni would never return them their share of land and kingdom. It was futile to expect any change of heart. War would be the last solution; and prepared they must be for such an eventuality.

Jaidratha and Keechaka's Misdeeds

One day the Pandavas were not in their hermitage. They had gone for hunting, leaving Draupadi and Dhaumya alone. The king of Sindhu, Jaidratha, was riding through the forest on his way to Shalva's kingdom. Draupadi was leisurely picking up fruits dropped from the trees outside her hut. As Jaidratha passed by, he accidentally glanced at her. He was awe-struck by her beauty.

He stopped and asked one of his men to find about her. "I am on my way to get a bride for myself, but I don't think I need to go any further. Go and ask who she is, and if she will marry me, the king of Sindhu."

"Young lady, who are you? Whose daughter are you? Are you an apsara or a goddess? Kindly introduce yourself. The king of Sindhu is here and he wants to know about you," Jaidratha's attendant asked her in a polite manner.

It was quite unconventional those days for a woman to speak to strangers. "It is not right to speak to strangers," said Draupadi, "but, I will answer your questions since I am alone here. I am Draupadi, daughter of King Drupada and wife of the Pandavas. They are not here. They have gone out for hunting. Your king is my brother-in-law. He is a welcome guest at our hermitage."

The messenger went back to Jaidratha and conveyed the message of Draupadi to him. The king of Sindhu was a vain man. He was attracted to Draupadi, and therefore determined to make her his wife. He completely overlooked the fact that Draupadi was already wedded to the Pandavas. He decided to go into the hermitage.

Draupadi greeted him, had him seated and offered water to wash his feet. "My husbands are out in the forest, but should be coming soon. Yudhishthira will be really happy to see you here. He loves to entertain his guests."

Jaidratha was, no doubt, happy at the absence of the Pandavas. He found, in their absence, an opportunity to entice her. "Hospitality from you is all I am looking forward to. How can a delicate, beautiful woman like you live this wretched life? How can a beautiful lady brought up in royal fortunes live with them? Come with me and I will make you the queen of Sindhu," he offered.

Draupadi was stunned, but she took care to maintain her poise and said, "Don't repeat those words again. Our sister Dushala is already your queen. As far as I am aware, your forefathers were known for their morality and ethics. But you have proved them otherwise today. Remember, my husbands Bheema and Arjuna are not only strong enough to protect me, but also to send you to your heavenly abode."

"I do not fear your husbands. I belong to one of the seventeen top kshatriya clans and therefore, am socially superior to your husbands. They are no better than beggars now," said Jaidratha, and forcibly dragged her to his chariot.

Draupadi screamed and Dhaumya came running out. Dhaumya tried to protect Draupadi but Jaidratha thrust him aside. Next moment, he raced off with Draupadi in his chariot, followed by his retinue.

The Pandavas were returning to the hermitage. The eldest Pandava had a premonition of some mishap. "Let us hurry back," he said, "I feel everything is not quite well." They arrived fast only to find Draupadi missing. Only her maid was in the hermitage, weeping inconsolably.

"The king of Sindhu has taken her forcibly," she said sobbing, "He couldn't have gone very far. The chariot wheel marks must still be fresh. Go after him and protect Panchali's honour," she said, wailing loudly.

The Pandavas rushed after Jaidratha. On finding Draupadi in his chariot, they could hardly restrain themselves. Bheema roared at Jaidratha, while the latter tried to run away as speedily as he could.

Draupadi noticed Jaidratha trembling in fear. "You, disgraceful man! I told you to keep away from me. Now my husbands are here. They will send you to the abode of Yama."

Jaidratha ordered his men to attack and stop the advancing Pandavas, who were furious and unkind to the hurdles coming in their way. Jaidratha's men dropped like dead autumn leaves when faced with Arjuna's swift volley of arrows. Bheema indiscriminately maced through them. Nakula was swift with his sword, sparing none coming in his way.

Jaidratha, scared for his life, quickly dropped Draupadi out of the chariot and rode fast. Dhaumya picked up Draupadi and seated her in Sahadeva's chariot.

Arjuna had been aiming at Jaidratha and on finding him escaping for his life, he shouted to Bheema, "Don't waste time in killing his men. Go after Jaidratha or he will escape."

Bheema, drawing his chariot closer to Yudhishthira's, said, "Take Draupadi to the hermitage. We will be back only after killing that brute."

Yudhishthira found Bheema's statement distasteful. "Forgive him. He is our sister Dushala's husband. You can't bring widowhood upon our sister. Jaidratha is our aunt Gandhari's son-in-law."

Draupadi was, however, seething in rage. "Don't have mercy for him," she screamed, "He deserves no leniency. Bheema! Arjuna! Go and kill him. That would be the best present that you can offer to me."

Yudhishthira returned to the hermitage with Draupadi and Dhaumya. The other Pandavas, ignoring Yudhishthira's command, raced after Jaidratha. He was almost two miles away when a bunch of arrows shot by Arjuna killed his horses and his chariot tumbled as the horses fell. The king of Sindhu jumped out and ran.

"You coward! Stand and fight if you're a man," shouted Arjuna. Bheema ran after him and caught the king. He threw aside his mace and held him by his hair. Even before the monarch could plead for mercy, Bheema thrashed him with his hammer-like fists. Bheema might have killed the king, had not Arjuna stopped him. "Yudhishthira, our elder brother, will never approve of killing him, even though he deserves to die."

Bheema dragged Jaidratha to his chariot and took him to his hermitage in the Kamyaka forest. Jaidratha trembled in fear. He knew, no one except the eldest Pandava could save his life.

As soon as the chariot stopped near the hermitage, Jaidratha jumped out of the chariot and prostrated himself at the feet of Yudhishthira, begging to be forgiven.

Yudhishthira could merely say, "It is only Panchali, not me, who can forgive you. You have committed a crime against her, therefore, the onus of whether or not to forgive you, lies with her."

Draupadi was still boiling with rage. Nothing less than Jaidratha's blood would satisfy her. "Did I marry the five kshatriya warriors to lead a humiliating life? None of you rose up to defend me when I was being dishonoured in the court at Hastinapur. And now when this man abducted me with evil intentions, you are expecting me to forgive him."

These words of Draupadi were enough to instigate Bheema to kill Jaidratha. As Bheema advanced menacingly towards Jaidratha, Yudhishthira said, "My brother, it's not proper to take decisions in a bad temper. Control your wrath! I am not against punishing him. He must be punished for his crime, but the punishment should be due. I am not in favour of killing him as he is related to us through our sister Dushala. This is a very sensitive relation, which has bound our hands. Would you ignore Dushala's request if she comes here begging for his life?"

Draupadi held the eldest Pandava high in esteem. Although she was still seething in rage, words of Yudhishthira restrained her.

"I shall spare his life," said Draupadi addressing Bheema, "but I will avenge my humiliation. Have him dragged to my feet and shave the hair off his head, leaving five tufts of hair on his bald pate."

Bheema unsheathed his sword and shaved off Jaidratha's hair with it. The five protruding tufts on his head made him a laughing stock.

Bheema roared, "Listen carefully to what I say. Everytime you enter a royal court, you must announce that you are the slave of the Pandavas. That's the done thing when a king is defeated in the battlefield. You too have been defeated. Now go and tell Draupadi, you are her slave." Jaidratha hastily complied with Bheema's command.

Jaidratha felt terribly humiliated and disgraced. He resolved to even out the disgrace meted out to him by the Pandavas. Vowing vengeance, Jaidratha left the hermitage for the banks of River Ganga. There he meditated hard to appease Lord Shiva to grant him the boon of being the instrument of Pandavas' destruction. He meditated deeply for months together. Lord Shiva was pleased with him and he appeared before him saying, "Jaidratha, I am pleased with your devotion. Ask for any boon you want. I will grant it."

"I want the destruction of Pandavas. I want to defeat and kill them along with their soldiers in the battlefield," Jaidratha requested.

"That would be impossible. The Pandavas are invincible. You would never be able to slay them, but you would defeat them in the war that is to come, except Arjuna. He has my mightiest weapon with him," Lord Shiva said and vanished. Jaidratha was satisfied with whatever Lord Shiva offered him and returned to his capital.

The unhappy event of Draupadi's abduction depressed Yudhishthira, and Kamyaka no longer appeared charming to him. The Pandavas shifted to Dvaitavana which abounded with jewel-like lakes and groves laden with fruit. They passed their time happily and peacefully in meditation, prayer and participation in Yajnas.

The Pond of Death and Yudhishthira's Wisdom

One day a brahmin rushed into the hermitage demanding assistance. "O, noble sons of Pandu, I have come here seeking assistance from you. I had two pieces of fire-sticks hung from a tree. Suddenly a stag appeared and rubbed its body against the tree to satisfy its itch. The sticks fell off the tree, and as a result got entangled in its horns. The frightened stag ran off with those sticks. How will I perform my *agnihotra* without the fire producing sticks? O, great kshatriyas, only you can get my fire producing sticks back from the stag so that I can perform my oblations."

The Pandavas rushed after the stag with their bows and arrows, as protection of brahmins was the foremost duty of the kshatriyas. The stag, which appeared within the range of Arjuna's arrows, disappeared at once. They ran around looking for the stag but it was nowhere to be seen. At last, exhausted and tired, they sat under the shade of a tree to rest for a while and to decide upon their next move. They were at the same time feeling sorry for failing to get back the brahmin's sticks.

The exhausted Pandavas were feeling thirsty. Yudhishthira said to Nakula, "Dear brother, we're all feeling very thirsty. There's not a drop of water in sight. Why don't you climb up this tree and look for a water point?"

Nakula quickly climbed up a tree and craned his neck to look around. "Yes, I spot a water point at some distance," replied Nakula as he quickly made his way down the tree.

"Take this quiver and get water for all of us to drink," Yudhishthira said to Nakula.

Nakula went with an empty quiver in that direction and found a fresh water lake. Nakula was thirsty himself, and as he bent down to drink water out of the pool, a voice thundered, "Stop! You cannot drink water out of this pool, unless you answer my questions."

Nakula hardly bothered about the thundering command from the heaven, as he was very thirsty. He bent down and as he scooped a handful of water to his parched mouth, he dropped dead.

The Pandavas waited for a considerable length of time for their brother Nakula to return, but he didn't. Then they sent Sahadeva to find Nakula. When Sahadeva reached the lake, he was horrified to find his brother dead. But he was so thirsty at the same time that he was naturally driven to drink water out of the lake. As he was about to drink the water, the same voice commanded him not to drink water unless he answered the questions. Sahadeva was too thirsty to bother about those questions. As the first drop of water touched his parched throat, he too lay dead like his twin Nakula.

When the twins didn't turn up, the three Pandavas, the sons of Kunti, grew worried. Yudhishthira sent Arjuna after them. Arjuna found his brothers lying dead on the shore. Sorrow and anger clouded his emotion. He shouted, "Who is responsible for my brothers' condition? Come before me and I will show you who I am." There was no response. Arjuna was instinctively drawn towards the lake to quench his thirst. But as soon as Arjuna tried to drink water, the same voice shouted a warning, "Stop short! I am the master of this pool. No one is allowed to drink water out of it. You can drink water only when you answer my questions. If you ignore my warning you too will meet the same fate."

Arjuna ignored the warning and met the same fate as his brothers.

Yudhishthira's apprehension grew deeper when Arjuna too didn't turn up. He sent Bheema to find out what had happened. Bheema went to the lake and found his brothers lying dead. Tears rolled down his blood-shot eyes. "It must be the misdeed of a powerful rakshasa," thought Bheema, "as no ordinary human being was capable of killing Arjuna. I will send that rakshasa to hell, but let me first quench my thirst."

The same voice warned Bheema of the dire consequences if he drank water without answering the questions. Bheema too, like his brothers, paid no heed to the warning and met the same fate as his brothers.

When Bheema too, like others, failed to show up, Yudhishthira grew restless and worried. He decided to go himself. On reaching the lake, the sight of his dead brothers broke his heart. He bewailed their untimely departure without fulfilling their duties and promises. "Who could have killed the mighty Bheema?" he wondered. "How could Arjuna leave so suddenly when the Gods had proclaimed him invincible in war?" he wept. "Only Yama could have taken their lives," he cried hoarse. "Why didn't I die before having to see the dead faces of the twins," he wailed bitterly.

He could not bear his thirst and proceeded towards the lake. As he bent down to scoop water, he noticed a crane perched on the reeds. Yudhishthira was quite surprised when the crane spoke in human voice. "Stop, you can't drink water out of this lake unless you answer my questions. I own this lake and if you disregard my warning you will meet the same fate as your brothers."

"Who are you?" asked Yudhishthira as water dropped out of his cupped hands, "Are you a God or a demi-God? No ordinary crane could have killed my brothers."

The crane, in the next instant, changed into a Yaksha. "I am a Yaksha. I killed your brothers because they disregarded my warning. If you want to drink, answer my questions first."

"Ask your questions. I will answer them as best as I can," Yudhishthira said, bowing humbly to the Yaksha.

The Yaksha looked mysteriously into the eyes of Yudhishthira and metamorphosed into a crane before shooting his questions. These were the questions and the answers:

Q: Who causes sun to rise, who keeps it company and what causes it to set?
A: Brahma causes sun to rise, the Gods keep it company and dharma causes it to set.

Q: What makes a man great and who is a man's true friend?
A: Meditation makes a man great, and patience is his true friend.

Q: In what lies the greatness of a brahmin and how is he like the others?
A: A brahmin's greatness lies in meditation and study of scriptures, but like other men, he too must die one day.

Q: In what does the strength of the kshatriya lie? Which acts of theirs are said to be pious, which sinful, and in what does their weakness lie?
A: Their strength lies in their weapons, their sacrifice to Gods is pious, their refusal to protect someone is sinful, and in fear lies their weakness.

Q: What is important to a farmer, to a trader and to a householder?
A: Rain is important to a farmer, collecting money is important to a trader, and a son is important for a householder.

Q: Which person is living but as good as dead?
A: He who does not feed Gods, guests; he is alive but is as good as dead.

Q: What is greater than the earth, higher than the skies, faster than the wind and more numerous than blades of grass?
A: A mother is greater than the earth, a father higher than the heavens, the mental speed is faster than the wind, and thoughts are more numerous than blades of grass.

Q: What sleeps with its eyes open, what does not move after birth, what has no heart and what grows with its own impetus?
A: A fish does not close its eyes even while sleeping, an egg does not move after birth, a stone has no heart, and a river swells with its own impetus.

Q: Who is a friend to an alien, to a native, to a patient and to a dying man?
A: A co-passenger is an alien's friend, wife is a native's friend, a doctor is a patient's friend and charity done on death-bed is a dying man's friend.

Q: In what do virtue, fame, heaven and happiness lie?
A: Virtue lies in sagacity, fame lies in charity, heaven lies in truth and happiness lies in right conduct.

Q: Who is a man's soul, and who is his true friend?
A: A man's son is his soul and his wife is his true friend.

Q: What is the best of all laudable things, what is the most valuable of all possessions, what is the best of all gain and which is the highest form of happiness?
A: Skill is the best of all laudable things, knowledge best of all possessions, health best of all gains and contentment is the best of all happiness.

Q: What is the highest duty, which virtue always bears fruit; what, if controlled, leads to no regrets, and who are they with whom an alliance can never break?
A: The highest duty is to refrain from injuring anyone, following the strictures of the Vedas always bears fruit. The mind, if controlled, leads to no regrets, and an alliance with the noble never breaks.

Q: What envelops the world and why are friends forsaken?
A: Darkness envelops the world, and friends are forsaken because of avarice.

Q: What is the best of all knowledge, and in what does mercy lie?
A: The best of all knowledge is that of the supreme, and mercy lies in desiring the happiness of all.

Q: What is grief, and what is charity?
A: Ignorance is grief, and protection of all creatures is charity.

Q: Which man is erudite, who is an atheist, and what causes grief?
A: One who knows his duties is erudite, an atheist is one who is ignorant of the supreme being, and envy brings grief.

Q: Loss of what makes a man popular and loss of what keeps away sorrow? Loss of what brings in happiness?
A: Loss of pride makes one popular, loss of anger keeps away sorrow while loss of greed brings in happiness.

Q: Why is charity given to brahmins, to servants, to entertainers and to kings?
A: Charity is given to brahmins for salvation, to servants for their upkeep, to entertainers for fame, and to kings out of fear.

Q: Which person is considered to be dead? Which nation is considered to be dead and which Yajna is useless?
A: A penniless person is practically dead. A nation without a king is a dead nation and a Yajna with unpaid gratification is useless.

Q: What is knowledge and what is peace? Which is the best form of mercy and what is simplicity?
A: Knowing the spirit is real knowledge. Peace means undisturbed mind. Goodwill for all is the best form of mercy while simplicity comes from seeing all things with one eye.

Q: Who is man's worst enemy? What is an endless disease? And who is a true saint?
A: Anger is the worst enemy of man, and greed is an endless disease, while a philanthropic person is a true saint.

Q: What are attachment, pride, and laziness?
A: False love is attachment, false vanity is pride, ignoring one's duty is laziness.

Q: Who is called a scholar and who is an atheist? What is lust?
A: He who truly understands dharma is a scholar. An ignorant person is an atheist. And uncontrolled desire is lust.

Q: What sort of person suffers constantly in hell?
A: A person who calls a beggar to give alms but returns him empty handed suffers constantly in hell. A person, who despite having money, neither spends it on family nor gives it in a charity also constantly suffers in hell.

Q: What kind of man becomes popular and what kind of man is successful?
A: A man of sweet words becomes popular and a man who thinks before acting gains success in whatever he does.

Q: Who is really happy?
A: A man who has no debt to pay is really happy.

Q: What is the most strange thing?
A: Every day countless men die, but those who live do not see their end coming.

The Yaksha was pleased. "I am satisfied with your answers. You can ask for the life of one brother since you answered all my questions correctly," he smiled.

It was a tough choice for Yudhishthira but he said, "If that be your will, then please give life to Nakula."

"Why choose Nakula, your half brother, instead of Bheema or Arjuna, whom you love no less?" the Yaksha asked.

"Because my father had two wives, Madri and Kunti. Nakula is Madri's son while I am Kunti's son. Since I am alive, it is only a matter of justice that one of the two sons of Madri be alive. That's why I choose Nakula."

The Yaksha was delighted with response. "You are exemplary in upholding moral values, O, son of Kunti. All your brothers shall live." As Yaksha uttered those words, the four Pandavas rose up bewildered.

"Although you appear as a bird and admit you are a Yaksha, but I doubt it. Tell me, who are you?" Yudhishthira asked.

"I am Dharmaraja, my child," said the crane as it vanished, and in its place, appeared Yama, the Lord of dharma and death, of justice and morality, righteousness and virtue and the ruler of Yama Lok.

Dharmaraja also informed Yudhishthira that he was testing his virtue and knowledge and was delighted at his wisdom and moral values. The Death God, pleased with Yudhishthira, offered him to ask for a boon.

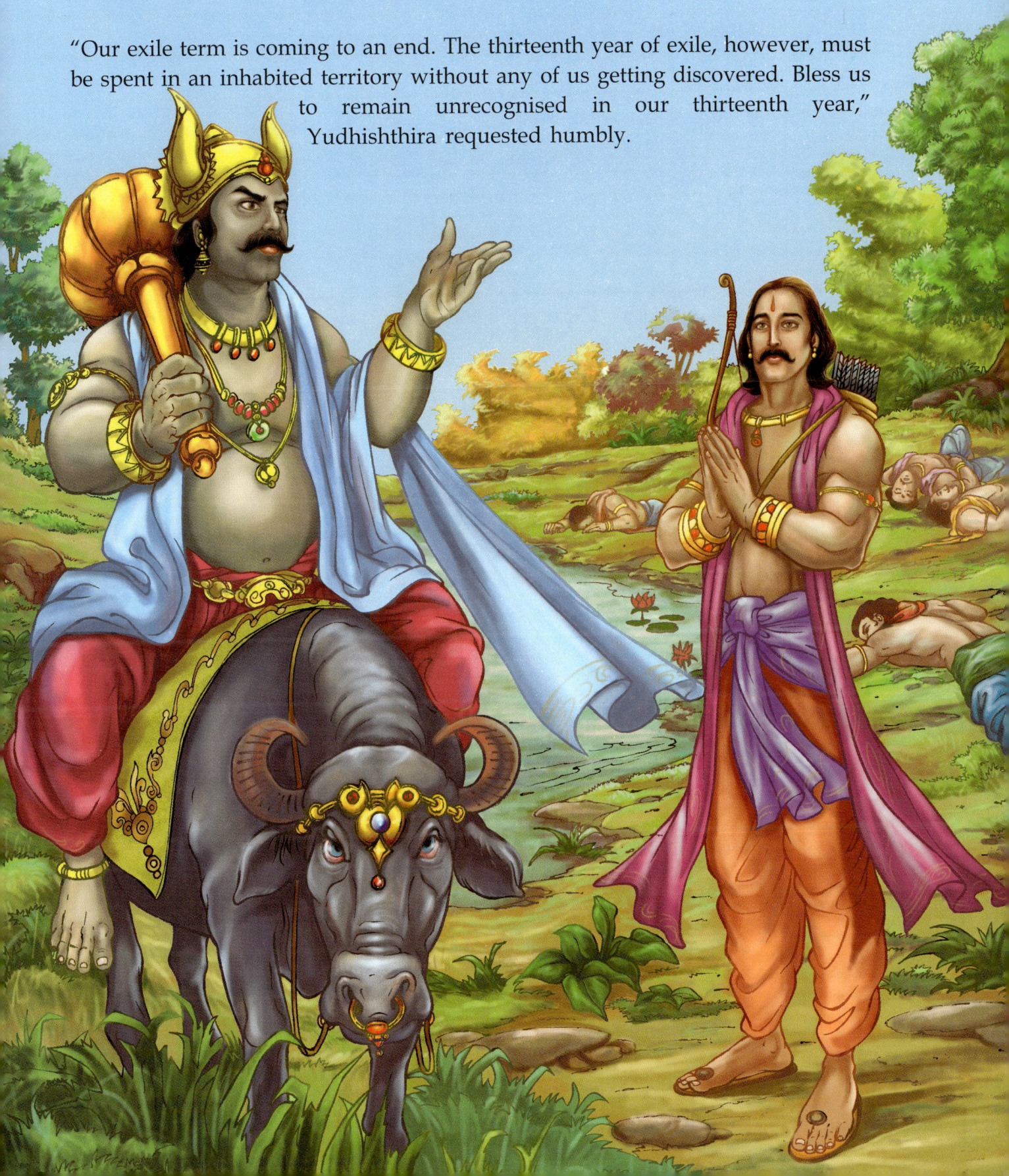

"Our exile term is coming to an end. The thirteenth year of exile, however, must be spent in an inhabited territory without any of us getting discovered. Bless us to remain unrecognised in our thirteenth year," Yudhishthira requested humbly.

"Go to the court at Viratnagar. You will remain undetected there in the thirteenth year," Yama said, and asked him to ask for another boon.

"May I never deviate from the path of virtue and right conduct," Yudhishthira requested humbly.

"Your wish will be granted," said Yama, and vanished.

The Pandavas returned to the hermitage with the fire sticks and gave them to the brahmin. They were happy that their greatest worry, of where to spend their thirteenth year, was settled.

The Pandavas' forest term was coming to an end, so they charted out their course for the thirteenth year. Yudhishthira decided to approach Virata as a brahmin skilled in dice, who had once been Yudhishthira's friend.

Bheema decided to approach the king as a wrestler-cum-cook, and claim he was a cook and wrestler at Yudhishthira's court.

Arjuna planned to disguise himself as a eunuch. Uravashi's curse served him well. He could quote his experience as having served Draupadi and Satyabhama before.

Nakula disguised himself as a horse-trainer and Sahadeva thought that he would do well as a cowherd. All of them had decided to refer their previous employment in the court of Yudhishthira until his exile.

Draupadi decided the role of *sairandhri* or hairdresser for herself. As a *sairandhri* she would be serving queen Sudeshana.

Yudhishthira sent the royal attendants and cooks to Drupada's capital with a request that they should be looked after well. He sent his charioteer Indrasena to Dwaraka. He instructed his men to express ignorance about them saying the last they saw the Pandavas was in Dvaitavana.

Before Dhaumya left for Panchala, he instructed Yudhishthira to take special care of Draupadi, as Draupadi, being immensely beautiful, could be subjected to unpleasant attention. He also advised them to understand their roles well, as servility and humility would not come easily to them. The king was required to be handled carefully because kings are very particular about their dignity.

While Dhaumya left for Panchala kingdom along with Yudhishthira's attendants, the Pandavas set out for Matsya where King Virata ruled. On reaching the outskirts of the city, they split, so as not to appear connected.

The Pandavas decided to hide their weapons before approaching the king. Looking around, Arjuna could spot a huge banyan tree in a crematorium and thought that was the best place to hide their weapons. They wrapped their weapons in soft leather and tied it to a branch hidden in the huge tree. To ensure no one even approached the tree, they hung a corpse on the branch. Its stench was bound to keep people away.

Yudhishthira went to Virata's court and introduced himself as Kanaka, a brahmin and an expert in the game of dice. Virata was impressed by his noble bearing and instantly hired him as his personal advisor. Yudhishthira put two conditions before he joined the king's court. First, he would not involve himself in any dispute that could arise over a game of dice, and if he won, he would not return whatever he won out of the game.

A few days later, Bheema walked in, while Virata wondered who the powerful, tall young man was. He introduced himself as Vallabha, King Yudhishthira's cook. Virata was sympathetic to the Pandavas. He hired Bheema.

The next day Draupadi arrived as a *sairandhri*. She introduced herself as Malini, a maid who waited on Draupadi and Satyabhama. Queen Sudeshana thought she was so beautiful that she could lose her husband. Draupadi allayed her fears saying that she was always guarded by her five Gandharva husbands. They would kill any man who dared to approach her. The queen felt reassured and hired her as her hairdresser.

Before joining, Draupadi said, "I have one condition. I would neither eat the leftovers nor wash anyone's utensils." The queen agreed to the conditions.

Next, King Virata hired a horse trainer by the name Granthika. He was Nakula. Sahadeva joined under the name Tautipala. He took up service as the royal cowherd. Arjuna, as a eunuch, was appointed as a dance and music teacher for princess Uttara and her friends. He was called Brihanalla. The Pandavas thus enjoyed and felt safe in anonymity.

Pandavas had already spent ten months in Virata's court without any incident of significance. One day queen Sudeshana's brother Keechaka, also the commander of the king's forces, happened to see Draupadi accidentally while visiting his sister.

"Who is she?" Keechaka asked his sister, pointing at Draupadi. Sudeshana smiled mischievously, saying, "Why don't you ask yourself?"

Keechaka couldn't hold himself and entered her apartment. "Who are you, young lady? A goddess or an apsara? What are you doing here? You don't deserve to be a maid. I would rather have you as my queen. You will have nothing wanting, should you accept to be my queen."

Draupadi controlled her temper. She held her head low. "I am a poor maid, a *sairandhri*. I am a wife of five Gandharva husbands." Draupadi's response was formal and emotionless. Keechaka thought, being a lady she was coy.

"I am the commander of Virata's army and responsible for the safety of his kingdom," Keechaka asserted boldly, "accept me and you will rule over this kingdom."

Draupadi sternly refused his offer, warning him to stay away from her or her husbands, the five powerful Gandharvas, would not think twice before killing him.

Keechaka went straight to Sudeshana and pleaded with her to send Malini to his palace on some pretext. The queen had to agree, as Keechaka was not only her brother whom she pampered, but also because he was responsible for the safety of Virata, the king and his kingdom.

Soon an opportunity presented itself. A royal festival was to be held, for which necessary articles had to be collected. The queen needed them for Lord Shiva's worship. She summoned Malini and said, "I would be needing some objects necessary for the worship of Lord Shiva. I shall be happy if you can go to Keechaka's palace and get me those things he has with him. Do it tonight itself because tomorrow morning I would be sitting for the worship."

Draupadi hesitated. "It would be better if someone else went in my place. His intention is not fair towards me. I fear trouble if I go there and the consequences could be worse because my five Gandharva husbands are merciless to anyone who troubles me."

"Do as I command," said Sudheshana, "My brother knows how to conduct himself."

Draupadi went to Keechaka's chamber fearing his ill intention. As she knocked at his door, Keechaka opened it. He stared at her and smiled. His evil intentions were writ large on his face. "Come, this is a special night for us. I will cover you in silk and rubies and we will drink honey and wine together," Keechaka said, trying to pull her in.

"But I am here to get some objects of worship!" Draupadi resisted strongly.

"Oh, come on! Your errand is not all that important!" Keechaka said and tried to draw her closer to his body.

Draupadi trembled in fear and rage. "I have never been unfaithful to my husbands. My husbands will be satisfied with nothing less than your death." Draupadi wrenched herself free as Keechaka, trying to grab her by her clothes, fell down. She ran without stopping to look behind and rushed to the court where Yudhishthira and Bheema were playing dice with the king. They looked up at her with surprise and found Keechaka chasing her. Keechaka grabbed her hair and pinned her down before kicking her animatedly. Wild with fury, Draupadi lashed out and knocked him down. When Bheema advanced towards Keechaka in rage, Yudhishthira held him mildly and indicated him to stop.

Later that night, Draupadi sobbed in Bheema's chamber as she complained to him. Bheema could hardly bear the tears in her eyes. He promised to do away with Keechaka secretly. He asked Draupadi to lure him to the dancing hall next night where Bheema would end this story once and for all.

The next day Draupadi, finding an opportune moment, spoke to Keechaka. Bowing her head and lowering her eyes, she hushed, "I am sorry for yesterday's unfortunate incident. Let us meet in the dancing hall tonight, when there would be no one."

"I will be there," said Keechaka," and don't worry, no one would be there."

Bheema draped himself in a woman's garment. He lay down on a couch covering himself. Keechaka mistook Bheema for *sairandhri*. Bheema rose up, caught him by his hands and flung him on the floor. He thrashed him mercilessly to death. Although Keechaka was a strong warrior himself, he could not resist the might of the furious Bheema.

As soon as Bheema left after murdering Keechaka, Draupadi raised an alarm. "My Gandharva husbands could not see me dishonoured and have therefore, killed the commander-in-chief," she said in a matter-of-fact tone.

Virata, the king, and Sudeshana, the queen, got worried about the safety of their kingdom after Keechaka's death. The Queen was so scared of the *sairandhri's* five Gandharva husbands that she decided to terminate the services of Malini. Draupadi requested that she should be allowed to be in their service for the next thirteen days, promising that no harm would come to anybody during her stay.

The Peace Mission Fails

Duryodhana turned restless after the start of the thirteenth year of the Pandavas' exile. He sent for his best spies and ordered them to spread out in all directions so as to spot the Pandavas.

News of Keechaka's death reached Duryodhana. His network of spies had sent word that the Pandavas were not to be traced in the Matsya kingdom, but the death of Keechaka was mysterious. This was especially so because Keechaka was one amongst the four invincible warriors. The four warriors were Balarama, Bheema, Shalya and Keechaka.

Duryodhana was still not sure whether Keechaka's murder was linked to Bheema or not. However, he had been planning to annexe Matsya kingdom for a long time and thought this was the right opportunity to attack. Dushasana guessed, "The Pandavas have probably been eaten up by wild beasts or perished of hunger."

"Don't even make the mistake of thinking that," Guru Drona warned him contemptuously, "Pandu's sons cannot die easily out of hunger or hardship."

Bhishma agreed with Drona. "Don't take the Pandavas so lightly. They are capable of defeating the three worlds. Give them their dues back when they come, if you do not want a defeat for yourself," he warned.

The king of the Trigartas, Susharma, was also present there. He was more interested in the consequences of the death of Matsya's commander-in-chief than in the fate of the Pandavas.

"Virata is in a vulnerable position after the death of Keechaka," Susharma said, "We ought to make the best use of this opportunity to attack and conquer the Matsya kingdom." Virata was an old enemy at whose hands Susharma had suffered several defeats, and now was the time for revenge. "We can easily defeat Virata with our combined forces and annexe his kingdom to our advantage," Susharma suggested enthusiastically.

Karna favoured the scheme. He suggested that they march immediately instead of worrying about the sons of Pandu. Duryodhana, agreeing with Karna, summoned Dushasana and asked him to get the forces ready to mount an attack on the Matsya kingdom.

Both the armies, the Trigartas as well as the Kauravas, marched a day after each other, from Hastinapur. On the seventh day, the Trigartas mounted an attack on the south eastern border of Matsya. The Kauravas attacked the cattle stations, seizing the herd.

Virata mustered his army, and marched to the battlefield. Yudhishthira, Bheema and the twins also joined the army, as it was an obligation they felt, they needed to fulfill. Only Arjuna, as he was disguised as a eunuch, could not join them in the war.

The king met the opposing Trigarta forces on a great plain outside the city. The fierce battle raised enough dust storm to almost blind the warring men even as the sun disappeared behind the cloud of arrows. Virata battled through bravely, surrounded by his guards, but Susharma was able to successfully raid through the ranks and capture the Matsya king.

When Yudhishthira saw the king being taken captive, he shouted to Bheema to rush and rescue the king. Bheema instantly uprooted a huge tree, which alarmed Yudhishthira. "Don't do that!" he warned Bheema, "It will draw everyone's attention to you and we shall be spotted. Fight with a sword or mace, like others."

Bheema, along with Nakula and Sahadeva, went after Susharma, killing his rear guards. They smashed his chariot and killed the charioteer. Susharma jumped out and ran but Bheema caught him and punched him with his savage blows. The Trigarta soldiers ran helter skelter in panic.

Bheema dragged the Trigarta king before Virata and Yudhishthira. He was hell-bent upon killing Susharma but Yudhishthira let him go. Virata expressed his heartfelt gratitude to Yudhishthira.

When Virata was engaged with the Trigartas, Duryodhana attacked his cattle stations and captured sixty thousand cattle herds along with the herdsmen. Only one cowherd sneaked through to arrive at the palace, where only one male member, prince Bhumijanya was there. The others were all ladies, including princess Uttara. The cowherd informed the prince of the unfortunate incident of the capture of sixty thousand cattle herds by the Kauravas and requested the prince to do something immediately. Prince Bhumijanya sighed, "If only I had a good charioteer, I could have easily handled Bhishma and Drona."

Arjuna whispered in Draupadi's ear, "Tell him Brihanalla would man his chariot. Tell him he was Arjuna's charioteer." When Draupadi conveyed the message to the prince, he was shocked, "I can't ask a eunuch to be my charioteer." However, when Uttara insisted on behalf of Brihanalla, the prince reluctantly agreed.

The two of them mounted the chariot and drove to the battlefield. Bhumijanya, who only moments ago was full of confidence, panicked when he saw the huge Kaurava army. "Drive the chariot back, Brihanalla. I am alone. I can't take on the mighty warriors like Bhishma, Drona, Duryodhana and Karna," he requested fearfully.

Arjuna refused to listen. "No, I can't. I don't want to return to the palace and hear the palace women laughing mockingly at us. The *sairandhri* has spoken of my antecedents as Arjuna's charioteer. I do not want to be laughed and mocked at." The prince jumped out of the chariot, in fright, and ran backwards. Arjuna rushed after him. When the Kauravas saw that a eunuch was the prince's charioteer, they went mad laughing.

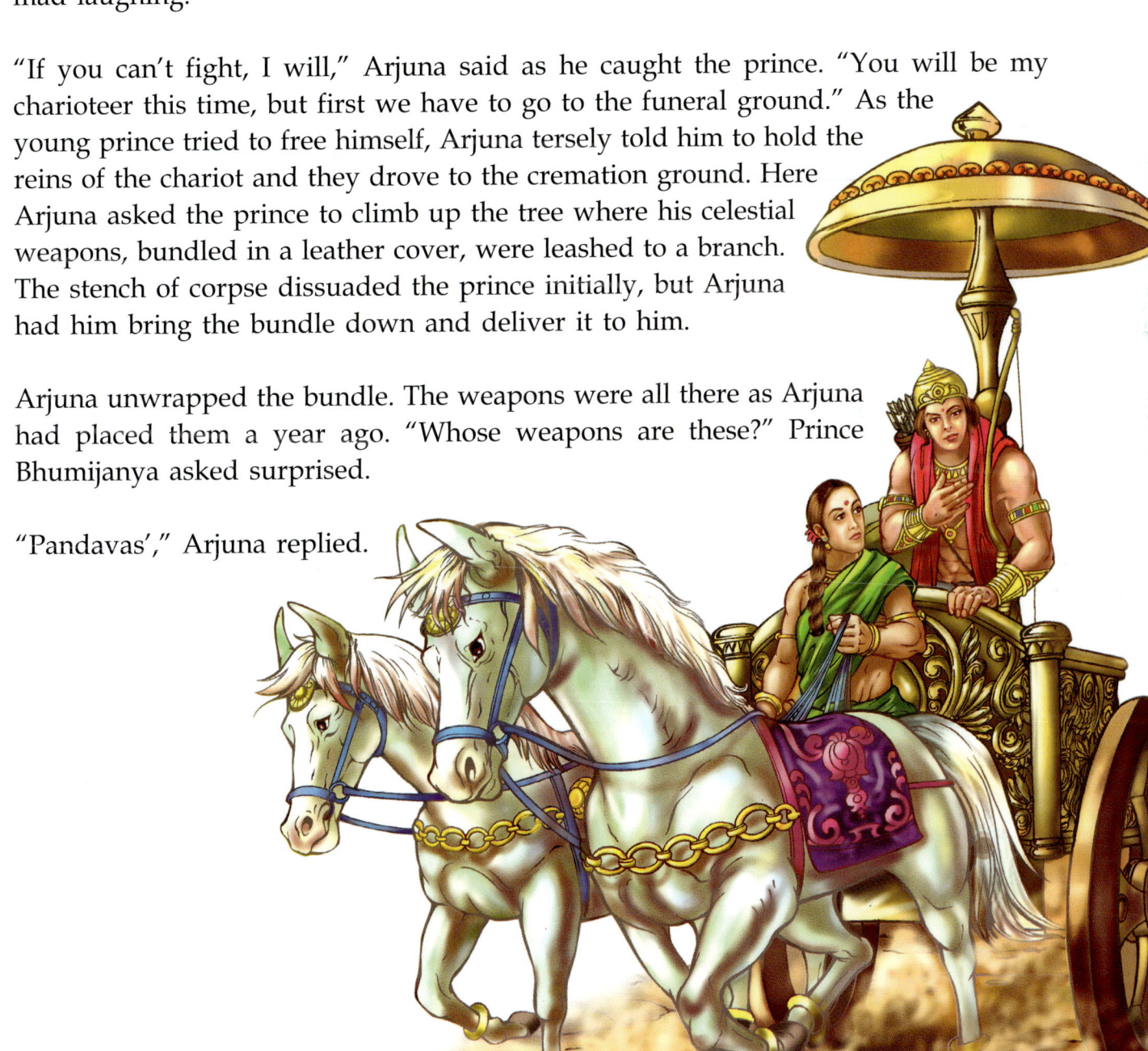

"If you can't fight, I will," Arjuna said as he caught the prince. "You will be my charioteer this time, but first we have to go to the funeral ground." As the young prince tried to free himself, Arjuna tersely told him to hold the reins of the chariot and they drove to the cremation ground. Here Arjuna asked the prince to climb up the tree where his celestial weapons, bundled in a leather cover, were leashed to a branch. The stench of corpse dissuaded the prince initially, but Arjuna had him bring the bundle down and deliver it to him.

Arjuna unwrapped the bundle. The weapons were all there as Arjuna had placed them a year ago. "Whose weapons are these?" Prince Bhumijanya asked surprised.

"Pandavas'," Arjuna replied.

"You're lying. Where are they and why are you taking their weapons?" Bhumijanya queried, even more surprised.

"I am taking what belongs to me," Arjuna smiled, "I am Arjuna. The brahmin who plays dice with your father is Yudhishthira, the one who cooks is Bheema, his cowherd is Sahadeva and his horse trainer Nakula. The Queen's hair-maid is our wife Draupadi."

"I don't believe you," Bhumijanya said, "If you all are really Pandavas and you are Arjuna then tell me why are you known as Phalguna, Savyasachi and Dhananjaya?"

"I am known as Phalguna because I was born under the constellation of Phalguna, people called me Savyasachi because I am ambidextrous and they call me Dhananjaya because I return with the treasure of the king I defeat," Arjuna grinned broadly. The prince no longer doubted the words of Arjuna. He bowed humbly to his hero, his palms joined in reverence.

Both Arjuna and Bhumijanya mounted the chariot. Arjuna held his Gandiva, while Bhumijanya held the reins. "How did you become a eunuch?" asked Bhumijanya.

Brihanalla Fights The Battle For Virata

"I was cursed," Arjuna replied, "but now the period of curse is over. It was for one year." Arjuna slung his Gandiva and sounded the conch 'Devdutta', as he entered the battlefield. He also twanged his bow-string and the reverberating echoes rippled over the Kaurava army.

Duryodhana, recognising the sound, jumped in joy saying, "It is none else but Arjuna. The Pandavas are discovered before the completion of the thirteenth year. Now they will have to go in exile for the next twelve years."

"Not so. Arjuna has revealed himself only after the expiry of his term. Isn't it?" Drona looked at Bhishma for confirmation.

"According to my calculation, the period of exile is over," Bhishma replied, "To arrive at the correct hour, two months must be added to the calendar every five years because of the fractional differences caused by the movement of the heavenly bodies.

Taking that calculation into account the extra five months and twelve days must be reckoned, which means the term of 13 years has expired today. That is why, he has emerged today."

Bhishma asked Duryodhana, who was not prepared to do justice to the Pandavas, to return to Hastinapur with the cattle, and some troops to guard him.

Arjuna was quick to spot Duryodhana missing from the battlefield. He asked Bhumijanya to turn his chariot towards Duryodhana and pursue him till he came within his arrows' range. Arjuna saw the dust raised by the cattle and he shot a volley of arrows towards his rearguard. But Duryodhana's brother Vikarna and Karna came ahead to check Arjuna's advance. Arjuna killed Vikarna's horses and destroyed his chariot. He now shot a volley of arrows at Karna. Karna, no ordinary warrior himself, intercepted them mid-air.

Drona and Bhishma rushed ahead to defend Karna, who successfully killed Arjuna's horses and destroyed his chariot. Arjuna's next set of arrows plunged deep into Karna's thighs and chest, and blood gushed out of his body. Karna was compelled to retreat. Arjuna once again turned his attention towards Duryodhana.

One by one, Arjuna dealt similarly with Drona, Bhishma and Ashvathama. He used Sammohanastra, a missile bestowed to him by Indra, which burst over the Kaurava army, immobilising them. Soldiers dropped unconscious. Arjuna asked Bhumijanya to collect the upper garments of Kuru generals including Drona, Karna, Duryodhana and Ashvathama. Only Bhishma was impervious to Sammohanastra and therefore, Bhumijanya was advised to be aware of Bhishma.

Arjuna was victorious. The Kauravas were defeated. Arjuna twanged his bow which reverberated through the unconscious Kaurava army and they rose up. With their heads bowed and palms joined, they acknowledged their defeat. "We are your slaves," they admitted according to the custom, but Arjuna asked them not to fear and go their way.

The Kauravas retreated, leaving the cattle behind. Arjuna asked Bhumijanya not to reveal his identity to the king and take the credit for victory on himself. They drove to the cremation grounds, where Arjuna hid his weapons once again as before. "Mount the chariot," he asked the prince, "I will drive you back."

King Virata had already defeated Susharma, the ruler of Trigarta, with the help of Vallabha (Bheema). The king was informed by the ladies of the household that the brave prince had gone all alone to fight the Kauravas, with Brihanalla as his charioteer.

Virata was worried about his son. "I dread to think what the Kauravas might have done to my son," Virata expressed his fear.

Yudhishthira, who was also present there, assured the king, "There's nothing to fear if the prince has Brihanalla as his charioteer. He can defeat Yakshas and Gandharvas and bring back your cattle safely."

Just then a messenger came running to the king and informed them, "The prince has defeated the Kauarva army." Yudhishthira smiled, "There's nothing surprising about it as Brihanalla was his charioteer."

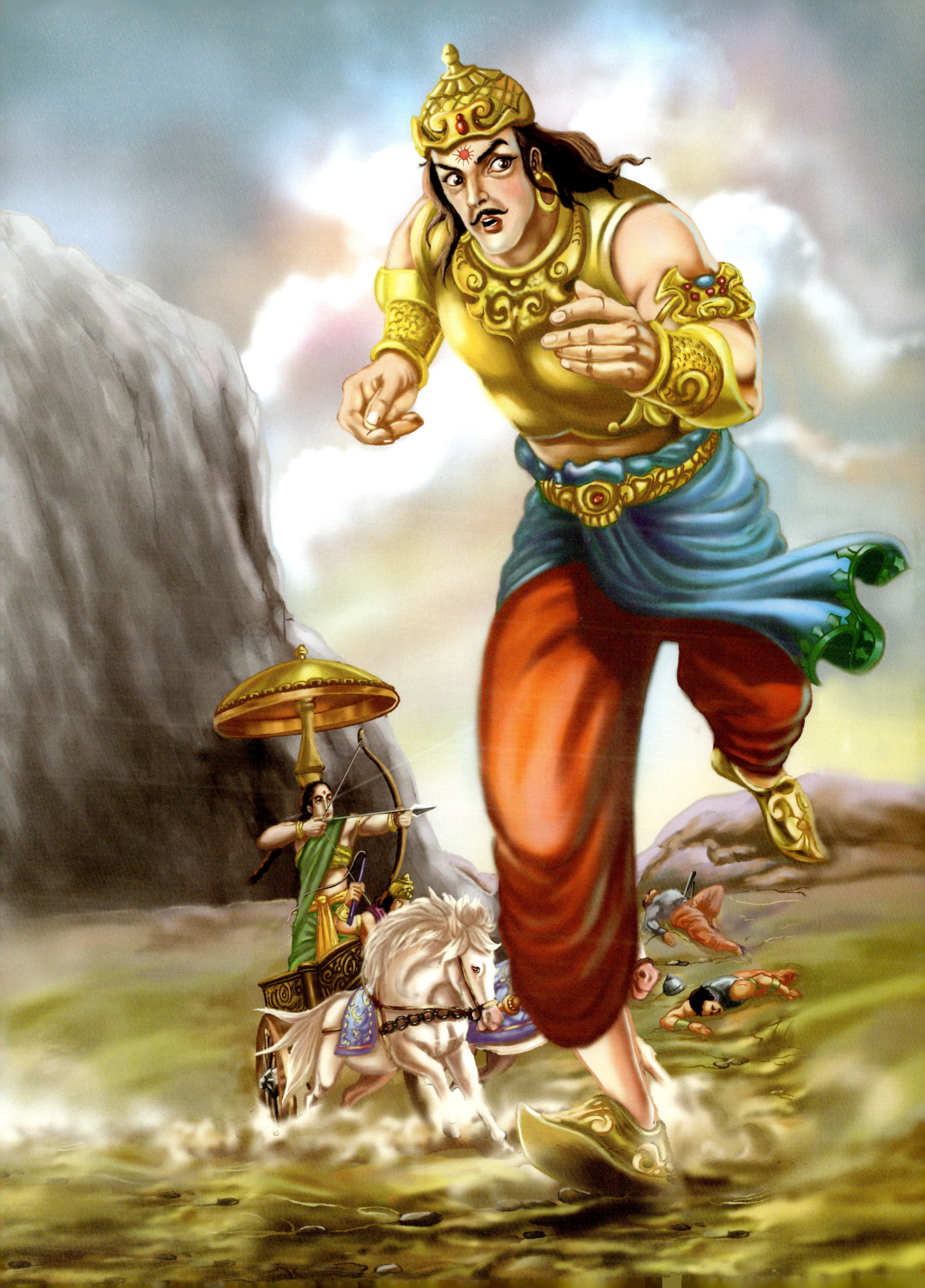

Virata was so overwhelmed by the news of his son's victory that he hardly cared for the words of Yudhishthira. The king ordered a grand reception for his son and asked the city to be decorated. He turned to Yudhishthira, inviting him to a game of dice while he waited for his son's arrival.

The game began as the dice rolled, while the king was in high spirits. He started the conversation, "Look Kanaka, how brave my son is! He has defeated Bhishma, Drona, Karna, Duryodhana, all mighty warriors single handedly."

"It had to happen," said Yudhishthira mildly amused, "with Brihanalla as his charioteer."

Virata flared in rage, "How dare you praise a eunuch's valour above my son's? I have been tolerating you for long. Ever since we heard that Brihanalla accompanied my son as charioteer, you have been praising none but him." The king flung the dice at Yudhshthira's face as he said these words.

Yudhishthira remained calm even as drops of blood oozed out of his nose. Draupadi looked at the bleeding Yudhishthira with a painful rage, but she lowered her eyes, veiling anger and rushed forward to nurse his wound.

A guard bowing to the king announced, "Your son and Brihanalla have come."

"Let them come," the king ordered joyfully. Yudhishthira briefly interrupted the guard saying, "Send in the prince first, ahead of Brihanalla." Yudhishthira knew Arjuna won't be able to tolerate his bleeding nose.

As Bhumijanya walked in, he noticed Yudhishthira bleeding. "Who did this to Kanaka?" he asked in consternation.

"I did it," the king replied, "this stupid brahmin dared to praise the eunuch over your valour."

A little later, Arjuna entered and bowed to the king. By then Yudhishthira's nose had stopped bleeding. The king was so thrilled by his son's victory that he hardly noticed the entry of Arjuna.

"You defeated the mighty Kurus all alone. I can't imagine how you could have defeated great warriors like Bhishma, Drona and Karna alone. I am proud of you, my son." Virata exuded happiness.

The prince admitted that he had no role in victory. It was a God's son, who fought on his behalf and won the battle for him. He vanished soon after.

Arjuna, with the king's permission, presented Uttara with the clothes of the Kaurava warriors, as in her childlike banter she had asked her brother Bhumijanya to get the clothes of defeated Kauravas.

Two days later, the Pandavas disclosed their identity to the king and his counsellors as they took to the thrones meant for royal guests.

Virata was shocked at their mannerism and questioned them. The prince then told his father the truth about the victory attributed to him. "It was Arjuna, who defeated the Kurus," he admitted.

"Where are the other Pandavas and Panchali?" asked the king. The prince disclosed everything and the Pandavas corroborated what the prince said.

The guilt-ridden king could not dare to meet his eyes with those of Yudhishthira, whom he had insulted in his ignorance. He rushed to embrace them, "My kingdom is yours. I owe my victory to you," he said to the Pandavas. Then he rushed to the Queen's apartment and blessed Malini, calling her his daughter. The Queen was equally surprised and thrilled when she came to know about the truth of the Pandavas.

Uttara Marries Abhimanyu

"Tell me, what can I do for you?" asked Virata, "but let me first pledge to bestow Uttara to Arjuna," he beamed with delight as he declared his wish to marry off princess Uttara to Arjuna.

"I am also in favour of an alliance between the Bharatas and the Matsyas. I would also be happy to receive the princess, not as my wife but as my daughter-in-law," Arjuna declared.

"Why do you refuse my offer," asked Virata, offended and surprised.

"I have been Uttara's tutor and lived in her apartment for a year. If I marry her, others will be suspicious of our character, but if on the other hand, she marries Abhimanyu, no one will have any doubt about her chastity and strength of character. Abhimanyu is young, brave and as handsome as a God. He would be an ideal match for her." Arjuna's reply was wise and reasonable.

Virata was satisfied with Arjuna's response, as it was the right and proper thing to do. Messengers were sent across to different regions including Dwaraka, where the Pandavas' son lived. Krishna, Balarama and the Vrishnis were specially invited. The Panchalas were also invited to the wedding. The town of Upaplavya was offered to the Pandavas to stay and entertain the guests. Krishna and Drupada arrived with an *akshavahini* force each.

On the auspicious day, Abhimanyu and Uttara were married to each other. The visiting kings and princes presented the young couple lavishly with horses, elephants, gold and silver. Yudhishthira gave donations to brahmins generously, from the wealth that Lord Krishna had brought for the occasion.

The exile of Pandavas had ended, and Uttara was married to Abhimanyu. After the wedding, all the kings and princes congregated in Virata's court. The Pandavas' future had to be decided upon. Krishna rose and addressed the assembly, "The Pandavas were cheated by Duryodhana and Shakuni, but they kept quiet. They could have easily killed the Kauravas and it would have been justified, but they didn't, because they are honourable gentlemen. The Pandavas have kept their part of the bargain. They lived in forest and underwent hardships of having to perform the menial tasks, without ever complaining once. Duryodhana's spies did their combing in every direction, but they could not identify the Pandavas. It is only fair now that the Kauravas return them their kingdom. It is within their power to snatch what rightfully belongs to them. But they will not. We cannot make any decision right now because we do not know what Duryodhana is planning to do. I suggest we send an emissary to their court."

King Drupada was convinced with the views expressed by Lord Krishna. "Krishna has very aptly, truly, impartially and accurately placed all the facts before us. He is well regarded by everyone for his justice and righteousness. We accept his views and therefore we shall strive to achieve justice for the Pandavas," he said.

Balarama did not harbour very generous attitude towards the Pandavas. Krishna's extreme affection for Arjuna also did not go down well with him. He never reconciled with Arjuna since the day he abducted Subhadra with the help of Krishna and heaped immense disgrace upon the Yadavas.

Balarma stood up and said, "Duryodhana ought to return their kingdom. If he does so without violence, it would be better. We can send the mediator but great restraint must be exercised when dealing with the Kurus. Yudhishthira lost to Shakuni for no fault of his. He could have chosen to play with any other player. It would be better to seek settlement with the Kurus instead of war, because they hold the kingdom."

Satyaki stood up aggressively in support of the Pandavas. "I don't see how Yudhishthira is to be blamed. He was outrightly cheated. Moreover, Yudhishthira had fulfilled the conditions laid down at the time of the game. Why should he beg for what rightfully belongs to him? A kshatriya never begs for his right. He takes it. If it comes to war, I am with the Pandavas. We aren't deprived of warriors. We have Drupada, Abhimanyu, Dhrishtadyumna and Shikhandi. Karna and the Kauravas will not pose us any challenge."

Drupada didn't mince words in expressing that Duryodhana being malicious, vindictive and without any sense of honour will not easily give up what he acquired through foul means. Moreover, he would be impervious to reasoning or fact and diplomacy. Therefore, Drupada suggested that the best course was to begin mobilising the allies like Shalya of Madra, Dhrishtaketu of the Panchalas, Jayatsena of the Kekayas and the others.

Sanjaya, the royal priest of King Drupada, was entrusted with the job of going as a messenger of the Pandavas. Lord Krishna advised that the messenger must bear in mind that their prime objective was the reinstatement of the Pandavas.

After Krishna and the Vrishnis departed, Virata, Drupada and Yudhishthira dispatched messengers to their allies. In Hastinapur, Duryodhana was merrily engaged in the preparation of war.

Arjuna Gets Narayan, Duryodhana Gets Narayani Sena

Drupada called his family priest and explained to him in detail what assignment he was expected to carry out in his role as a messenger. "Try to convince Dhritarashtra to return the kingdom without the need for a war. You may encounter difficulty in convincing him of the same, but Bhishma, Kripa, Drona and Vidura already see our point. Woo them to your side. Your presence in Hastinapur will dissuade Duryodhana in his war efforts since war has not been officially declared," the king told the emissary.

As Drupada's priest went to Hastinapur, Arjuna left for Dwaraka. When Duryodhana's spies informed him of Arjuna's intention to meet Krishna, perhaps with the aim of mobilising his war resources, he too rushed to Dwaraka and entered Krishna's chamber. When he arrived, Krishna was sleeping. Duryodhana arrogantly brushed Arjuna aside, and sat by Krishna's pillow, where his head lay. Arjuna stood humbly at Krishna's feet. When Krishna opened his eyes, he noticed Arjuna first and smiled. Next, he noticed Duryodhana who rose up from behind.

"Arjuna and I have arrived to seek your assistance. Since I arrived before Arjuna, I should be given the first priority," Duryodhana said.

"As far as I am concerned, I will not take up arms in this war. Your choice is between me on one side, or my strong Narayani army on the other," Krishna offered them the option.

"I will take you," Arjuna said promptly, to the secret delight of Duryodhana. He couldn't have asked for more. He had come precisely for Krishna's army. Having got what he wanted, he rushed to Balarama to seek his assistance. Balarama had already made a decision to keep away from the war. That didn't matter to Duryodhana because if Balarama was not helping him, he was not helping the Pandavas either. Kritavarma was another Vrishni hero, whom Duryodhana met with a plea for assistance. Kritavarma offered to fight for him along with one *akshavahini* army.

Shalya, the king of Madra, marched to Upaplavya when he heard about the mobilisation of troops for the coming war, so as to assist his nephews. The king on his way to Matsya, was pleasantly surprised on finding banners, pavillions and refreshments laid out for him and his men on the way. Shalya, thinking that it must be Yudhishthira who has been so hospitable to him, was highly impressed.

Shalya asked an attendant to inform whosoever had been so nice to him, to present himself before the king. He announced his intentions to reward his host. The king was shocked to find Duryodhana emerge before him, but he couldn't go back on his words now. Embracing him, he asked, "How can I reward you?"

"By offering your men and material in our war efforts," Duryodhana said politely.

"Yes, I will," assured Shalya, "but first I will meet Yudhishthira at Upaplavya and discuss it with him, before my commitment."

The Pandavas received the king at Upaplavya with utmost honour. "Son, I cannot fight for you," Shalya addressed Yudhishthira, "Duryodhana set a neat trap and got a favour promised from me. He has asked me for my support to him in the war."

"It's alright," Yudhishthira said, "I would not want you to go back on your promise. But I have one request. You are as good a charioteer as Krishna. You would be asked to hold the reins of Karna's chariot. There's bound to be straight combat between Karna and Arjuna. When they fight, do all you can to take the fight out of Karna, demoralise him. I know it's not quite moral, but I want Arjuna safe."

"I will. I will strip that suta's son of his arrogance," Shalya promised.

War preparations were going on, on both the sides. Upaplavya was turning into a military centre with the stock piling of war machineries and armouries. The Pandavas mustered the strength of seven *akshavahinis*, which included the contributions of Satyaki and the king of Chedi with an *akshavahini* each. The others like Jayatsena of Magadh, the king of Coastal Pandya and the Satvatas also swelled the number of the Pandavas' army.

Duryodhana's army was numerically much stronger, with eleven *askhavahinis* contributed by Bhagdatta of Pragryotisha, Bhurishrava, Kritavarma, Shalya, Jaidratha of the Sindhus, the princes of Avanti and many other kings.

Emissary Brings Pandavas' Message to The Kauravas

Sanjaya, on reaching Hastinapur, greeted Dhritarashtra, and conveyed to him the message he had brought as a messenger of the Pandavas. "You are familiar with the laws of inheritance. Dhritarashtra's and Pandu's sons inherit equally, but why have the Pandu's sons been denied theirs? You permitted a game of dice between unequals and condemned Pandu's sons to thirteen years of exile. Duryodhana tried to kill them a number of times, but they never retaliated. They don't want a war, although they are capable of fighting and defeating your sons," Sanjaya said.

Bhishma, Drona and the other Kuru elders favoured a peaceful settlement, while Duryodhana and Karna as usual were belligerent and rude. Dhritarashtra vacillated

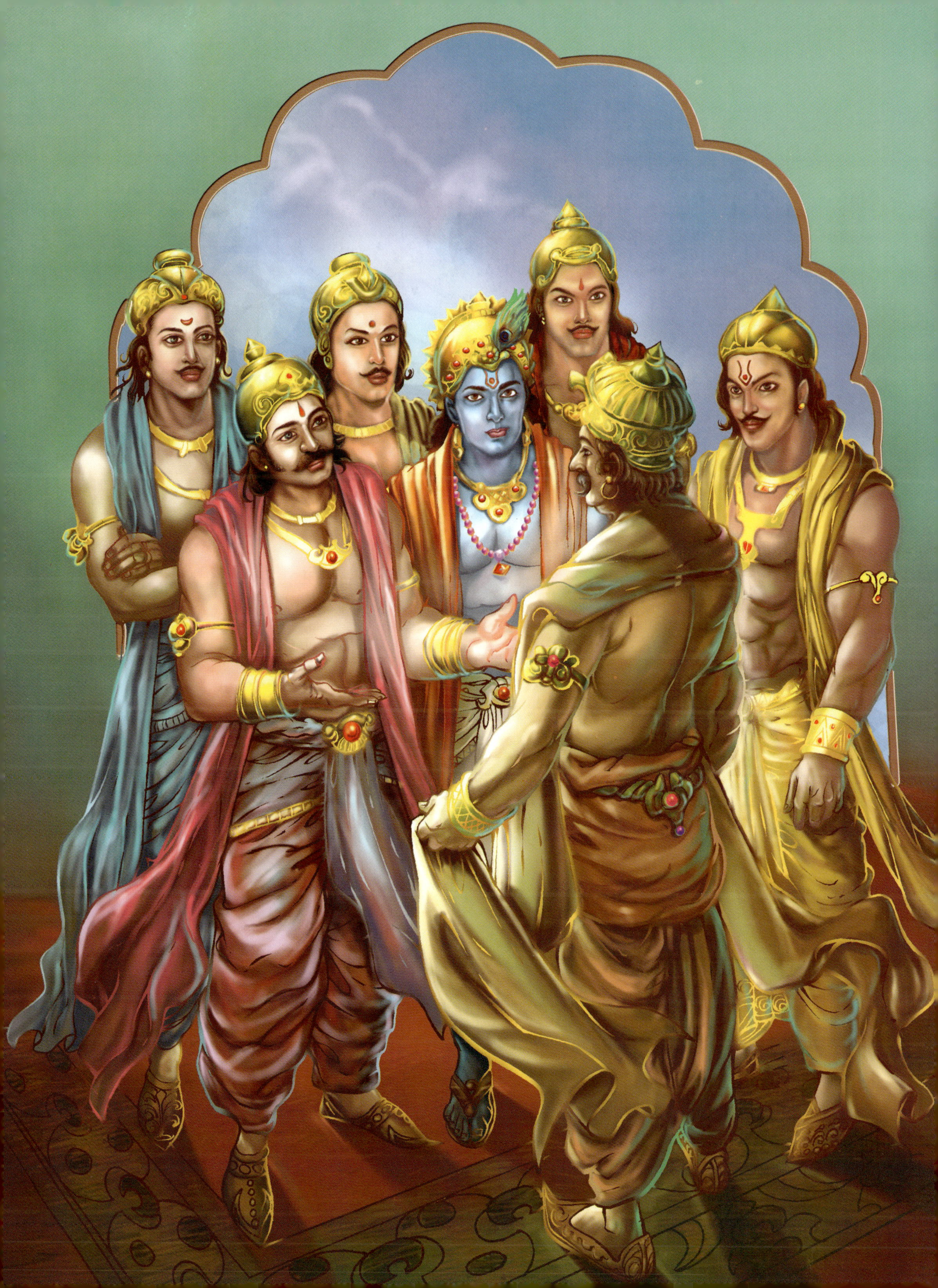

between the two sets of opinions. Dhritarashtra sent Sanjaya with the message that he favoured peace, but he very cleverly made no mention of the patrimony that should have gone to the Pandavas after the end of their thirteen years of exile.

Sanjaya came back with Dhritarashtra's message of peace, but that didn't please Yudhishthira since no mention of doing justice to the Pandavas, by giving them their dues, was made.

Yudhishthira said, "One has to follow the tenets of one's order. What is right for a brahmin may not be right for a kshatriya and vice versa. The duty of a brahmin is to acquire knowledge, while that of kshatriya is to act. I am only doing what my duty dictates me. I see no way for us but war, unless our kingdom is returned to us."

Lord Krishna spoke with much greater determination. "Kurus have unlawfully acquired another's kingdom. That's disdainful. That need not just be condemned, but the thieves must be punished. Dhritarashtra's sons are thieves. The Kuru elders have no authority to preach morality and honour when they did not stop their sons from humiliating Draupadi. She was dragged to the court and Dushasana tried to strip her naked. They didn't speak anything."

Sanjaya was once again sent to Hastinapur. He was to give the message to Duryodhana that asking for peace and not doing justice to the Pandavas were contrary. "We withstood vilification of Draupadi, several attempts to kill us not because we could not avenge but because we didn't want the Kurus dead. I am patient and prefer peace to war. That does not mean I cannot fight," was what Sanjaya had to say on Yudhishthira's behalf in Hastinapur.

Sanjaya spoke with brutal frankness, when he met Dhritarashtra alone in his chamber. "You have done injustice to Pandu's sons. You have cheated them of their kingdom. If Kurus are destroyed, the fault will lie with you. Return them their kingdom. Pandu's sons still honour you. I will deliver Yudhishthira's message in the court tomorrow. I am quite tired today," Sanjaya took his leave after a brief conversation.

Dhritarashtra lost his peace of mind at the veiled threat of Sanjaya. He summoned Vidura and told him that he was feeling miserable. He wanted Vidura to console him.

Vidura minced no words in telling him that he was responsible for whatever was happening to him. If he really wanted to regain his peace of mind, he should give

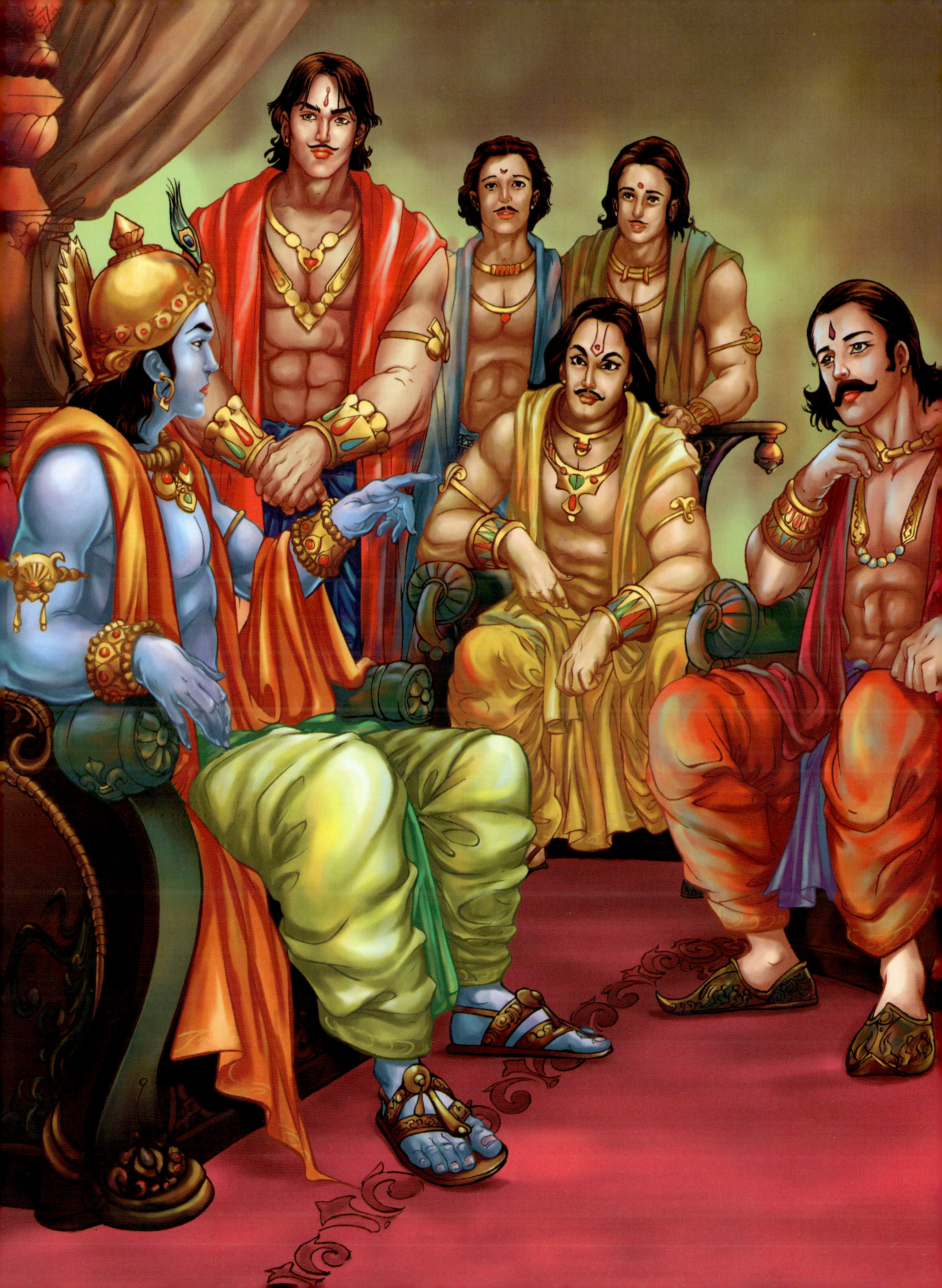

back the kingdom to the sons of Pandu. He should do justice to them. It was due to his greed and excessive love for his children that he had lost his peace of mind. Finally Vidura said, "I can do only one thing for you. I will invoke the presence of the immortal Sage Sunatsujata, who will clear all your doubts."

The sage appeared and clarified the doubts of Dhritarashtra. He said, "Attachment to worldly pleasure is another name of death. Detachment, truth, simplicity, humility and self-control are the weapons that keep away death. Self-control or continence is the most potent means to overcome the fear of death." The words of the sage were comforting enough for Dhritarashtra. He attained his peace of mind and the sage vanished.

The next day, Sanjaya appeared before the Kurus and allies, and announced, "I have Yudhishthira's message. The Pandavas bow and touch the feet of elders and express greetings to their friends and cousins. Arjuna has asked me to speak in presence of Duryodhana and Karna that if they want peace, they will have peace; but if they want war, they shall get a bitter war. Arjuna says, 'Yudhishthira's hardships will be nothing in comparison to the fate that Dhritarashtra's sons will meet, if the war takes place. Presence of Krishna with me ensures my victory. My Gandiva will speak in war. I will fight and win my kingdom. I will fight till a single Kaurava exists in the battlefield.'"

Bhishma didn't favour a war. He tried to appeal to Duryodhana's understanding, saying Arjuna and Krishna were Nara and Narayana who could never be defeated. He also said that no one, except Duryodhana, Karna son of a suta cursed by Parashurama, Shakuni, Suvalas and his evil brother Dushasana were in favour of a war.

Karna felt offended and replied tersely, "I have always been loyal to Dhritarashtra and his sons. So, how does that make me evil? If it comes to war, I will kill the Pandavas."

"You have repeatedly claimed that when it comes to war, you will kill the Pandavas. But let me know if you have defeated them even once? When fighting with Gandharvas, you ran away. It was Arjuna who rescued his cousins."

Drona too was against a war and advised Dhritarashtra against it, but Dhritarashtra, expressing his helplessness, blamed fate for everything. He tried to reason with Duryodhana, but his son was adamant. "I would rather lose life, wealth and kingdom than live with the Pandavas! I would not give them even a scrap of land," Duryodhana vowed.

Dhritarashtra sighed, "Then I see no hope for you. I grieve for you and all those who will embrace death with you." Duryodhana felt insulted by the lack of confidence in him. "I am no less in prowess than Pandavas. Let Gods come to their rescue, but I say I will kill them. I can split each of them into two. I have been taught by Bhishma, Drona and Kripa and know no less about war and weapons than Arjuna," Duryodhana spoke furiously.

Karna, aggrieved by Bhishma's tirade against him, said, "I know I have been cursed by Parashurama, but I can still face the Pandavas single handed. I can kill them as easily as one can split a gourd. I still have the *astra*."

Bhishma caustically remarked, "Arjuna defeated Indra and gave Khandava to Agni with only Krishna to support. No one can touch Arjuna so long as Lord Krishna is with him. That weapon you have will perish with you."

Karna, insulted by Bhishma's remarks, swore, "I have had enough of your insults! I vow not to raise arms in the battle till Bhishma leads the army."

Vyasa too arrived in Hastinapur and tried to reason with Duryodhana without success. Gandhari chided Duryodhana for his foolishness and tried her best to show reason to his son, but that too didn't have any impact. Duryodhana simply refused to see reason. When advised by Sanjaya and Dhritarashtra to speak to Krishna, who was impartial, he insolently remarked that it was below his dignity to seek advice from a person who was friendly to the Pandavas.

The first peace mission by Sanjaya failed miserably.

Yudhishthira was not in favour of a war. On one hand, he had to be a witness to the destruction of the Kurus, if he permitted war, while on the other, war was a necessity. He was not prepared to cede his rights meekly to his cousins. He could not decide what he ought to do.

"If you want, I can personally go to Hastinapur and negotiate for peace without sacrificing your interest, of course," Krishna offered to mediate.

Duryodhana Tries to Capture Krishna

While the other Pandavas were debating upon the inevitability or otherwise of war, Sahadeva was in favour of war and an end of Duryodhana. His views were supported by Satyaki. He reminded the Pandavas of the injustice done to them.

Yudhishthira was worried about the safety of Krishna as their messenger to Hastinapur. However, Lord Krishna assured Yudhishthira that nothing could happen to him there, although Duryodhana was mean and vicious.

As Krishna was about to leave, Draupadi went up to him and complained, "We were robbed of our kingdom, of our happiness. Sanjaya's plea was rejected. All we asked for, were the five villages — Avisthala, Brihannala, Makondi and Varnavata, leaving the fifth to be decided by them and you know their answer. Keshava! Remember my unkempt hair when you meet Duryodhana. I have known no peace for the last thirteen years. Peace will be distant to me unless I see Duryodhana dead and Dushasana's chest torn. Only his blood will quench my misery. If you and the Pandavas go for peace, I know where to turn to. My old but brave father, brothers and sons will avenge me. They will do for me what my husbands couldn't," Draupadi spoke furiously as tears streamed down her cheeks.

"Kuru ladies will weep as you do today. That is my promise. Your husbands will regain their kingdom and Kurus will be destroyed," Krishna assured Panchali and left for Hastinapur.

When Dhritarashtra came to know of Krishna's departure for Hastinapur, he ordered pavillions to be raised in his honour. Krishna, on the other hand, didn't accept even a glass of water and rode through his way.

Dhritarashtra bid expensive gifts, gold and silver to be presented to Krishna. Vidura, however scorned at the idea of bribing Krishna as nothing could separate Krishna from Arjuna.

Bhishma warned Duryodhana to choose his words with care when Krishna arrived and to return his kingdom. The very mention of return of kingdom enraged Duryodhana. "No, I will not return the kingdom. Instead I will imprison Krishna. This will bring the Vrishnis and the Pandavas to their size," Duryodhana said furiously.

Bhishma, turning to Dhritarashtra, rued, "Your son is vindictive and foolish. Do as he says and we will be utterly destroyed." Bhishma left the court distastefully. Krishna was accorded a full ceremonial honour on his arrival and led to a jewel-encrusted throne, but he politely refused the offers and went straight to meet Kunti at Vidura's house.

Kunti enquired about her sons and Draupadi as she met Krishna. With pain in her heart and tear-soaked red eyes, she grieved for her sons and Panchali. Finally she said, "I have a message for my sons. Tell Yudhishthira to act with honour. Death is preferable to a kingdom gained through fraud and deceit. Losing the kingdom meant nothing to me, but my heart ached when I came to know how Draupadi was humiliated."

"You are a widow and the mother of heroes. Your sons and daughter-in-law touch your feet and send you their regards. I promise they will rule the earth." Krishna assured Kunti and went to Duryodhana's palace.

Krishna was offered the highest welcome and hospitality but Krishna spurned them, saying that as a messenger he could not accept their hospitality. Karna and Duryodhana felt slighted at his refusal and they asked him why he was behaving so when he was a relative of both Pandu's and Dhritarashtra's sons. Krishna said he was not there in his capacity as a kin but as a messenger. He refused to even eat, saying one eats because of either love for the person offering the food or because of hunger, and he had neither.

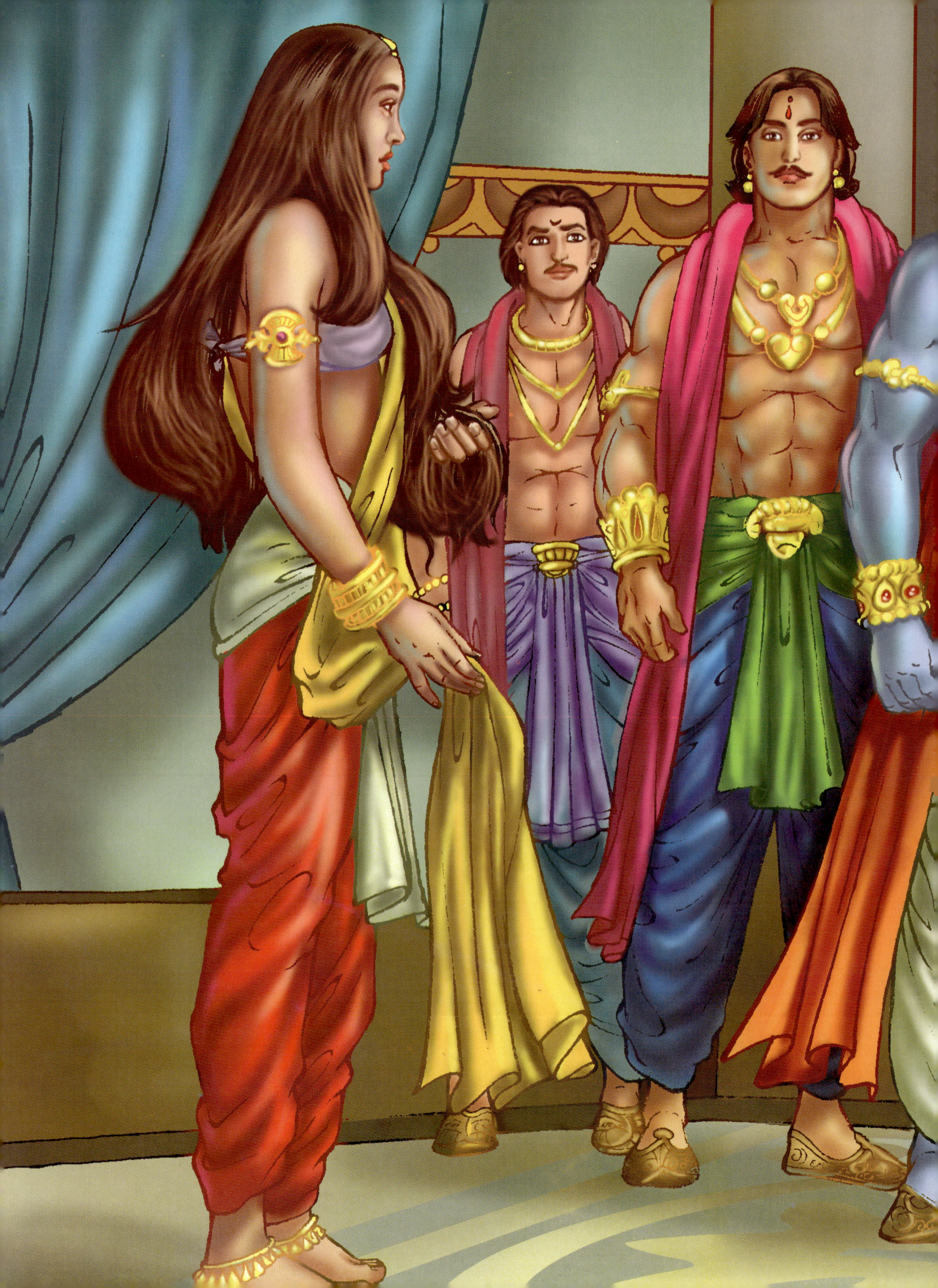

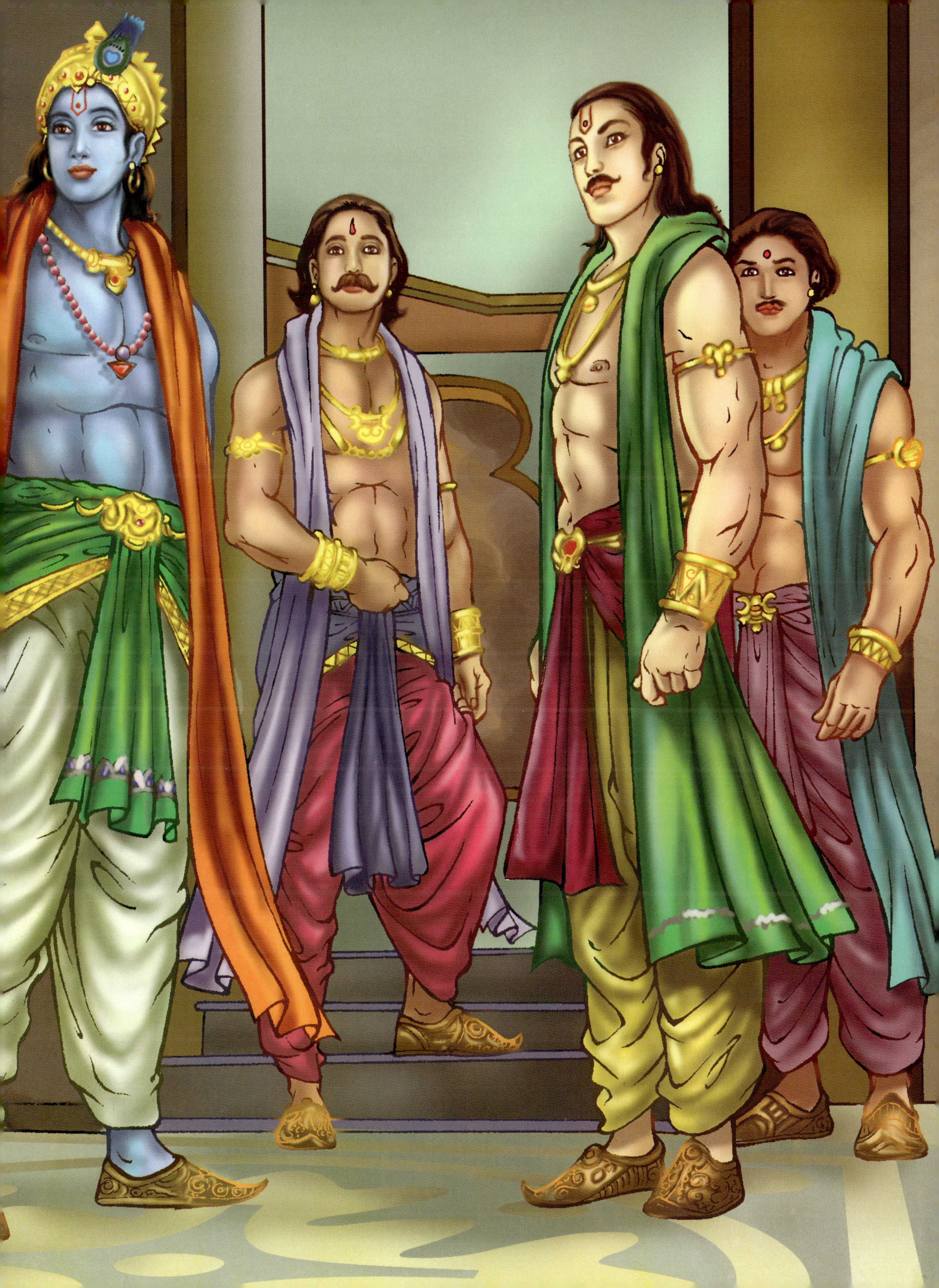

The next day, Krishna pleaded the Pandavas' case in the Hastinapur court in the presence of the Kuru elders and the immortal rishis Parashurama, Narada, Kanva and Vyasa. Krishna spoke eloquently, urging Dhritarashtra to restrain his foolish, unruly, avaricious and mean son. The Pandavas had fulfilled their obligation and led a miserable life for thirteen years in forest. Now, it was the time for Dhritarashtra and his sons to fulfill their part. "The kingdom must be returned to them. Yudhishthira has never sought to harm you or your sons. He treats you as a father figure and expects you will do justice to him," Krishna spoke softly but firmly to Dhritarashtra.

Dhritarashtra pleaded with his son but Duryodhana haughtily disregarded them. "Krishna! I sincerely pray for peace but my sons are being misled by Shakuni and Karna. Tell me, what can I do?"

Krishna, Bhishma and Drona each pleaded with Duryodhana but he stubbornly held on to his opinion. "Keshava! How am I to be blamed if Yudhishthira lost the game? Why does everybody blame me? Why do the Pandavas always threaten us with war? If they want a war, I am not afraid of it," Duryodhana directed his ire at Krishna.

Krishna stood up addressing the court, "We all have tried our best to avert a war. It is Duryodhana alone who wants nothing but war. If one individual is a source of constant trouble for a family, he must be disregarded."

Dhritarashtra asked Vidura to call Gandhari, hoping she would be able to restrain her son, but even her words failed to have the desired effect. Duryodhana simply walked out to hatch his next move in the company of Shakuni, Karna and Dushasana. Duryodhana informed them of all that had transpired in the court.

The general consensus was to capture Krishna. Satyaki heard of the plot and quickly dispatched Kritavarma to mobilise his men. He informed Krishna of the plot, at which Krishna laughed. Satyaki's disclosure shocked Vidura who instantly informed Dhritarashtra about the foolhardy plan hatched by his son.

Krishna's voice intervened, "Let them do it. I will snatch the entire kingdom and hand it over to Pandava's sons. Take my word, when I say I can, it means I can."

The Kuru elders chided Duryodhana in unison as he was summoned to the assembly. Vidura reminded Duryodhana of Krishna's valour. He was a boy and beheaded Shishupala in the presence of all the kings.

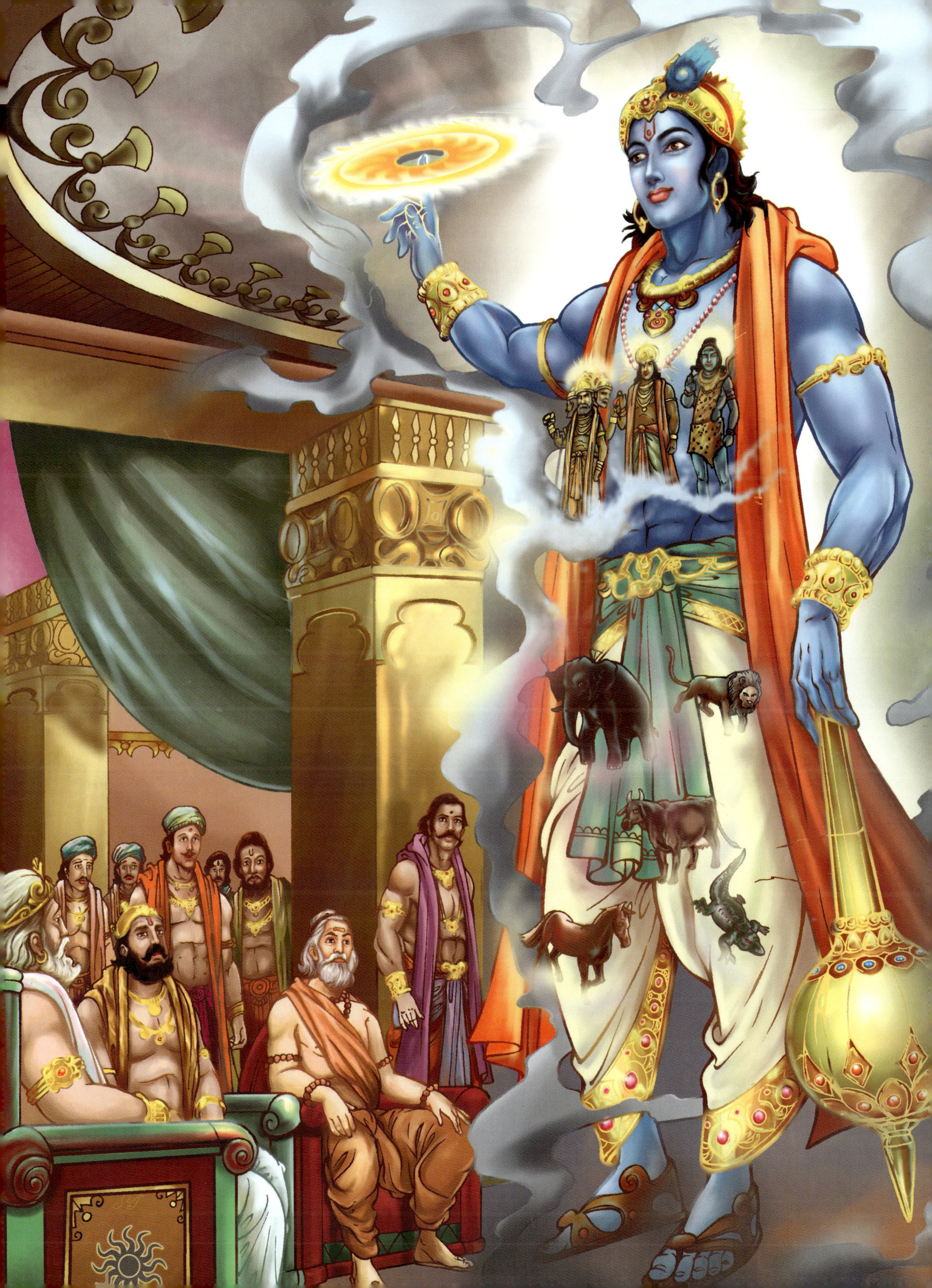

Lord Krishna assumed his cosmic form (Virata rupa) and his magnificence, with unearthly radiance, blinded everyone. "You think I am alone," said Krishna, "Look within and you will find the universe in me. How can you capture me?" None except Bhishma, Drona, Vidura and Sanjaya could look into that brightness.

As the vision faded, Krishna walked out along with Satyaki and Kritavarma even as the Kurus rushed after him. Krishna went straight to Vidura's house and informed Kunti that his mission was not successful and asked what message she had for her sons. Kunti said, "Tell them, so far they have behaved like anything but kshatriyas. Now, they must act like kshatriyas and fight to end for their rights. They must fight like kings and bring honour to their ancestors."

The War Clouds Gather and Sermon of Gita

Krishna bid farewell to Kunti and rode through the city, with his charioteer Daruka. On the way he came across Karna, whom he asked to accompany him for a while. Krishna watched Karna, speculatively in silence for a few moments before starting the conversation.

Krishna said, "You are a nice and honest person, Karna, but envy and evil company have blinded you to reason. You are well versed in scriptures and Vedas, and must be aware that there are two types of sons — Kanina and Sahodara. A Kanina is a son born to an unwed mother. You are a Kanina, born to Kunti and not Radha. So you are our kin and a brother to the Pandavas. Come with me to Upaplavya. The Pandavas will touch your feet once they come to know that you are their eldest brother. The princes will wash your feet and anoint you with water kept in the golden vessel. Draupadi will be your wife too as the common wife of the Pandavas. Yudhishthira will be your heir, obedient to your every command."

Karna replied, "I am aware of my antecedents. I am Kunti's son by Surya, but she abandoned me after my birth. The suta Adhiratha took me home. Radha fed me with her own breast-milk. For all practical purposes, they are my parents and I am a suta-putra. How can I rob them of a son? Adhiratha gave me my name, Vasushena, performed ceremonies for me and chose my wives. I have spent my life among sutas and I am a suta. My children and relatives, kith and kin are sutas. Neither fear nor greed will make me break those bonds. Duryodhana offered me his friendship and liberally gave me a kingdom. I am living on his charity. He trusts me. How can I turn a traitor? Nothing will compel me to abandon him. Let Pandavas never know the secret of my birth. If Yudhishthira has the slightest suspicion that I am his brother, he will refuse the kingdom and offer it to me instead. I, on my part, will hand it over to Duryodhana without a second thought." Karna's words reflected an honest person speaking with conviction.

Krishna's attempt to lure Karna to Pandavas' side failed. He even predicted in no uncertain terms that the war will end in victory for the Pandavas, but Karna didn't reply, as he himself perhaps knew the result of the war. Finally, Krishna told Karna as he alighted from the chariot to pass on a message to Bhishma and Drona at Hastinapur, "Today everything appears fine. The weather is comfortable, trees are laden with fruits, granaries are full, but seven days after the new moon, all these will no longer remain the same due to the devastations brought about by war."

After Krishna's departure from Hastinapur, Vidura went to see Kunti. "I have tried my best to avert the impending doom in the form of a war that is bound to witness the end of the Kurus. Dhritarashtra is making no efforts to rein in his sons. I am scared to imagine the consequences."

Kunti thought she would go to Karna, who would not disobey her, as he was her son. "Karna will come to my fold if I reveal to him the secret of his birth," Kunti thought.

Kunti Meets Her Eldest Son

Every morning Karna prayed to Sun God near the bank of Ganga. Kunti came there to meet him and saw him absorbed in his prayer, facing east. She waited in silence for Karna to finish his prayer.

Karna was surprised to see Kunti standing before him when he opened his eyes. He bowed his head and saluted her with his palms joined together. "Tell me what this son of Radha can do for you, lady? What makes you come here to meet me?" asked Karna formally.

"You are not Radha's son, but mine. Nor is Adhiratha your father. You were born to me, blessed by Surya. That is why you were born with the golden armour and earrings. You are my son, elder to Yudhishthira. The scriptures declare one's highest duty is towards one's parents, yet you display your allegiance towards Dhritarashtra's sons. Come to me, your own mother, help your brothers regain their kingdom. I owe you my injustice that I did to you, for the fear of infamy."

Kunti added, "You are a first-born. Why bear the stigma of a suta? Like rest of my sons, you are Partha, son of Pritha. When Kauravas are defeated, you will be the legal heir to the throne."

A heavenly voice was heard as soon as Kunti finished speaking. "Pritha speaks the truth. Do as your mother says."

Karna ignored the disembodied voice. "Revered kshatriya lady! I don't agree that my highest duty ought to be towards you, who abandoned me, as soon as I was born, to the mercy of the flowing river. No one could have done more harm to me. You took away the little fame and glory I inherited by virtue of my birth. I came to be called a suta for all time to come. Radha brought me up with love and care, yet today you have come here to offer me your affection. Kindly tell me, what brings you here?" Karna vented out his grievance.

"Son, what I did is unpardonable, but that doesn't take away a mother's feelings for her firstborn son. How can a mother see her sons trying to kill one another? War is inevitable, with Duryodhana turning down the offers of peace. He has turned down the pleas of Kuru elders, and worse still, of his own father and mother. You are his friend. Why don't you advise him to honour his words, like a kshatriya, and refrain from fratricidal war?" Kunti spoke compassionately to her son.

"A mother always desires happiness for her sons, but you have come to me not out of affection for me, but for a selfish reason. But I would be a coward if I switch my sides now. The world doesn't know my relationship with the Pandavas. If on the eve of this war, I suddenly claim kinship with them and switch over my loyalties, I will be dishonoured. Everyone would think of me as coward. All I am today and all I have, is due to Duryodhana. How can I desert him now to join the enemy camp? He relies on me. He trusts me. He has confidence and faith in me. How can I betray him?

"Bhishma and Dronacharya can't go against him. Bhishma is duty bound to protect the Kuru throne. Dronacharya is dependant on the patronage of Hastinapur court. I have to be true to him, especially because I owe him everything. I must repay my debts, even if it means sacrificing my life. I know I stand to gain if I join the Pandavas, but I cannot." Karna spoke in a polite but straight language. He rejected his mother's plea. Therefore, to soothe her, Karna said, "Although I have not agreed to your pleas, but let me assure you, your visit to me will not be completely futile. I can make at least one promise to you. I will not harm any of the Pandavas except Arjuna. The two of us have a bitter rivalry, and we are bound to come face to face in the battlefield. One of us will surely fall in the battle. In either case, you will have five sons," Karna promised.

"Remember your promise when you raise arms against my sons," Kunti felt reassured at the promise.

Karna bowed in respect with palms joined and went his way, while Kunti stood looking at him as he went. Krishna came back to Upaplavya only to inform the Pandavas regretfully that he had failed in his peace mission. He said he tried his best to reason with Duryodhana, who even Gandhari, Dhritarashtra, Vidura, Bhishma and Parashurama could not convince, to refrain from the destructive war. He could not be convinced of peace as a better option. What was worse, said Krishna, was that Duryodhana's eleven *akshavahinis* were on march even as death awaited them in the plains of Kurukshetra, which they refused to see.

The Armies March In

Yudhishthira asked his seven *akshavahinis* to be assembled. The seven generals for the seven *akshavhinis* were chosen. They were Drupada, Virata, Dhrishtadyumna, Shikhandi, Satyaki, Chekitana and Bheema.

Dhrishtadyumna headed the army as its commander-in-chief and the Pandava army was ready for action. It marched to the plains of Kurukshetra. The army was prepared in every way with stores and provisions, fodder, food, cattle, war machines, surgeon's stores and physicians accompanying them.

The Pandavas camped on a level plain with easy access to fuel and water but at a distance from the main battlefield. The generals had their tents pitched in high security area so as not to be ambushed easily. To ensure further safety, Krishna had a moat dug around the camp which was filled with water diverted from the river Hirnavati. The armoury was filled to the brim with all kinds of missiles and weapons. The surgeons and physicians had their tents at a considerable distance from the camp, protected by armed sentries.

Duryodhana had left no stone unturned in his war preparation. He meticulously selected his generals and the fighting corps. They were the best of men prepared for any situation. Camps were pitched near the forest, out of the reach of the enemy's missiles. The supply routes were heavily guarded. The divisions had a balanced combination of veterans and raw recruits. The best of charioteers and mahouts were appointed to man chariots and elephants. Workshops were set up for the repair of chariots, and reserves of elephants and horses were stationed within the camp. Reserves of army comprised five hundred chariot warriors, five hundred elephant warriors, two thousand five hundred infantry men and one thousand five hundred cavalry men.

Duryodhana's spies had informed him of the activities going on in the Pandavas' camp. He approached Bhishma and humbly requested him to assume the command of the Kaurava army. "You are invincible. You cannot be defeated. You are the greatest warrior in the world. Kindly take the charge of my eleven *akshavahinis*," Duryodhana requested.

Bhishma spoke straight. "I have two conditions for leading your troops, I will not kill Pandu's sons. I love them as much as I love you. I gave you my word and I will fight for you but their happiness and well being are at the core of my heart. I will, however, kill their army. I will kill at least ten thousand soldiers every day so long as I survive in the battle. Secondly, as long as I am in command of the army, Karna will not enter the field of the battle. He may be dear to you but he has always been disrespectful to me."

Karna stood up in anger and left the tent, saying, "I will wait for Ganga's son to fall before I take up arms in this battle."

As the preparations for the war were going on, Balarama and Pradyumna arrived in the Pandava camp. Balarama touched Drupada's and Virata's feet and accepted the Pandava's offering of water to wash his feet. He blessed the Pandavas when they touched his feet but looked disapprovingly at them. Turning to Krishna, he said, "There's no way the war can be avoided now and I hope your friends survive the war. I asked you to stay neutral since both the warring parties are related to us, but you paid no heed to my words."

Balarama himself had chosen to be neutral and he conveyed his decision to Yudhishthira. "Krishna loves Arjuna and so he cannot remain unaffected by your cause. He is with you and that's why you will be victorious. I am also with you because I cannot stay opposed to Krishna. Without Krishna, I have no worth. Since both Bheema and Duryodhana are my disciples, I cannot choose one over the other. Therefore, I have decided not to raise arms and to stay neutral. Since I cannot watch the bloody carnage indifferently, I have decided to go on a pilgrimage so long as this war goes on." Saying so, Balarama left the camp.

After Balarama, the king of the Bhojaktas and Krishna's brother-in-law, Rukmi arrived. Rukmi was a great warrior. He was a disciple of Dronacharya and had with him

Indra's bow, the Vijaya, which was no less powerful than Arjuna's Gandiva. He prided himself as a warrior to the extent of being arrogant.

Rukmi came to Yudhishthira's tent with the confidence that in this hour of need, the Pandavas would welcome him more than any other warrior. Krishna was also present in the camp when Rukmi arrived. Yudhishthira was aware of the animosity between Rukmi and Krishna. Therefore, he greeted him coldly. Krishna had abducted Rukmini, the sister of Rukmi, and defeated the forces led by him, before carrying her away to Dwaraka.

Rukmi offered the Pandavas his assistance pompously. "I will send the Kauravas to hell despite Drona, Kripa and Bhishma, if you are afraid of them. I have an *akshavahini* of mighty warriors, who will conquer the earth for you. You just sit back and watch us in action."

Arjuna's forehead creased. "I am a Kuru, the son of mighty King Pandu. I have my Gandiva with me as also Krishna, my friend and brother. I am afraid of none, not even Duryodhana. I alone am enough for him. I don't need your assistance. Your support makes no difference to me. Stay or leave as you please."

Rukmi left the Pandava camp humiliated, only to offer his assistance to Duryodhana. But Duryodhana too turned him away as he considered it below his dignity to accept a warrior, who had been rejected by the Pandavas, as an ally. Rukmi left Kurukshetra along with his men.

On the battle-eve, every kshatriya, with the exception of Rukmi, Pradyumna and Balarama, was present in Kurukshetra, ready to pounce upon the enemy at the sound of the conch.

Duryodhana summoned Uluka, Shakuni's son that night and asked him to deliver a message to the Pandavas. "Give this message to Yudhishthira in presence of Krishna," he insisted with malicious laughter. "You claim yourself as virtuous but indulge in a war. I rejected your plea for granting you five villages only to instigate war. We tried to burn you down in Varnavata. Avenge yourself if you can. We are mighty kshatriyas trained by Drona and Kripa, why do you then rely only on Krishna, who is neither a kshatriya nor half as powerful as you?"

"Tell Krishna that the Pandavas have mustered the courage to attack me only because he is there. But you can do nothing more than the charlatan's trick you performed in the court. Fight me if you have the courage. Where are the Gods in you? If you could create illusions, I too can do the same. It was nothing but a common conjurer's act. The one who is the Supreme Being ordains his will and does not subjugate people by charlatan's acts. You said you would kill Dhritarashtra's sons and give the kingdom to the Pandavas. Do it now if you can. Fight in this war if you are a man. Eunuchs are more manly than you. All your claim to fame is dubious. A monarch would consider it below his dignity to cross swords with you." Duryodhana's words, full of hatred and vengeance, to be carried as message by Uluka made him fearful.

Duryodhana, however continued with his tirade, "Tell Bheema he is a fool. All he knows is cooking. He is a glutton. He is just like a bull without horns. He said he would drink Dushasana's blood. Now is the time for it. Tell him to do that if he can. Fighting in a war is no cooking. The oaths he took after that game are as hollow as reed. Tell Nakula and Sahadeva to recall the humiliation of Draupadi and avenge her insult, if they can."

Duryodhana roared with laughter even as Uluka felt extremely frightened. He didn't stop at that. His tirade against Arjuna was no less venomous, which he wanted to be delivered through Uluka, "Tell Arjuna to remember his miserable days in the forest. Tell him to prove his claims of being a brave kshatriya warrior. Let him remember how I made him my slave and dragged his wife in the Kuru assembly. Can he ever hope to defeat Bhishma and Drona? Can mount Sumeru be crushed by wind? Tell him, he is a man of small vision who cannot see my huge army."

"Repeat my words, Uluka, to him ensuring you do not miss anything. Tell him, 'You can't breach my army and my elephant corps, always guarding me. Show me what you can do with your Gandiva and Agni's chariot. Hollow threats are just that, hollow threats! If they could do any damage, any loud mouth weakling could conquer the world. I reigned over your kingdom for the last thirteen years, while you rotted in the forest. I will kill all of you and continue to rule. Where was your Gandiva when Draupadi was being dragged and stripped? Where was Bheema's might, then? Neither your Gandiva nor his strength could save you against me. You are as hollow as your words. Shame on your manhood! You wore bracelets and braided your hair in Virata's palace. Can a eunuch music teacher fight a kshatriya? I cannot give up the kingdom. Take it out of me, if you can. Not even a hundred Arjunas and Krishna can force me to do that."

With great reluctance and fear, Uluka carried the message to the Pandava camp. Yudhishthira noticed fear in his eyes and tried to soothe him, "Tell us frankly, what Duryodhana had to say. Don't fear! You are only a bearer of the message. You have nothing to fear. Tell us now fearlessly what you have to."

Uluka repeated the message verbatim. The Pandavas heard him silently without taking any offence at the provocative words used against them. However, Uluka's nervousness grew even worse at their silence.

Bheema could barely restrain himself and burst out, "You, gambler's son! What are you waiting here for now? Just go away before I lose my control." As Uluka rose to leave, Bheema shouted at him to stop and take back his message as well, "Tell Duryodhana we have got his message, and take mine. Tell him we are no fools like him to be instigated by provocative words. We tolerated his mischief and evil ways only because we honour the words of our eldest brother. He is lucky to have survived because of our elder brother. But if he is so keen to visit Yama's court, tell him to see me tomorrow. Tell him, the Pandavas still remember the oaths they took in the assembly, only more vividly now. I will drink Dushasana's blood, as the time for it has arrived."

Arjuna interrupted Bheema in an attempt to comfort the terror stricken son of Shakuni, "Every one is aware of your strength, no one doubts it. The son of Shakuni is only a poor messenger." Turning to Uluka, he said, "Tell him my arrows will answer him tomorrow as a man is known by his deeds. Only eunuchs use words as weapons."

Yudhishthira, temperamentally calm, was not so this time. "A kshatriya king can never tolerate himself meekly submitting to reviling words. Tell Duryodhana, he mistreated us and yet we tolerated. Now our patience is wearing out. He is immoral and stupid enough not to see where his misdeeds would lead him. If he is a man, tell him to face us directly and not place our beloved ones at the head of his army. A kshatriya relies on his own strength."

Bheema felt he had not spoken out his heart and had to say more. "I swear by the Lord of the universe that I will drink Dushasana's blood, kill Dhritarashtra's sons and break Duryodhana's thigh before placing my foot on his head."

Uluka hastily left the Pandavas' camp to deliver the messages to the Kauravas.

At about the same time, back in Hastinapur, Dhritarashtra was quiet and alone in his misery, when the wise sage Vyasa arrived there.

Vyasa Gives Divine Vision to Sanjaya

Vyasa tried to cheer up the sagging morale of the old blind king. "It's no use lamenting now, my son," he said, "I can grant you the divine vision for the duration of this war so that you can see and hear everything that takes place in Kurukshetra."

The miserable king shook is head in negation and said, "I have no desire to see the death of my own sons, but I would like to hear about every detail of the war."

Sage Vyasa decide to grant the same boon to Sanjaya. "The vision granted to Sanjaya will enable him to see and hear everything about the war, day or night, manifest or concealed, word or thought. Weapons will not injure him, neither will fatigue affect him," Vyasa pronounced.

"I will assure the fame of Kurus spreads to all the three worlds. They will live forever. Do not grieve for circumstances beyond your control. As for victory, it always goes to the righteous," Vyasa said.

Dhritarashtra thought over Vyasa's enunciation about victory, somewhat unconvinced, but the sage went on speaking, "Nothing is eternal or permanent. Time destroys everything, but you have it in you to prevent this war. You can restrain your sons and compel them to do justice to Pandu's sons. Duryodhana would be responsible for the end of your dynasty. Exile him now and avert the doom."

Dhritarashtra grimly heard the words of the wise sage, but appeared not quite interested in reining in his son. All he was interested in was the outcome of the war. Whether his sons or Pandu's sons would be victorious in the war was all he wanted to know. Vyasa, too, made no further attempt to make his son, Dhritarashtra, see sense. Nevertheless, he answered the query of his son, who was too curious to know who would be victorious.

"An army, whether big or small, but loyal and contented will emerge victorious," Vyasa replied briefly as he continued cryptically, "Strength in numbers doesn't necessarily imply victory. As for victory, there can be defeat in victory and victory in defeat." The sage blessed his son and left.

When Sanjaya came in, Dhritarashtra told him of his being blessed with divine eyes for the duration of the war. "You would be able to see and hear all. Tell me whatever you see and hear and what the kshatriya kings are doing in the battlefield."

Sanjaya faithfully narrated everything that he saw and heard of the war in Kurukshetra for the next eighteen days. He was impartial in his description, but at the end of each day he never forgot to remind the king that it was he who was responsible for the bloody carnage.

Both the armies stood facing each other in the field of Kurukshetra. A code for the war was agreed upon by both the warring parties. The major rules were:

1. Suspension of the war at sunset.

2. Not to attack an unarmed person.

3. Not to attack any warrior who had surrendered.

4. Not to attack messengers and transporters of weapons, provisions, medicines and other war-material to the battlefield.

5. Not to raid the medical camps for the treatment of the wounded.

6. A fair and just fight in every respect.

As the two armies stood facing each other, the silence was broken by the blasts of hundreds of conches, beating of kettledrums, neighing of horses and trumpeting of elephants. The first rays of the sun saw the two armies alert and ready in their battle gear.

Bhishma, the commander-in-chief of the Kaurava army, addressed them briefly. "War is the only mission of a true kshatriya. Doors of heaven remain open for a kshatriya dying in the battlefield or the victory. There's no other alternative for him. There's no better glory than death in a battlefield. Those who die of disease or old age are pitied. Move ahead fearlessly. Fear nothing."

Yudhishthira, at the centre of his army, guarded by elephants and cavalry divisions, hopelessly noticed the huge Kaurava army, almost double the size of his. "How can we defeat that army?" he expressed his apprehensions to Arjuna, "Our grandfather is their commander-in-chief, who can reduce us to dust this very moment, if he wants."

Arjuna stood fearlessly. Turning towards his elder brother, he replied, "Victory has nothing to do with greater numbers. It has everything to do with courage and conviction in one's cause. Our victory is certain, for our cause is just, and Krishna is with us."

Krishna smiled, "Bhishma and his army are ready to fight. Recite the hymn to Durga and ask her to bless you with victory."

Yudhishthira, on noticing the huge Kaurava army, which gave the impression of a much greater strength, asked Arjuna to arrange their army in the needlepoint form. When the two armies were ready, Krishna blew the Panchjanya, and Arjuna his Devdutta. Duryodhana responded by blowing his conch. Krishna moved the chariot to a position from where Arjuna could see the Kuru warriors.

Krishna Imparts The Knowledge of Gita to Arjuna

Arjuna saw Bhishma, Dronacharya, Ashvathama, Kripacharya, Shalya, and other near and dear ones and a darkness settled over his heart. His shoulders stooped, the grip on his Gandiva loosened. "I tremble with nervousness and my mouth goes dry when I see my beloved gurus and other familiar faces," Arjuna bemoaned.

"My thinking fails. Oh Krishna, I don't want victory, I don't want kingdom. Sovereignty will bring me no pleasure. I can see my grandfather, teachers, uncles, and friends. They are here with the intention of killing me, but I can't kill them, even if I am offered the kingdom of the three worlds. Dhritarashtra's sons are my cousins. How can I kill them? Can fratricide ever bring me happiness? My cousins are blinded by greed, and so is my uncle. They cannot see evil in fratricide. But you and I can. How can I commit this sin? We must do all we can to prevent it."

"When a race dies, anarchy and evil prevails, because the custom and code, culture and tradition die with it and nothing remains to guide the people. I cannot bear the responsibility of committing this sin. I would prefer Duryodhana killing me rather than I committing the sins of fratricide and genocide." Arjuna felt listless and aggrieved. He dropped the Gandiva and crouched in his chariot. His eyes were wet and his head rested on his knees.

Lord Krishna tried to inspire him. "What you are saying and doing, doesn't go with your kshatriya creed. The gates of heaven are barred for a weakling. Get up, son of Kunti. This is no time to allow any weakness to enter your heart."

"Tell me Krishna, how can I face my grandfather and my gurus with weapons in my hand? These hands are there to worship my gurus. I would rather live on alms than kill my gurus. Oh Krishna, what shall I do? I neither want kingdom nor heaven. I cannot stain my hands with the blood of my near and dear ones. I can't decide anything, Krishna. I don't know anything, Krishna. I don't know what difference does it make whether they or we are victorious. I don't know what my duty is. I am your disciple. Teach me Krishna. Tell me what to do. Tell me what I can do to alleviate my misery. I will not fight, Krishna," Arjuna spoke his heart out and fell silent.

"What are you worried about, Arjuna? Your worries are futile. The wise ones do not grieve. Those who grieve neither for the living nor for the dead, are truly wise. The kings you see over there have always been there. It's not that they were not here before or will never be here again. Everything changes. Nothing remains the same. Even we undergo changes, passing through childhood, adolescence, youth and old age. All things have a beginning and an end, but a truly emancipated man remains untouched by them. The soul remains permanent. It pervades the universe and is eternal. It can never be destroyed. Only body, the embodiment of soul, is finite and destructible."

"Partha! Get up now and hold your Gandiva."

"He who thinks soul can be destroyed, is unwise. Soul can neither slay nor be slain. Soul does not perish with the body. The man who knows this knows he can neither kill nor be killed. There is nothing called death. He simply casts away his worn-out garment to don a new one. The soul discards bodies, but is itself indestructible. Weapons can't slash it, fire can't burn it, water can't drench it, nor can wind touch it. Recognise the soul for what it really is and do not mourn these people who are here, ready to die."

"Those who are born must die one day, as those who die must take a re-birth. This is a plain truth, the natural order. There's nothing extraordinary about it. Many know this truth but don't understand it, so they grieve. Do your duty as commanded by your kshatriya code. For a kshatriya nothing is better than a battle fought with complete dedication. Do your duty without vacillating. You will be wanting in the performance of your duty if you refuse to fight. People will talk of your cowardice, which will bring you infamy and infamy is worse than death. If slain, you will attain

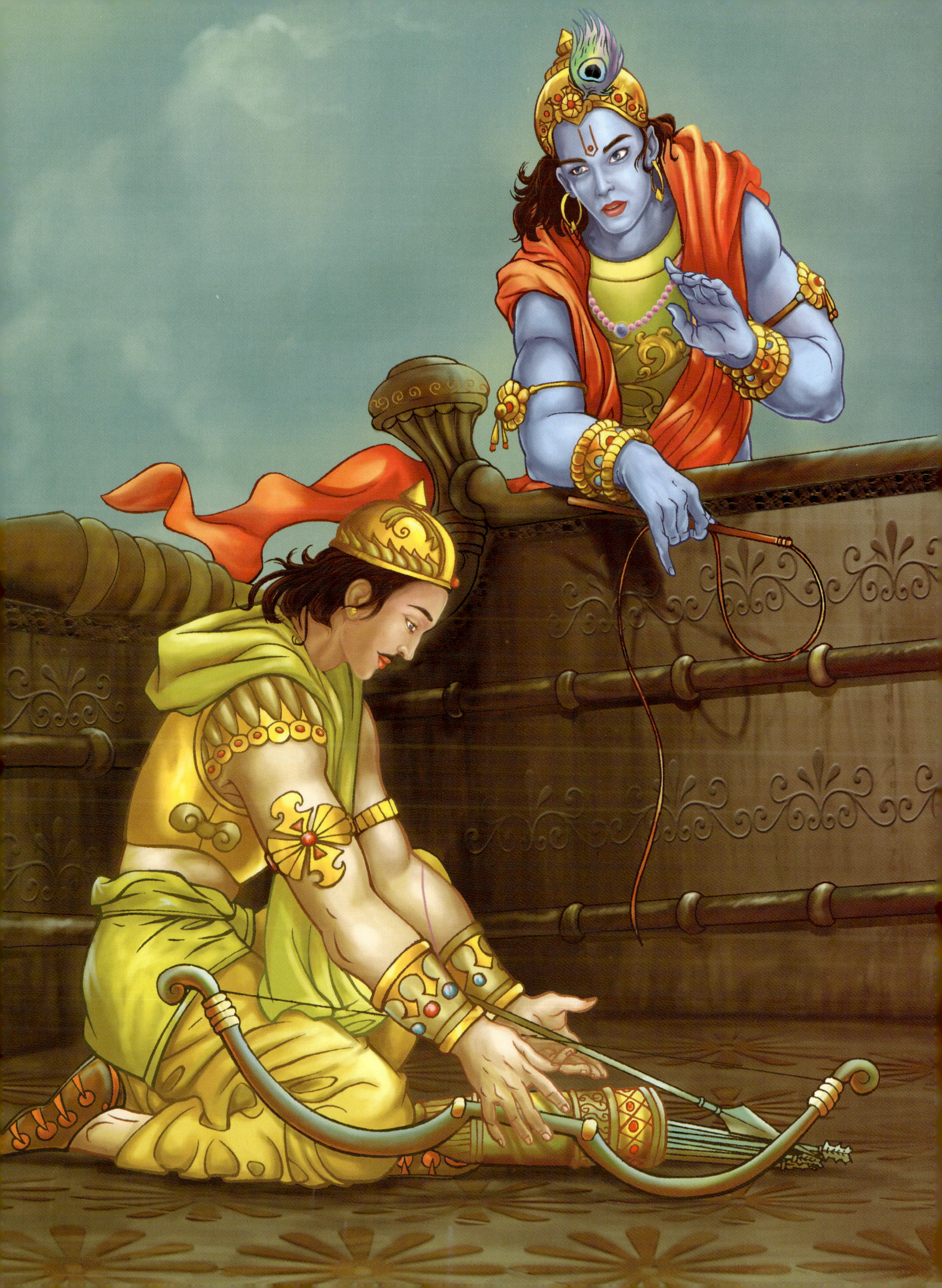

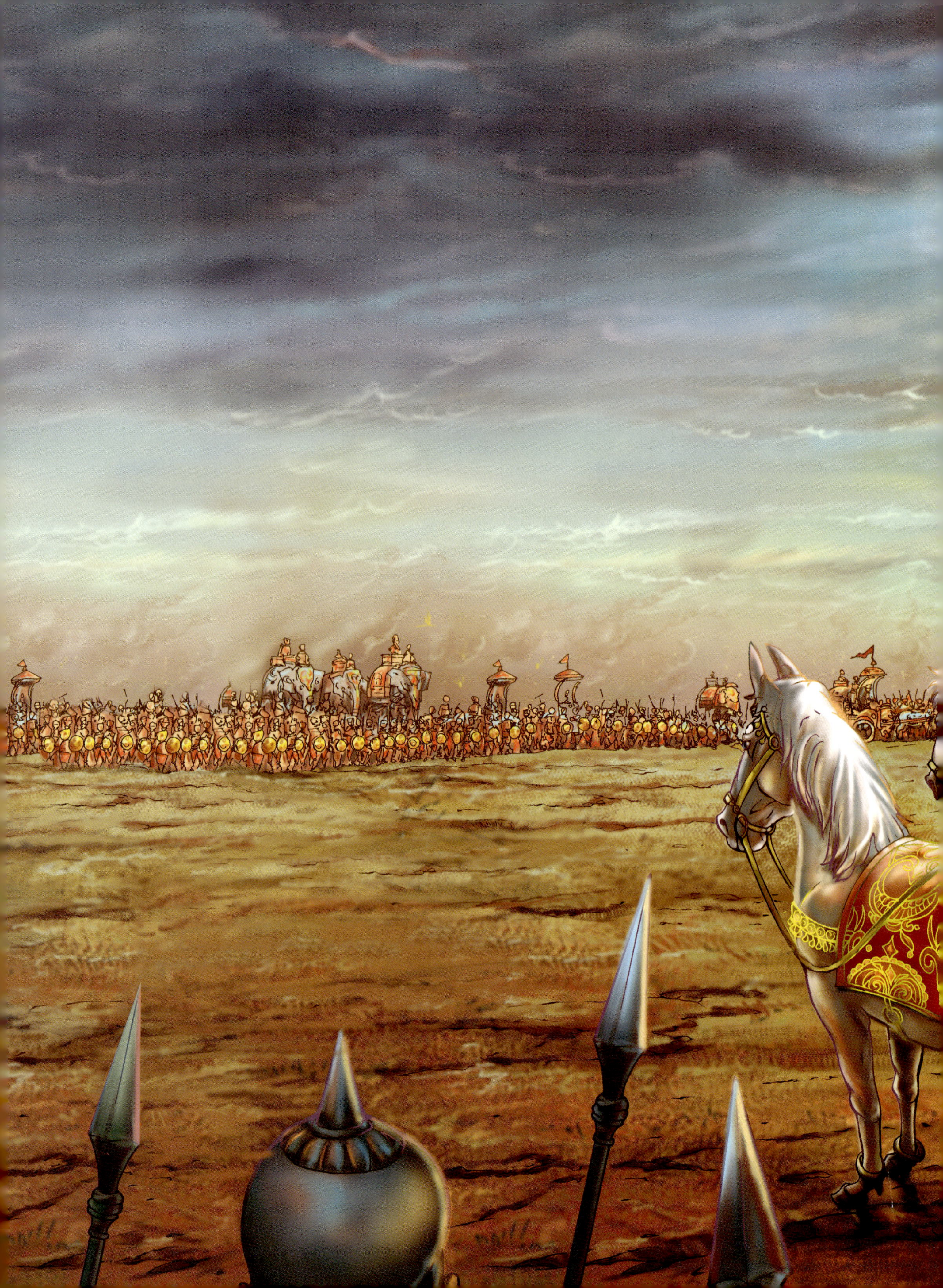

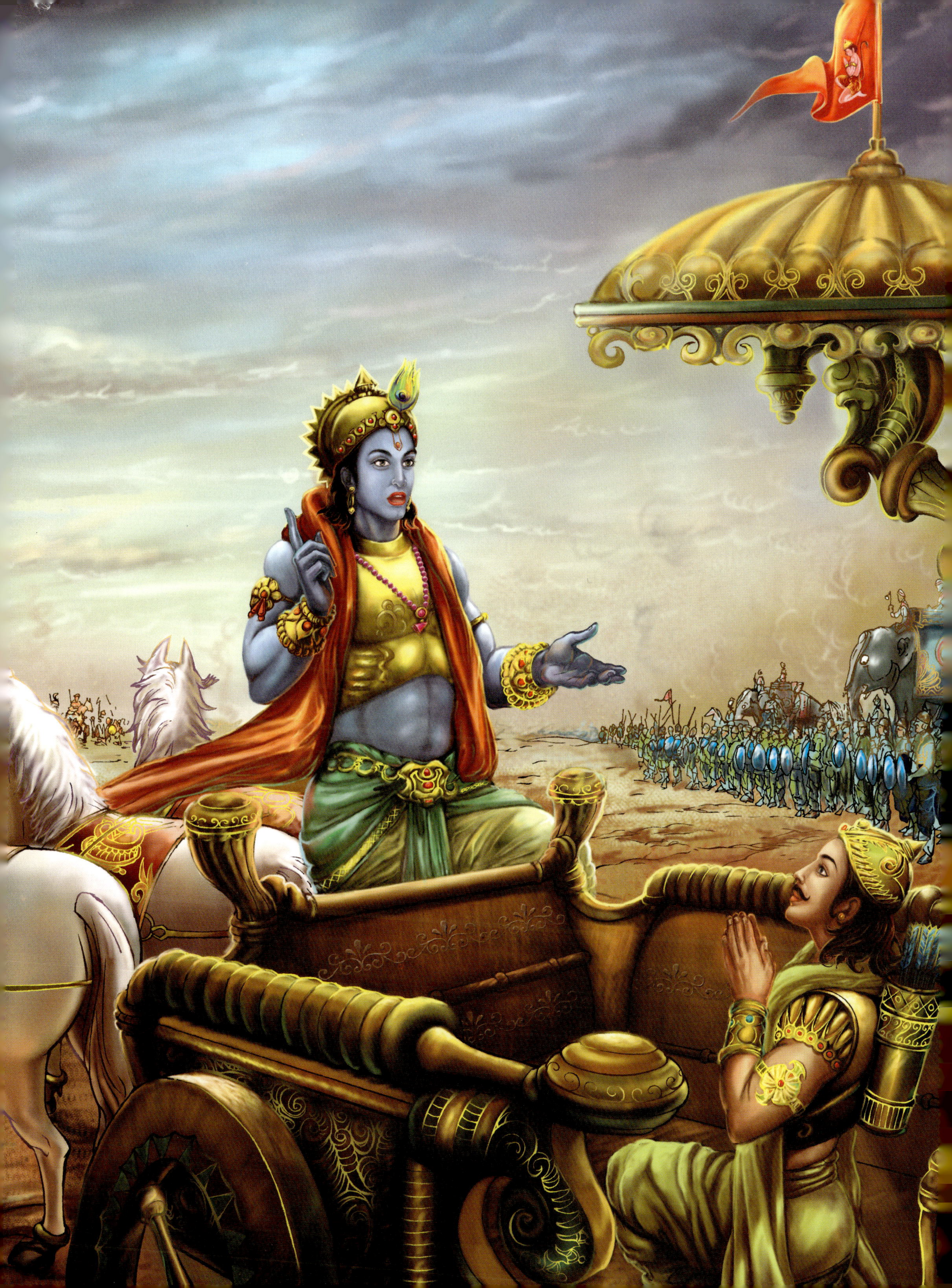

heaven; if victorious, you will gain earth. You have nothing to lose. So pick up your Gandiva and fight, Partha!"

"Fight because you must. You have no other option. Get over victory or defeat, pain or pleasure, gain or loss, and fight. Perform your duty for what it is — duty and do not bother yourself with the end result — the fruit. Loss or gain will be purely an appendage to what are the first and the last ends — duty. Do your duty for the sake of duty. This is what Sankhya yoga teaches. It is the yoga of reason and understanding. He who practises this yoga faces no impediment while performing duty."

"Transcend the opposites — pleasure, pain; heat, cold; victory, defeat; happiness, sorrow, to realise your true self, the end of all knowledge contained in the Vedas. Your object and goal is to act, not the consequences of action. To act is all you have in you and the motivation should not come from the fruits or rewards that you would get out of your action. Do your duty without personal involvement, that is, by remaining unattached to it. Do what is to be done by you, irrespective of whether it results in success or failure. Devotion is but the name of this equanimity in the face of pleasure and pain, victory or defeat. A devotee remains his usual self, mentally calm and steadfast in every circumstance. Devotion has to do with action, not with its result. Your mind should be calm and peaceful in any adversity. It should crave neither pleasure nor success and should get over the negative emotions like fear and anger."

"Mental poise and one's ability remain unwavering when the senses are brought under control. A man whose senses have been brought under control feels unagitated by either positive or negative emotions. He suffers no extremes of feelings. It is only the man whose senses are under control, who enjoys perfect peace, for the agitating senses lead to misery. A man who knows no peace, knows no happiness. The senses, by their nature, rush out to seek outward pleasure. Draw them in like a tortoise draws in its limbs. Restrain them. The restrained senses will rid you of all desires. This is the state yogis attain. One merges with the supreme self after attaining this state, which is the divine state."

Even after Lord Krishna had spoken these words to Arjuna, his mental gloom and agony continued. He remained listless in the chariot. "You speak of devotion as a superior path to that of action. Why do you then want me to fight this war?" he asked.

Krishna replied, "There are two kinds of devotion. That of Sankhya yoga, which is through knowledge, and that of Karma yoga through action. Non-performance of duty doesn't free a man from action. Inactivity doesn't lead to emancipation, nor does renunciation of action lead to it. Life means action. To exist, one must act. No one can exist without action. Man must act, but without any regard for consequences, whether good or bad, success or failure. This is devotion. He who acts with devotion attains the supreme state. There is no way but for a man to act, otherwise the world will cease to exist. If you take my case, you will see, there is nothing that I desire, there is nothing that I need to do, yet I must act and that's what I am doing."

"The only difference between *agyani* and *gyani*, an ignorant man and a wise man is that while both of them act, the former acts with desire and attachment, while the latter acts without. Every action results in consequences, but a fool thinks it is he who acts and the results are his doing, the wise know better. All creatures have distinct nature, but are alike in responding to the objects with either aversion or affection, depending on whether they are accompanied by pain or pleasure. Performance is always better than non-performance even when the performance lacks perfection. Death as a course of duty is preferable to inaction."

Arjuna was beginning to feel at peace with himself. His curiosity was aroused and he asked, "How does a man sin?"

Krishna blamed desire and anger at the root of all sins men commit. "Desire and anger gobble all wisdom and learning. Desire is insatiable and senses diligently obey the command of desire. Unfulfilled desires give rise to wrath, which has a great destructive potential. You will never realise the Supreme unless you control the senses. You must conquer desire to win the world."

Arjuna wanted to know in greater detail with complete understanding, the import of Krishna's statement, "You were here before, are here now, and will be here again."

"Both you and I have gone through many ages before," Krishna said. "Though unborn and eternal, I take the bodily form whenever such a need arises to protect righteousness and destroy evil. I am born in every age to perform this task. Those who know me are perfect men, free from desire and anger. I accept all those who come to me irrespective of their caste, creed or guise, provided they come to me with devotion. But all must act, for life and prosperity come from action."

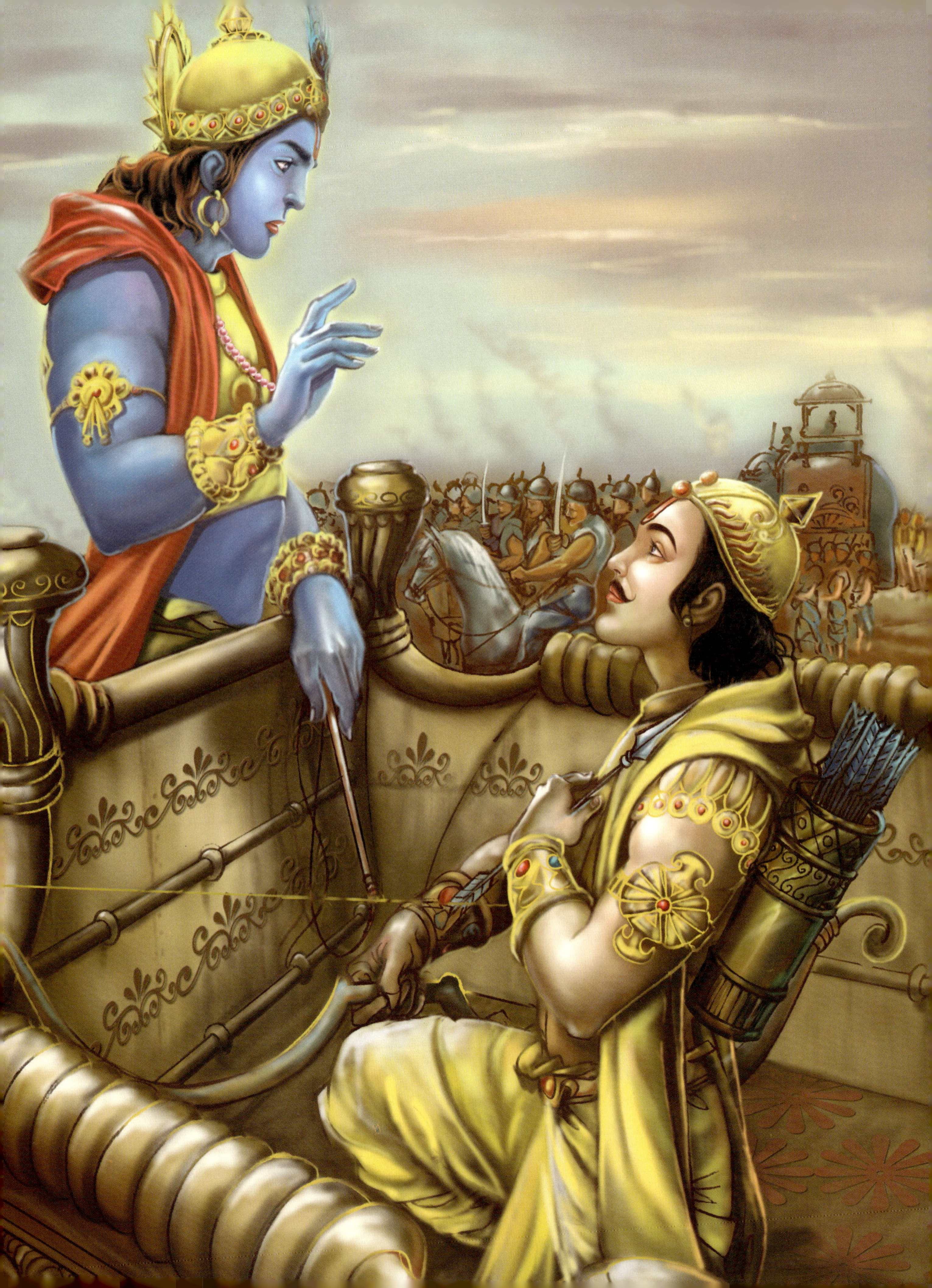

"What is the difference between action and inaction?" Arjuna asked.

Krishna replied, "He who sees action in inaction and inaction in action is truly wise. He who acts disinterestedly without the desire to preserve the body and soul cannot sin. The man who rises above the opposites goes beyond every desire, and remains untouched by success and failure, is never bound by action, though he acts. The wise know the truth and those who know the truth see the universe as me. Devotion brings success and knowledge purifies vision. Man without knowledge and devotion is lost in darkness. He sees truth neither in this world nor the next. Ignorant men are tied by the deeds they perform, but wise are not, for they do deeds without desire. They overcome desire through devotion and the restraint of their senses. Give up all actions with desire for fruit."

Arjuna felt puzzled by Lord Krishna's words. "I don't understand the contradiction you made. First you told me to renounce action and in the same breath you are telling me to do what I am supposed to do," he expressed his bewilderment.

"Both action and renunciation lead to emancipation. Renunciation should not be confused with inaction. A wise person is one who is above desire and hate. He is a true renunciate, not the one who is inactive. Gyan marga of Sankhya is not distinct from the Karma yoga. Only fools think Sankhya is distinct from Karma; action with awareness is not distinct from action with devotion. Practise any and you get the same result. One who realises this truth knows he does nothing even though he eats, drinks, sleeps, feels and walks. One who dedicates all his deeds to Brahma remains untouched by sin as lotus remains untouched by water. He knows he is not the doer, even though he acts. The wise see no difference in different creatures, from a brahmin to a *chandala*, and from a cow to swine, as he knows the supreme soul pervades them all. The wise are aware of desire and attachment as the cause of all misery and suffering. They act, therefore, independent of desire and attachment. They are moderate, devoid of extreme love or hate."

"Devotion as a quality remains unattained by those who either eat too much or abstain totally from food. Devotion remains equally elusive for those who either sleep too much or not at all. The wise ones do not sink to the depths of despair nor are over thrilled. They maintain their equanimity under all circumstances," Krishna replied.

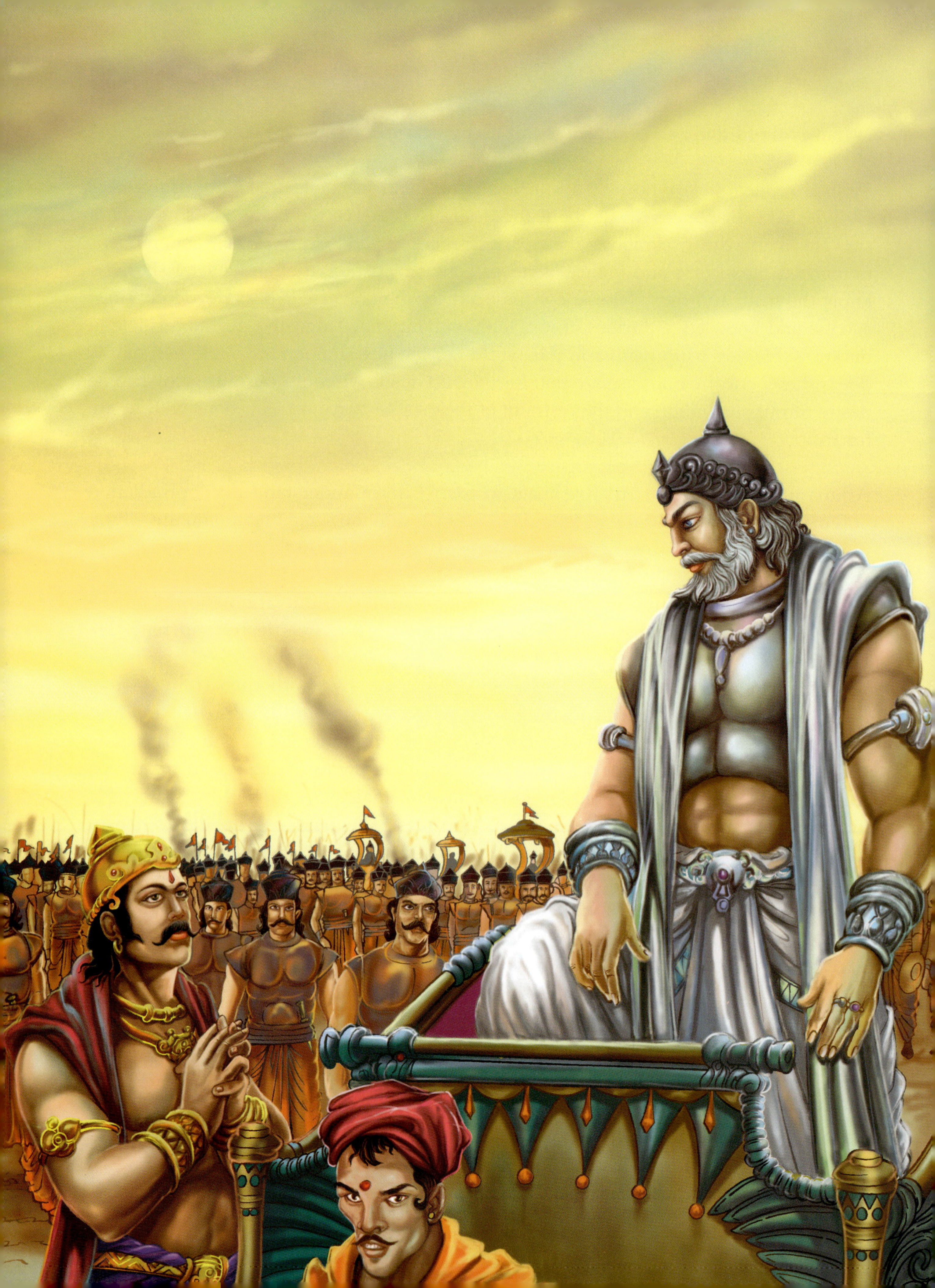

"How can you speak of peace and equanimity of mind, when by its very nature it is restless and unrestrained?" Arjuna's doubts were still unsettled.

"It is quite true that mind is restless but it can be restrained and controlled with practice, by rooting out desire and leading the life of devotion," Krishna answered.

When Lord Krishna had cleared all the doubts that Arjuna had, he felt blessed and satisfied. Finally Arjuna made one last request to Lord Krishna. "You have cleared all my doubts. Now I want to see your supreme form, that is, if you consider me blessed enough to behold your form," Arjuna requested.

"All right, behold!" Krishna smiled.

In the next instant Krishna assumed his Virata form, the magnificent form with the splendour of a thousand suns emanating from him. Arjuna saw the Gods, men and divine beings in the infinitely radiating effulgence. He bowed before the Lord of universe with folded hands.

When Krishna unfolded his magnificent form, Arjuna gathered his Gandiva and stood heroically on the chariot, ready to take on his enemies. The twang of Gandiva once more echoed dreadfully across the Kaurava army.

The two mighty armies stood ready to charge any moment, when to the surprise of all, the eldest Pandava came out of his chariot disarmed and began walking towards the hostile Kauravas. His brothers rushed after him perplexed.

They tried to stop him, but he walked unheeded. "Don't worry, he is going to salute his elders and gurus, which is the right conduct to be followed to ensure victory," Krishna smiled as he tried at alleviate Arjuna's apprehension.

Yudhishthira walked up to Bhishma with joined palms and head bowed low. "I salute you," he said, "I go to battle. Permit me and offer me your blessing."

"May you be victorious, my son," Bhishma said. "Had you not behaved as you did now, you would have been a victim of my curse and victory would never have been yours. Ask for a boon. Ask for anything except requesting me to fight for you," Bhishma said.

"I won't ask you not to fight for the Kauravas. Fight, you must for them, but if you have any love for me, enquire after me every day," Yudhishthira requested.

"That I will do, but tell me of what help I can be to you," Bhishma smiled, looking affectionately at the eldest son of Pandu.

Yudhishthira enquired from Bhishma as to how he could be defeated. Bhishma said, "I can't see anyone who could do it." Bhishma's reply was matter of fact. When Yudhishthira insisted upon knowing how his foes could kill him in the battle, Bhishma said his hour had not come, but asked him to come at a later time when he would reveal his manner of death.

Then Yudhishthira went to Dronacharya, Kripacharya and his maternal uncle Shalya in turn, asking for their permission and blessings. As Yudhishthira returned to his side, the Mahabharata war began.

The War of Mahabharata

As the war was about to begin, Yudhishthira announced in a loud voice, "Anyone who wants to join us may do so." Yuyutsu, who was Duryodhana's son by a Vaishya woman, crossed over towards the Pandavas' side saying, "I will fight for you, if you accept me."

As the generals of the sides issued commands, the battle began with earth-shaking roar of the two shouting armies.

The First Day
The War Begins

Dark clouds of arrows enveloped the sun as fathers fought sons, friends attacked friends like sworn enemies, and brothers fought brothers. The battle raged through the vast plains of Kurukshetra as the terrible haze of dust arose from earth.

Bhishma led a terrible attack on the Pandava forces. Pandava heroes, led by Abhimanyu, valiantly faced their great-grandfather and checked his further advance.

On the other front, a terrible battle waged between Prince Bhumijanya of Matsya, and Shalya. The prince, atop an elephant, attacked Shalya, fiercely killing all his four horses. Shalya was so enraged that he hurled a powerful spear at the Matsya prince, piercing his chest, and he fell down dead. The death of the prince alarmed his elder brother Shweta, who charged menacingly when Bhishma came in his way, leading to a fierce battle between the two great warriors. At last the elder prince too fell fighting. However, hundreds of Kaurava soldiers perished that day. No side had gained any significant advantage on day one and the men struggled back to their respective camps after the sunset.

The Second Day
Dhrishtadyumna Injures Drona

Although no side had gained any advantage on the first day, the Pandavas were looking for a quick victory. Arjuna and Dhrishtadyumna, the two commanders of the Pandava army, were ready to experiment with new strategies. So they encouraged their soldiers, motivating them to a yet higher level of performance and arrayed them in a typical formation called Vajravyooha.

The Kauravas were no less motivated. At Duryodhana's call, his men charged upon the enemy army, ferociously killing a number of them. Arjuna asked Krishna to lead the chariot towards Bhishma, the invincible warrior who would not let the Pandavas have any significant edge so long as he was commanding the enemy forces. The Gandiva's twangs echoed loudly as the two warriors clashed. Bhishma's deadly arrows pierced Arjuna in chest and arms but the brave Pandava remained unnerved, countering with his own volley of arrows that shattered Bhishma's chariot.

The way was now clear for the Pandavas' hero to penetrate into the Kaurava ranks, butchering the enemies with a vengeance. Duryodhana watched painfully as the Pandava hero unobtrusively made his way into their ranks even as the mightiest warrior on land, Bhishma watched helplessly.

Bheema, standing at the other end, charged like a bull with his mace breaking the Kaurava ranks. The mace of Bheema created such havoc in the Kaurava army that no warrior came to face him. Even Duryodhana fell down injured under the impact of Bheema's mace. His charioteer drove him out of the battlefield.

Dhrishtadyumna, the fire-born hero, headed for Drona's division with the single mission to kill his father's enemy. He was under a vow to kill the great guru, and did not want to give him any chance. Drona, with a single-winged arrow shattered Dhrishtadyumna's bow, but the great warrior quickly regained his composure and shot another arrow at the great guru wounding him grievously. Drona retreated from the battle for a while.

Since Bheema had caused a great havoc in the battlefield so Duryodhana was forced to send Karna's regiment to counter the onslaught. Karna himself was not fighting in the battle, but his forces were considered amongst the best fighting forces. Even his regiment could not resist the onslaught of Bheema. He routed the regiment and killed most of its soldiers. The Kaurava army having suffered huge loss, couldn't afford to suffer more, and Bhishma came ahead to check Bheema's advance. However Abhimanyu and Satyaki stood as strong pillars of obstruction, whom Bhishma could not overcome. The sun having set, the second day witnessed a clear advantage to the Pandavas.

The Third Day
Krishna Picks Up Arms

On the third day, Bhishma made a strategic change in the arrangement of his soldiers. Duryodhana was placed at the vanguard. He ensured that the Pandavas found it difficult to penetrate through the Kaurava lines. The Pandavas had arrayed their soldiers in a semi-circle with its ends under Bheema and Arjuna respectively.

As the sun rose, the two armies charged upon each other. The war was fierce and neither of the sides could penetrate into the other. Suddenly, Shakuni appeared with a strong regiment ready to back him, but Abhimanyu stood in his way and inflicted a crushing defeat on the Kaurava warrior.

Bheema once again found himself face to face with Duryodhana, a second time in the last three days, and came charging at him menacingly. He threw down Duryodhana in a direct clash and he lay unconscious when his charioteer drove him out of the battlefield. The Kauravas lost their ground to the Pandava men, who fought a deadly battle, where blood and gore turned to slush.

Duryodhana was perplexed at the loss and defeat he suffered at the hands of the Pandavas. He blamed Bhishma and Drona of holding back. "Why are the Pandavas still alive, when great warriors like you and Drona are warring against them? You said, you will not fight for the Pandavas, but since they are alive, it goes on to prove you have sympathy for them," Duryodhana spoke out his grievance.

"Haven't I told you a number of times about the invincibility of the Pandavas? They can't be defeated even by Gods. All I can do is ravage their armies and check their advance. No more," said Bhishma, laughing scornfully at Duryodhana.

The Pandavas had gained in the first half of the day. Bhishma's next charge by noon scattered the Pandava ranks, injuring Yudhishthira, who was forced to leave. Krishna drew Arjuna's attention to point to him the destruction caused by the Kauravas, who had masterfully dispelled the combined might of Arjuna, Bheema and Shikhandi.

Arjuna asked Krishna to wheel his chariot towards Bhishma. Krishna wheeled his horses, charging into Kaurava division. Bhishma rained lethal arrows on Arjuna, but Krishna handled the reins skilfully ducking the deadly arrows and thereby preventing any serious damage to Arjuna.

Pandu's son, the greatest archer of his time, aimed arrows straight at Bhishma's bow and broke two of his bows in succession. Meanwhile, Bhishma's elephant division had surrounded Arjuna, but Satyaki rushed to Arjuna's aid inflicting a crushing defeat on the Kaurava soldiers leaving men and elephants dead in his wake.

As the Kaurava soldiers retreated, Krishna shouted to Satyaki to go after them, and when he suddenly noticed the broken bow of Bhishma, Krishna shouted at Arjuna to kill him or else he will do that job.

Arjuna's hand trembled as he held his Gandiva with the thought of killing his grandfather. Krishna gave a look of scorn to Arjuna and jumped out of the chariot with his Sudarshan Chakra gleaming across the index finger of his raised right hand.

Bhishma looked at Krishna in wonder and welcomed him with open hands. "Welcome my Lord! I will attain heaven and my fame will spread to the three worlds, if I am slain by you."

Arjuna ran after him, pleading Keshava to come back, as he bound him in his muscular arms dragging him back. "Calm down, Keshava! You are our refuge. You promised not to raise your arm in the war. I have promised to wipe out the Kurus and I swear I will do it. Now, please hold yourself and come back."

Krishna calmed down and took up the reins of his chariot once again. The Gandiva screamed once again and Arjuna mercilessly killed the Kaurava men. At sunset, the battlefield was red with mutilated dead bodies over which red hawks and vultures hovered.

The Fourth Day
Bheema Faints

The fourth day again witnessed the might of the Pandavas. Arjuna presented a strong defence to Kaurava's frontal attack. In order to distract Arjuna, Duryodhana made a malicious plan. He sent his soldiers to surround and kill Abhimanyu. The young warrior, like his father, was more than a match for all of them.

On this day Bheema was in his best form as he went on to systematically decimate Duryodhana's elephant corps. Bheema was aware of his vow to kill the sons of Dhritarashtra. He killed eight of Duryodhana's brothers and his men as they came in defence of Duryodhana. The rest of his brothers fled. Bhagadatta saw the Kauravas under attack and he came to their rescue, shooting pointed arrows at Bheema, which wounded him grievously, and he fainted for a little while. Draupadi's five sons and Dhrishtadyumna, who were guarding him, came up to face Bhagadatta's attack, thereby affording a chance for Bheema to recover.

When Bheema recovered, he proceeded like a mad elephant to kill anyone who came in his way, shouting the war cry of victory. Bheema raged across the battlefield like a God of death ravaging men, horses, elephants and chariots alike. Before Bheema could bring about more destruction, Bhishma blew the siren for the battle of the day to end. At night, Duryodhana went to Bhishma's camp to express his worries and anguish about their successive defeats day after day. Bhishma as usual, advised him to patch up with the Pandavas who could not be defeated.

The Fifth Day
Satyaki's Ten Sons Killed

The Kauravas played defensive on the fifth day. Bhishma had organised the Kaurava soldiers in an array so as to prevent the Pandavas from piercing their ranks. The Pandavas, on the other hand, had arrayed their soldiers in such a way that they could easily break the Kaurava lines, breaching through the strategic points. Bheema was leading the Pandava soldiers along with Shikhandi, Satyaki and Dhrishtadyumna.

As the conch shells sounded, the two bloodthirsty armies began fighting with loud battle cries. Once again Bhishma and Arjuna were face to face. While Bhishma showered volleys of arrows in quick succession at Arjuna, he countered them with ease, as only a skilful archer like him could do. His deadly arrows dropped mid way, impotent and broken, as Arjuna's arrows cut them, quickly and sharply. Drona, coming to Bhishma's aid, could do little as Arjuna's defence was more deadly and sharp than the attacking might of the two greatest Kaurava heroes.

"Kill him, he is alone! If you can't do that, what's your worth?" Duryodhana shouted.

"We are doing our best and now don't disturb us, if you can't help us," Guru Drona retorted, highly irritated.

Dronacharya fell upon the Pandava army with ferocity enough to make the enemy shudder in fright. It took the combined strength of Bheema and Satyaki, as fearless as a lion, to check the advance of the great guru.

When Bhishma rushed in to assist Drona, Shikhandi suddenly appeared before him, forcing him to retreat as Bhishma was under a vow not to fight a eunuch or a woman.

A large number of soldiers perished on the fifth day as the battle raged on. Satyaki, the Vrishni hero, was the scourge of the Kauravas that day, cutting men like paddy with a scythe. Bhurishrava was a master swordsman, whom Duryodhana sent to rein in Satyaki. In the battle that followed Satyaki lay badly injured and his ten sons, who rushed to his help, were mercilessly butchered by Bhurishrava.

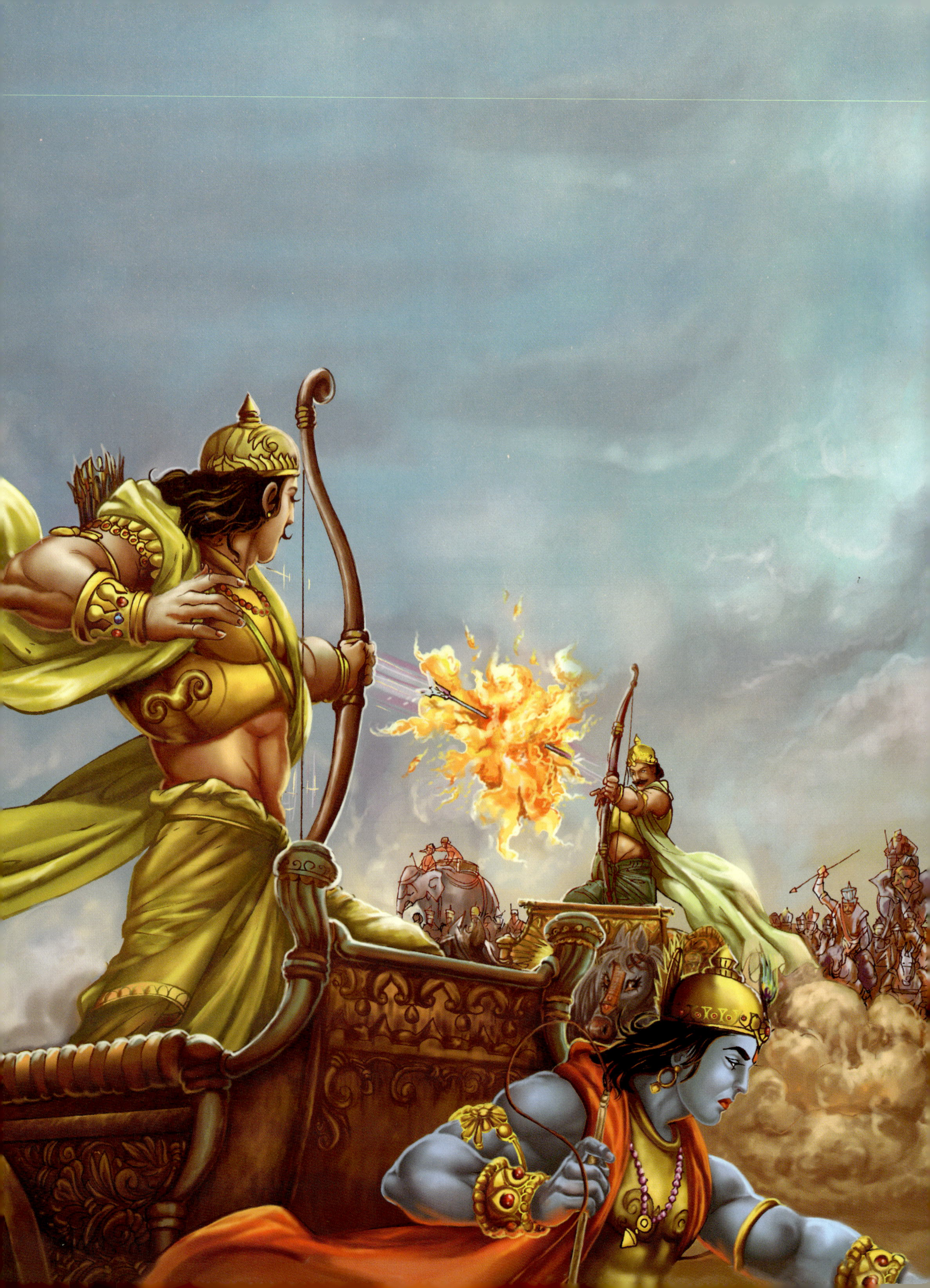

At another front, Arjuna killed thousands of Kauravas. The Pandava soldiers shouted a loud war cry echoing across the bloody plains of Kurukshetra. The sun was about to set and Bhishma ordered the day's battle to stop.

The Sixth Day
Bheema Injures Duryodhana

On the sixth day, Bheema went ferociously attacking the Kaurava men and entered into the vast crowd of Kaurava army. When Dhrishtadyumna noticed Bheema missing, he feared the worst and penetrated into the Kaurava army looking for Bheema apprehensively. He found Bheema ravaging the Kaurava army, to his great satisfaction.

When Duryodhana noticed Dhrishtadyumna at Bheema's side, he commanded his men to kill Panchala's son. They swooped upon Dhrishtadyumna, but before they could do any damage, the Panchala prince took a quick look at the men around to determine the magnitude of his counter attack required. The Kauravas dropped like autumn leaves, their weapons fell out of their hands as they lay unconscious. Bheema and Dhrishtadyumna made a killing field of the nerveless men in the plains of Kurukshetra. Then Bheema struck Duryodhana, wounding him grievously.

When the war came to an end for the day at sunset, Duryodhana rushed to Bhishma's tent without pausing to wash his wounds dripping in blood. "My troops were arrayed in impenetrable *makar* formation, yet Bheema pounded us thoroughly and killed my men in large numbers. It cannot go on like this. I want Pandu's sons dead before it drags on endlessly like this!" Duryodhana vented out his agony.

"Much as I would like to give you victory, my son," said Bhishma, "You must understand that the Pandavas cannot be defeated. Even Gods cannot defeat them when Arjuna and Krishna are together. Warriors like Drupada and his sons, Ghatotkacha and his rakshasa hordes, Satyaki and the king of Chedi do not know defeat or fatigue. I can do only what best lies in my power. But, let me get you treated first, my son, so that you are fit for the battle tomorrow," said Bhishma so as to comfort Duryodhana.

The Seventh Day
Abhimanyu Fights Valiantly

On the seventh day, Bhishma arranged his troops in the mandala formation, which was difficult for even the best armed forces to breach. Each elephant warrior was surrounded by seven chariot warriors and each chariot by seven cavalry men. Every cavalryman was guarded by seven archers and seven infantry men with lances and shields were there to guard every archer.

Yudhishthira countered the mandala formation of the Kauravas with the Vajra formation, with Bheema at the lead. The battle began at sunrise with the blaring of the conches.

Alambusha was a powerful Rakshasa and an ally of the Kauravas. He attacked Satyaki using the powers of his illusion and hurled lances and arrows at him materialising in the air. Satyaki remained calm and used a missile given to him by Arjuna, against the illusions of Alambusha.

In the next instant, the illusion vanished and the huge rakshasa cried out in pain as the pointed weapon struck him forcefully. Alambusha fled.

Arjuna faced Bhishma, while Drupada and Dronacharya battled each other. Bheema took on Duryodhana and his brothers. Nakula and Sahadeva crossed their swords against their maternal uncle Shalya. Drona defeated Drupada and killed his son Shankha, while Shikhandi was beaten by Ashvathama. Bheema wounded Duryodhana, Ghatotkacha was beaten by Bhagadatta, but Nakula and Sahadeva defeated Shalya who fell senseless and had to be driven out of the battlefield.

Abhimanyu, fighting on another front, found himself cut off from his troops and surrounded by Duryodhana's brothers. The mighty young warrior fought with all of them bravely, ensuring not to kill any of them as Bheema had vowed to kill them.

When Arjuna saw his son surrounded by the Kaurava warriors, he asked Krishna to take him where Abhimanyu was fighting alone with the Kauravas.

As Krishna led the chariot through the Kaurava ranks, Arjuna found himself under attack by Susharma, the king of the Trigartas. Arjuna promptly shot arrows out of Gandiva, whose first volley killed thirty-two men. However, despite the falling men, it hardly made

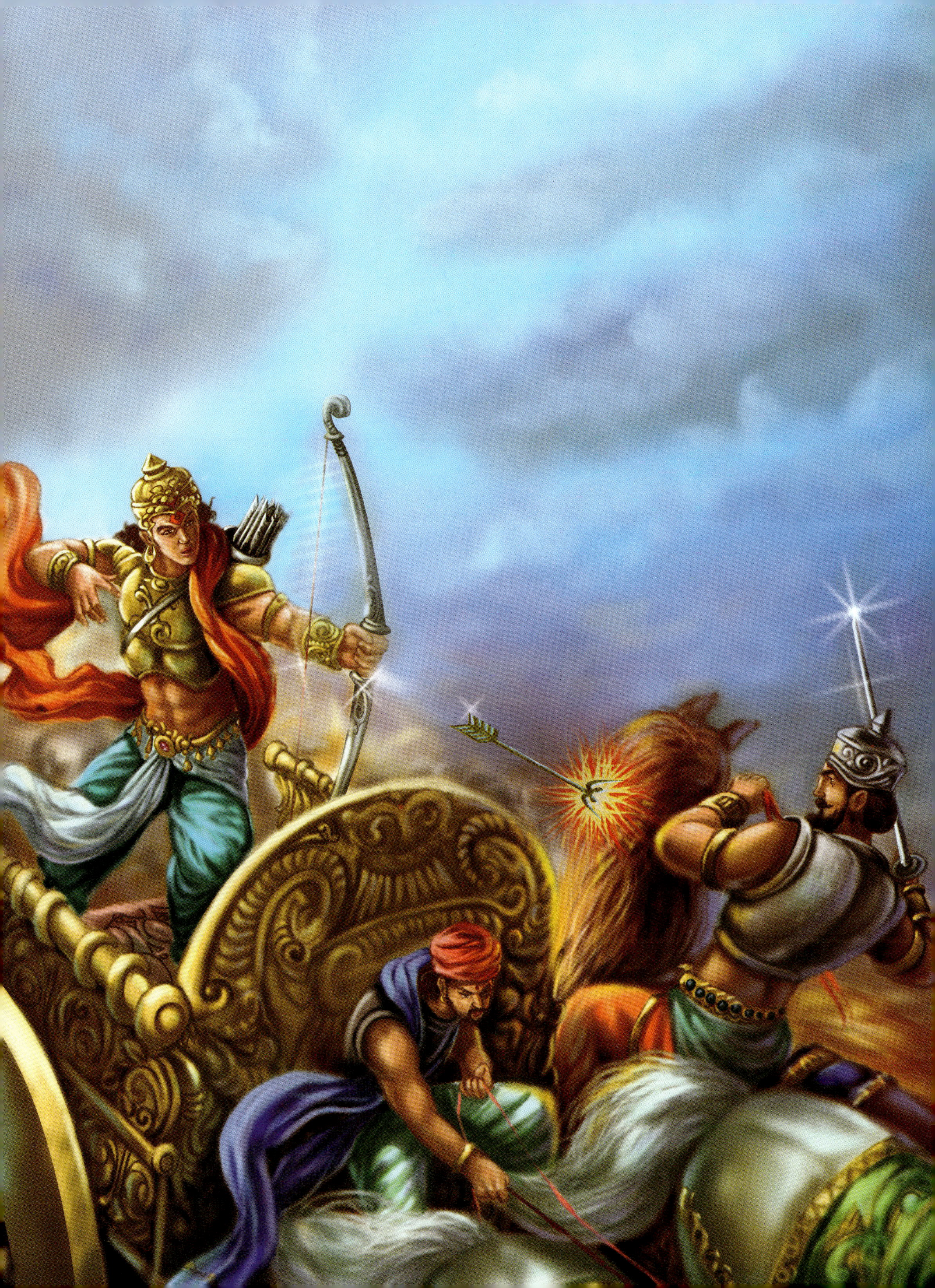

a dent in the number, as twice the men replaced the number of men falling dead each time. Arjuna managed to create a breach as volley after volley of raining arrows decimated Kaurava men. Krishna quickly drove the chariot through the breach, before it could be plugged. Arjuna was relieved to see Abhimanyu fighting like a lion against the Kauravas. The overall advantage clearly lay with the Pandavas on this day of the battle.

The Eighth Day
Iravat, Arjuna's Naga Son, is Killed

The eighth day saw a fierce battle, in which Bhishma launched a massive attack on the Pandava soldiers. He had arranged his soldiers in a turtle position and Dhrishtadyumna had arranged the Pandava soldiers on three fronts led by Bheema, Satyaki and Yudhishthira.

Bheema was able to check Bhishma's onslaught, driving him back, and penetrated through his guard. When he saw Duryodhana's brothers, his blood boiled and he killed six of them right in front of him. As Duryodhana saw his brothers falling, he commanded his men to kill Bheema.

Iravat, Arjuna's son by Ulupi, fell upon Shakuni and his cavalry with savage fury. He and his Naga warriors were great fighters. They knew only one thing — kill or die fighting. After a long battle, Shakuni's brothers killed Iravat's charioteer and horses. Brave Iravat leapt out of his chariot and began fighting with his sword. In a great show of his swordsmanship, he killed men and beasts coming within his striking range. Only one of Shakuni's brothers could escape with his life as of the rest of them lay dead.

When Duryodhana saw the fate of his men in the battle, he sent for Alambusha, a rakshasa who could counter Iravat through the means of illusion. In the very first brush with Iravat, Alambusha found his two thousand men dead. The great Naga warrior son of Arjuna rendered Alambusha armless after breaking his bow and javelins and wounding the rakshasa in chest and limbs. Alambusha kept changing his forms, while Iravat broke through his illusions, till he forced Iravat to take the form of Ananta, the great serpent coiled around the universe. Alambusha instantly took the shape of a huge and mighty Garuda, the serpent bird and attacked Iravat, severely injuring him. Iravat was very tired after a long and protracted battle and let his guard slip for a moment, when Alambusha cut off his head.

Ghatotkacha saw the fall of Iravat, and assuming a giant shape he fell upon Alambusha and his rakshasa horde, roaring in anger. Duryodhana rushed to the aid of Alambusha. Ghatotkacha attacked Duryodhana with mighty force. He hurled a deadly shaft at him, but Bhagadatta saw the hurtling shaft and quickly moved forward placing himself between the shaft and Duryodhana. The shaft pierced into Bhagadatta's elephant, killing the mammoth elephant on the spot, as a pool of blood gushed out. Duryodhana's men ran away to save their lives. Duryodhana was left alone to face the fury of Ghatotkacha. Soon Ghatotkacha's fierce war cries attracted the attention of Bhishma. He came rushing in with reinforcements. Ashvathama also joined Bhishma, mounting a combined attack and making their way through the Rakshasa army. Ghatotkacha redoubled his attack. His swift and piercing arrows broke Drona's bow and injured Kripacharya and Vikarna, Duryodhana's brother. Kauravas by hundreds lay dead while Ashvathama's chariot was shattered and Jaidratha's bow broken. Their troops were wiped out. But the Kaurava reinforcements kept pouring in.

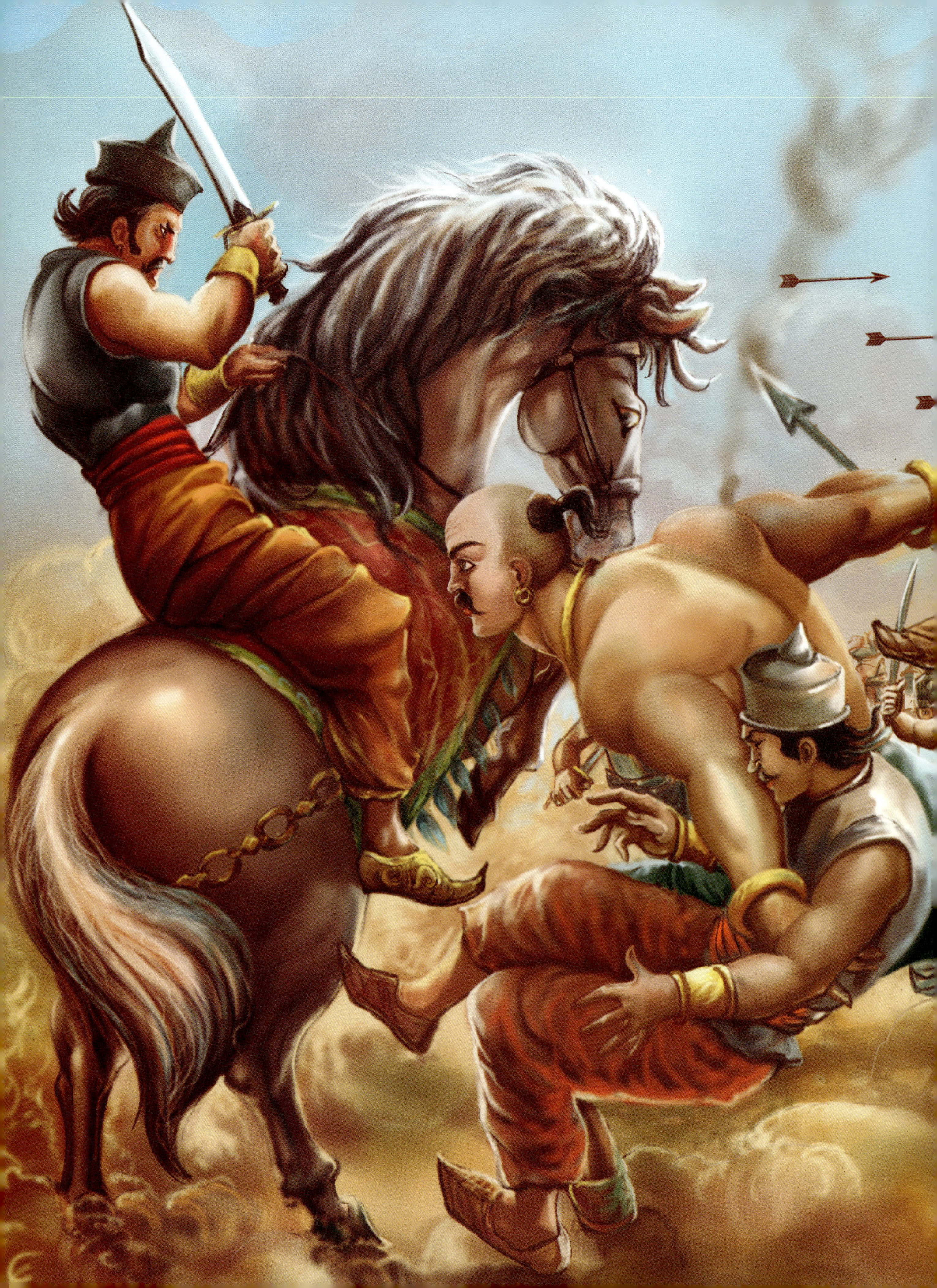

Ghatotkacha was tired and wounded fighting alone with horde after horde of Kaurava reinforcements, so he rose up in the air and let out a terrible scream. Yudhishthira heard the cry of Ghatotkacha and felt worried for him. He asked Bheema to help Ghatotkacha, who was fighting alone.

Bheema asked his charioteer to take him where Ghatotkacha was surrounded by the Kaurava forces. He was followed by Abhimanyu, Draupadi's five sons and Nila, king of the Hehayas. The brave Pandava men, racing swiftly through the Kaurava defence, left dead and mangled men, elephants, horses and chariots, in their trail before they found Ghatotkacha fighting alone. Ghatotkacha sadly informed Bheema of Iravat's death. Bheema raced to Arjuna involved in an intense battle with Bhishma, and informed him of Iravat's sad demise.

Arjuna's heart filled with bitter anguish at this sad news and he put aside his weapons. "Now I know, what Vidura meant when he said war brings nothing but misery. I have begun to understand why Yudhishthira was willing to settle for five paltry villages. What have we gained by killing our kinsmen?" Arjuna lamented, but the very next moment he determined, "The kshatriyas have only one duty — the duty to fight. I will be known as a coward if I put down my arms now. These weapons of mine will not rest till the Kauravas are wiped out."

At the end of the day, the war-zone was littered with corpses and vultures preyed upon the dead bodies, presenting a morbid sight.

Duryodhana consulted Shakuni and Karna to know why the Pandavas were not dead by now, but on the contrary, were killing the Kauravas in astronomical numbers. "It seems Bhishma, Drona, Kripa and Shalya do not have their hearts in the war," Duryodhana opined, regretting his losses. "Let me enter the war, if you want to see Arjuna dead, but for that to happen, ask Bhishma to stay out of the war," Karna suggested coldly.

Duryodhana sneaked into Bhishma's tent and made a humble request to him to stay out of the war to let Karna fight for him. Bhishma was enraged. He said, "I have told you again and again that the Pandavas are invincible but you are stupid enough not to understand it. Even our best efforts could not bring us the desired result because they are under the protection of Lord Krishna. You will find it impossible to defeat Arjuna so long as he is guarded by Lord Krishna himself. Since you instigated the war against our advice, so you must fight it out yourself. As for me, I have told you I will kill Panchalas and Somakas with the sole exception of Shikhandi."

"Why can't you kill Shikhandi?" Duryodhana asked with a look of surprise.

"Because, he was once a woman. In his last life, he was Amba, princess of Kashi, who swore to kill me. In the present life, she was born as Drupada's daughter. However, after a boon granted by a Yaksha, Drupada's daughter Shikhandi turned into a man. Since he was a woman once, I cannot fight against him, even if it means my death," Bhishma made his position clear.

The Ninth Day
Yudhishthira Asks Bhishma How He Could Be Killed

On the ninth day of the battle, Alambusha and Abhimanyu took on each other with deadly ferocity. The ferocious rakshasa was forced to retreat, faced with the might of Abhimanyu. Satyaki and Ashvathama were involved in an unending combat on another front.

Drona and Arjuna fought like strangers with only one mission — to put an end to the adversary. The Panchalas and the Matsyas, led by Drupada, Virata and Dhrishtadyumna, attacked Bhishma. The great general was more than a match for all of them together. He rendered them chariot-less. Then he butchered the leaderless men and forced the others to run for their lives. However, whenever he saw Shikhandi he refused to retaliate even at the expense of being shot by his arrows.

Krishna drew Arjuna's attention to Bhishma savagely killing Panchalas. "It's time you fulfilled your vow, Partha! Look how brutally Bhishma is decimating the Pandava forces. You had vowed in Virata's court to kill all the Kauravas including Bhishma and Drona. Kill Bhishma! Forget he is your grandfather," Krishna said to Arjuna.

"Take me there. I will do as you say," Arjuna replied.

Krishna quickly brought the chariot, skilfully avoiding the flying arrows, within the range of Bhishma. Arjuna shattered his grandfather's bow with a pointed arrow. Bhishma picked another bow and shot a volley of arrows hitting Krishna and Arjuna. Krishna noticed a half-hearted attempt on Arjuna's part, and threw down the reins in exasperation, and ran towards Bhishma holding the wheel in his hand. Arjuna quickly rushed to stop Krishna and persuaded him not to violate his promise of not taking up arms in this war.

Krishna once again took up the reins and the battle went on till sunset. Bhishma was clearly the hero of the day. His war efforts resulted in dead soldiers littered across the plains of Kurukshetra.

When the sun set, Yudhishthira felt relieved. On coming back to his tent, he was worried about the future course of the war, as he did not see victory coming to him. He blamed himself for everything that was happening to the Pandavas. He cursed himself for playing the dice, which resulted in the war and brought misery to everyone. "What shall I do, Madhava?," he lamented before Lord Krishna.

"You won't have victory so long as Bhishma is alive. If you ask me, I can kill Bhishma. But let Arjuna do this task, and he can do it," Krishna said.

When the night fell, Yudhishthira visited Bhishma along with Krishna and the other Pandavas. According to the requirements of protocol, they were unarmed and therefore, let in Bhishma's tent without any harm.

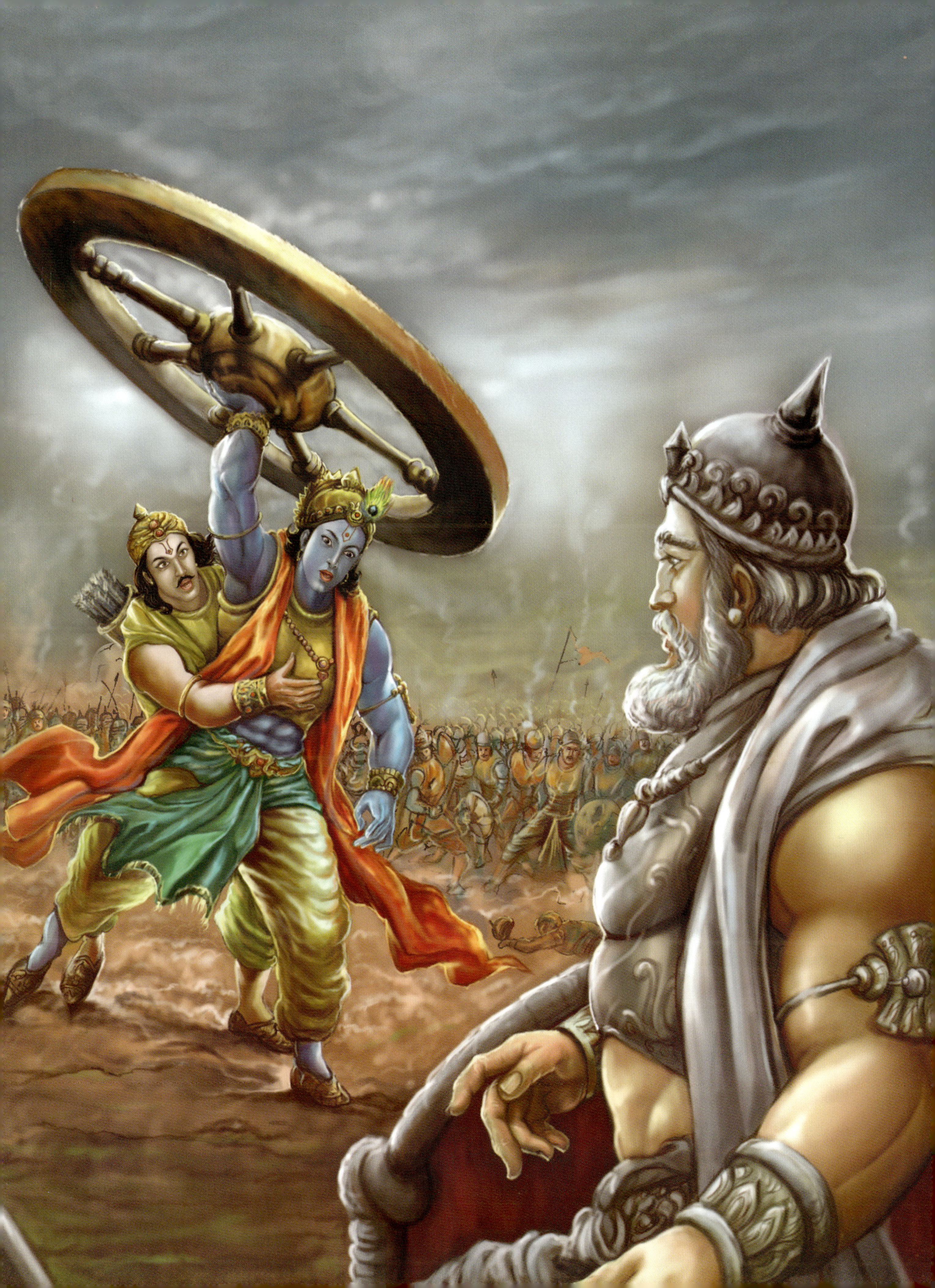

They wanted to know about the secret of Bhishma's defeat so that they could be victorious. "Victory never is yours, so long as I live, my sons! Therefore, put me to an end quickly if you want victory," Bhishma replied to them.

"But how can we put an end to someone who is invincible?" Yudhishthira put the question with a worried expression on his face.

"You can, provided you force me to disarm," Bhishma replied, "and there are only four ways to disarm me. I do not fight an unarmed warrior. I do not fight someone who is the only son. I do not fight men of low birth and I do not fight a woman or someone who has once been a woman, like Shikhandi. If you bring Shikhandi at the head of your army, followed by Arjuna, I will not fight and Arjuna can easily kill me then. Do as I say and you can easily defeat Dhritarashtra's sons." The Pandavas saluted their grandfather and walked out in silence.

The Tenth Day
Bhishma Falls

On the tenth day, Shikhandi was placed at the head, flanked by Arjuna and Bheema. Abhimanyu and Draupadi's five sons were positioned at the rear. Powerful warriors like Satyaki and Chekitana were positioned to guard the young warriors. Dhrishtadyumna was at the rear, flanked by the twins, Nakula and Sahadeva.

Kauravas were led by Bhishma, who in turn was guarded by Drona and Ashvathama. Bhagadatta and his elephant corps formed the rear guard.

Shikhandi charged upon Bhishma, shooting him with volley after volley of arrows, but he smiled without retaliating. Arjuna broke Duryodhana's mace and Dhrishtadyumna attacked his rearguard.

Abhimanyu, Dhrishtadyumna, Virata and Drupada combined forces and attacked Bhishma, but he was a determined general ready to face the Pandava might alone. Dushasana was under Arjuna's fiery arrows' range, but Bhishma protected him. Alambusha kept Satyaki engaged while Drona battled Virata's Matsyas and Ashvathama attacked Drupada, to cut him off from the Pandavas.

Virata and Drupada fought energetically, sending anyone coming into their way to the abode of death. Virata destroyed Ashvathama's arrows and wounded him grievously.

Bheema, who penetrated menacingly into the Kaurava ranks, suddenly found his advance checked by the joint forces of Bhagadatta, Kripa, Shalya, Kritavarma and the princes of Avanti. Shalya struck Bheema with nine arrows, but he didn't care a bit. He broke Kripa's bow, rendered Jaidratha and the princes of Avanti armless and knocked Shalya with his mace, ensuring that his uncle did not die. The Kaurava reinforcements kept pouring in till Bheema was tired and surrounded by them. Arjuna immediately rushed through the Kauravas to help his brother Bheema.

Bhishma had slaughtered a large number of men tirelessly and effortlessly, but the war did not interest him much. He surveyed the battlefield looking for Yudhishthira.

He asked his chariot to be driven near him. He said to Yudhishthira, "'I no longer wish to preserve this old body of mine. I have spent ages fighting and killing and I am tired of it. If you really want to do me a service, ask Arjuna and Shikhandi to spearhead the next assault."

Yudhishthira rearranged his troops with Shikhandi at the lead. Both Shikhandi and Arjuna rained volleys of arrows, but the great warrior Bhishma concentrated only on deflecting and countering Arjuna's arrows, disregarding Shikhandi contemptuously. Arrow after arrow pierced the old warrior, but he stood tall, firm and erect, and kept on incessantly killing the Pandava forces. Duryodhana effectively blocked Arjuna's target by placing a large number of Kaurava men ahead of Bhishma. Arjuna used one of his celestial weapons, enchanting it with appropriate mantra, and released it on Duryodhana's mounted elephant and cavalry unit. In the next instant thousands of men, elephants and horses lay dead and the earth was drenched in blood.

Dushasana, Shalya and Kripa spearheaded an attack against Arjuna, but he killed their charioteers and horses, thereby incapacitating the Kuru generals. Guard around Bhishma weakened as thousands of men died. Bhishma invoked a celestial weapon and was about to hurl it, when he saw Shikhandi and he checked himself but threw the weapon at Dhrishtadyumna's troops, killing ten thousand chariot warriors, and about the same number of infantry and cavalry men and the entire elephant army.

Krishna urged Arjuna to kill Bhishma so as to win the war. Arjuna acted on the advice and once again placed Shikhandi ahead of himself. Krishna raced through the army of Kauravas, with Arjuna killing everyone in the path. A number of Pandava warriors like Satyaki, Chekitana, Drupada, Dhrishtadyumna, Abhimanyu and Draupadi's five sons attacked Bhishma, but he easily repelled them all. Drawing a deadly weapon, he calmly hurled it upon the Pandava army, killing thousands of men. But he now decided that his hour had come. As he decided so, he heard the celestial voices of rishis and Vasus saying, "Your decision is right. We approve of it."

Arjuna kept on raining arrows on the old warrior even as he had decided to welcome his end. His body was riddled with arrows. As the sun set, Bhishma fell, but his body did not touch the ground. It remained suspended on a bed of arrows above the earth.

As Bhishma fell, he noticed the sun in the south, an inauspicious period to die in and the indomitable warrior decided not to give up his life till the sun returned to the north position.

The Kauravas were aghast and bewildered when they came to know of Bhishma's fall. Dronacharya blew his conch ordering the soldiers to lay down their weapons in honour of Ganga's son. The war came to a close. All the warriors came there to pay their final salute to Ganga's son. Krishna and Arjuna were also present to bid their final tearful farewell.

Bhishma lay above the ground on the bed of arrows while his head hung backwards unsupported. "Give me a pillow," Bhishma said, "to support my head." Duryodhana rushed to bring a pillow for him. Bhishma waved the pillow away saying, "This is not the pillow for a warrior. Give me a pillow fit for a hero's head."

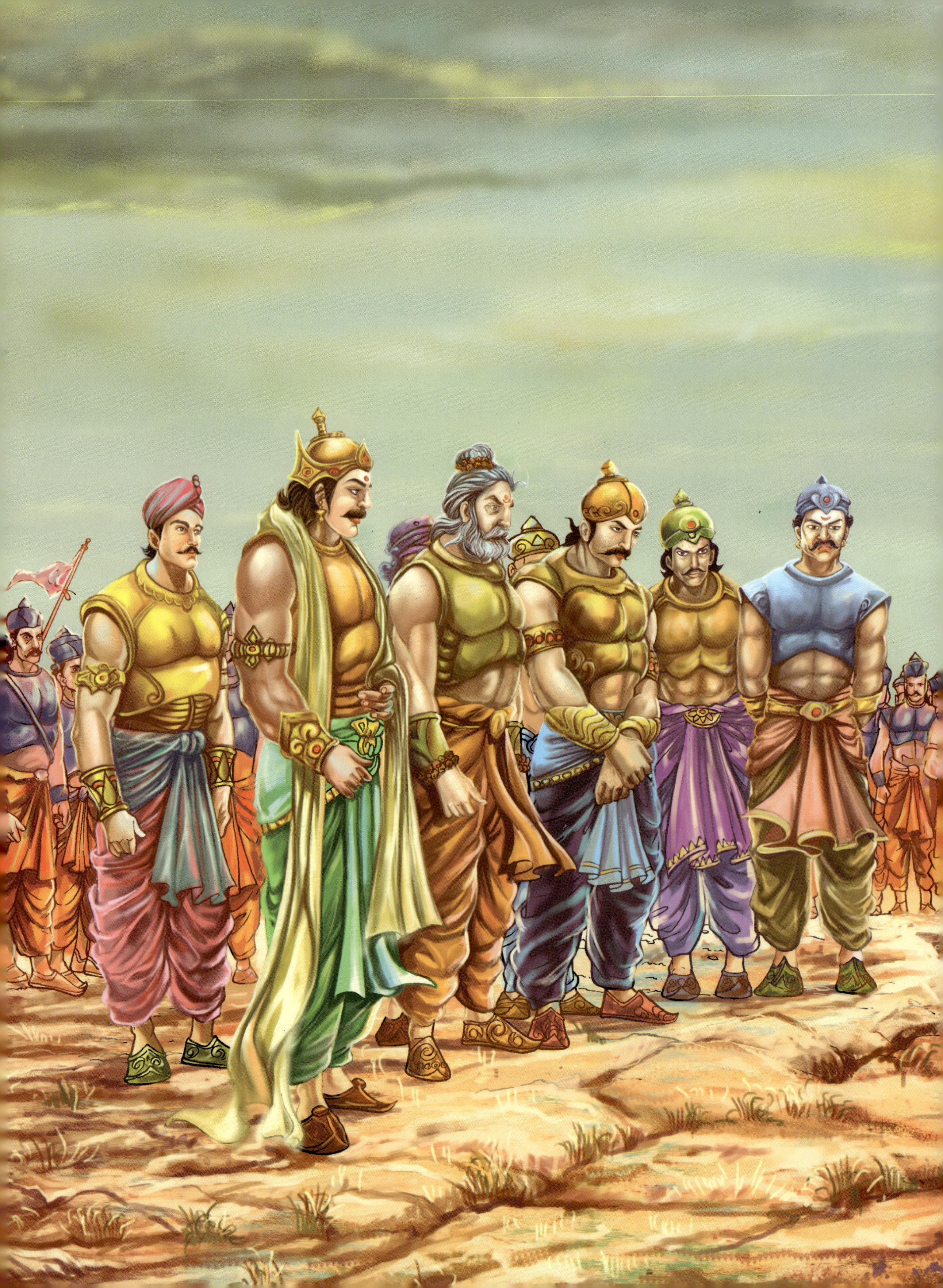

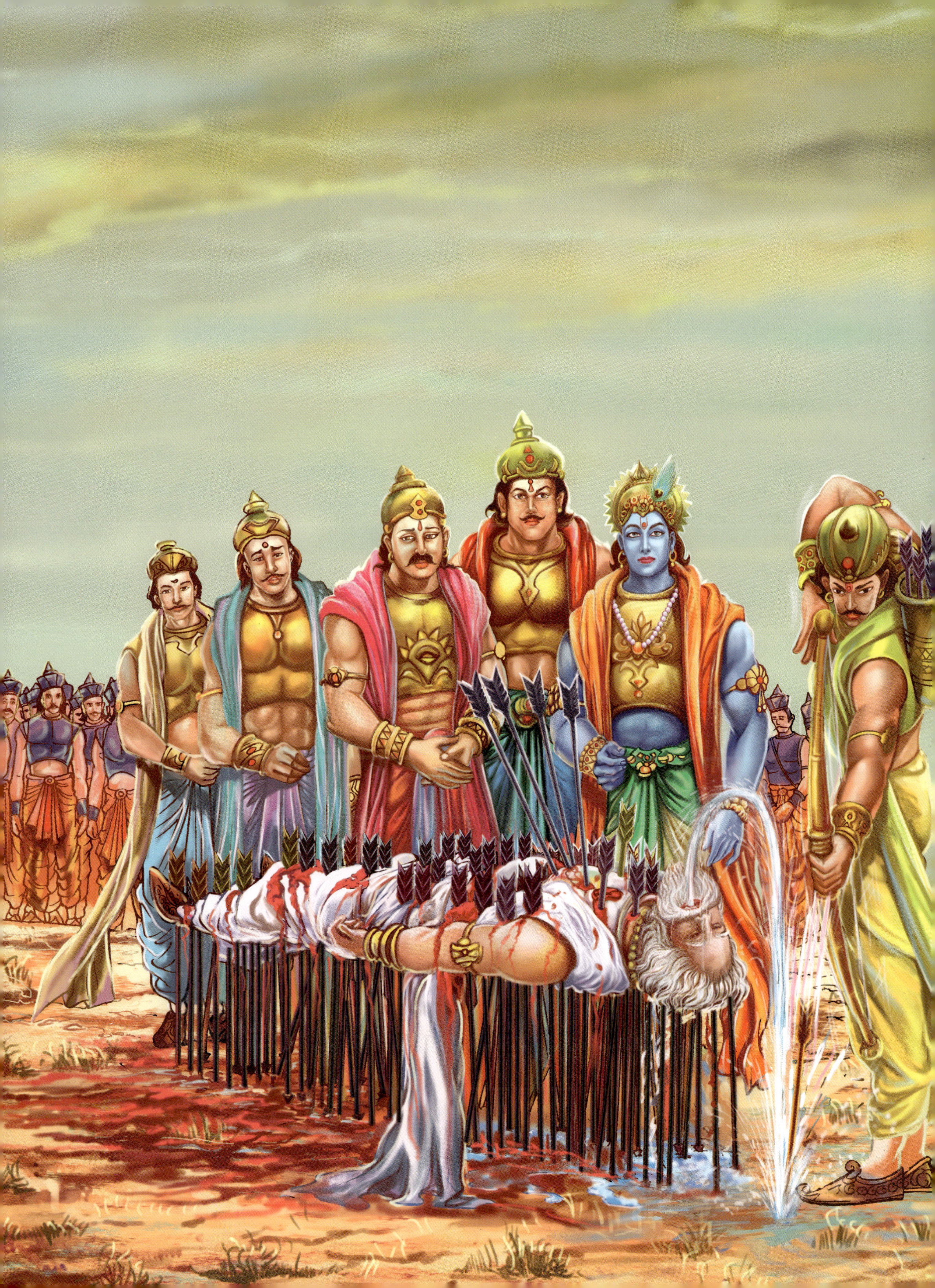

Arjuna understood what Bhishma meant. Taking his Gandiva and three arrows out of his quiver, he skilfully shot them in the ground in such a way as to prop up the old warrior's head. "Exactly! This is the pillow for a warrior sleeping on the bed of arrows. I will rest on this bed till the sun turns north."

The next morning, the kings returned to the battlefield to pay homage to the fallen hero. They came with the best of food and drink. Bhishma opened his eyes and surveying the kings and their offerings, said, "This is food for the living, not for me. Where is Arjuna?"

Arjuna came to him at his command. "My son, I am feeling very thirsty. Give me water to drink," Bhishma said.

Arjuna knew what his grandfather wanted. Raising his Gandiva, he shot an arrow into the ground so skilfully that it plunged into the earth forcefully and a cool sweet stream of water gushed out to fall straight into the parched, dry mouth of the grand patriarch.

Bhishma was highly pleased with Arjuna and declared him to be a matchless archer, who was none other than the ancient sage Nara. Then he called Duryodhana and advised him once again to patch up with the Pandavas so as to save the Kurus from extinction. But Duryodhana did not heed his grandfather's advice.

Karna too went to pay homage to the greatest warrior ever and stood there, weeping silently. Bhishma motioned him to come closer and spoke to him lovingly, "You are also my grandson. This was told to me long ago by Narada and Vyasa. I was harsh towards you only because you never tried to bring Duryodhana to the ways of gentlemen, but on the contrary you abetted and instigated him to adopt evil ways. Even now you can persuade him to adopt the right path."

But Karna showed his inability to do so since Duryodhana had done so many favours to Karna, as to make him ever obliged and indebted. He felt compelled and duty bound to serve and obey him.

Bhishma expected no other answer from him, but the oldest Kuru grandfather blessed Karna and asked him to do his duty to the best of his ability and said that for a kshatriya, there was no greater duty than to fight. Grandfather Bhishma also blessed him to lead the Kaurava army.

Duryodhana too wanted Karna to lead the army after Bhishma, because he was sure that only Karna could kill Arjuna. As Karna entered the battlefield armed with weapons on his chariot, the Kaurava men cheered him. When Duryodhana spoke his mind about Karna being the next commander-in-chief of the Kaurava army, Karna refused the offer. He advanced a better counsel instead, "This honour should be bestowed upon a warrior who is acceptable to one and all and I think Dronacharya is best suited for the job." Duryodhana agreed to the opinion of Karna and Dronacharya came to assume the leadership.

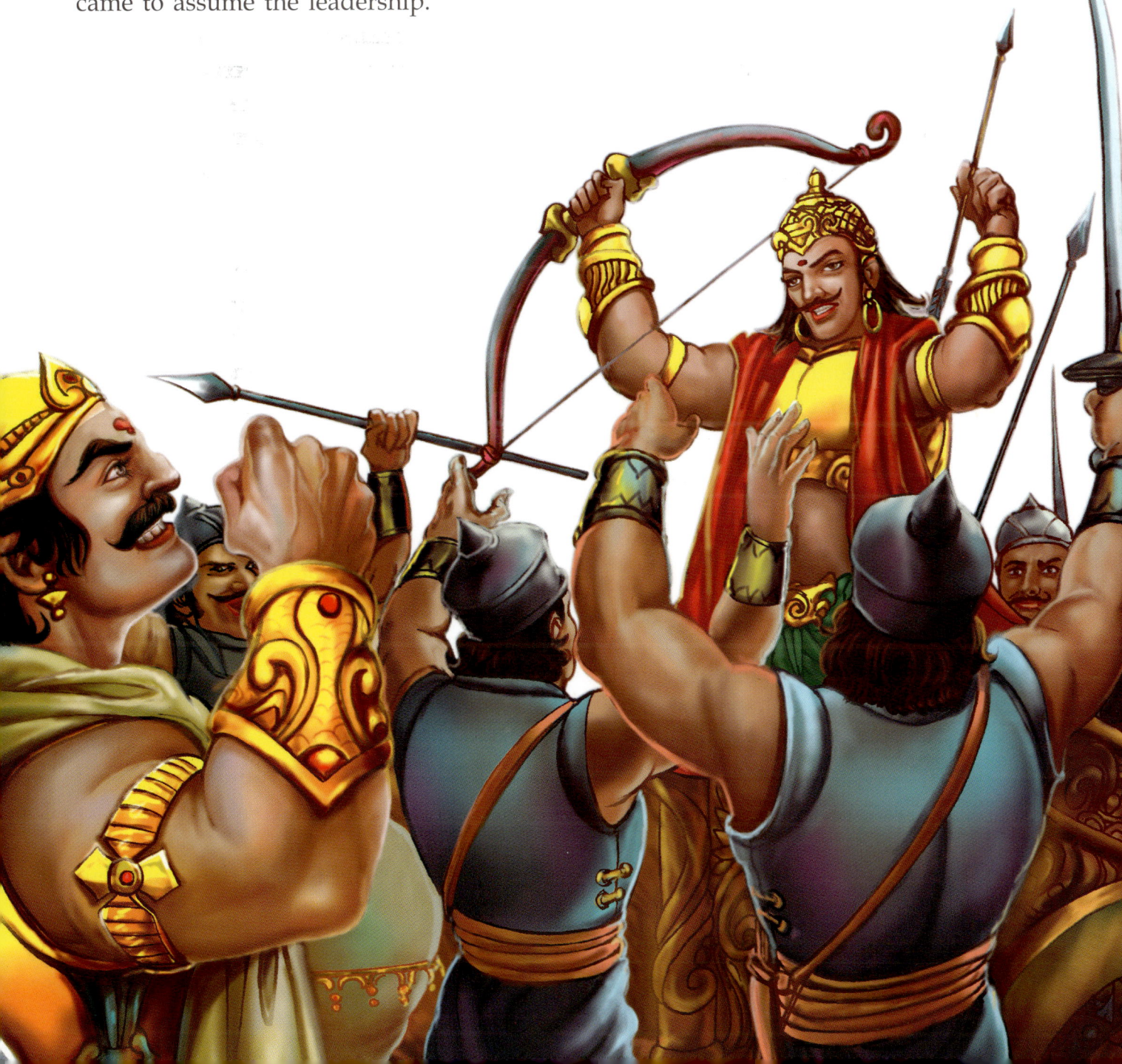

The Eleventh Day
Kauravas Plan to Capture Yudhishthira

For the next five days guru Dronacharya, tall, erect and 85 years old, led the Kaurava army. The eleventh day of the war was his first day as commander-in-chief.

Duryodhana asked the great guru to capture Yudhishthira alive. Guru Drona became suspicious at the request. "Why? Why do you want him alive when you would rather see him dead?" Drona asked.

"Because, if I have him killed, I will be the victim of Arjuna's wrath, who will have me, along with everyone related to me, killed in revenge. But if I have him captured alive, I can challenge him to play dice once again, which he won't refuse being a kshatriya, and force him to exile once again as before," Duryodhana replied.

"Not even Gods can capture Yudhishthira so long as Arjuna is with him. Take Arjuna away and I will give you Yudhishthira alive." Drona clearly spoke out his limitations.

Meanwhile, Pandava spies informed Yudhishthira of the Kaurava plot to capture him alive. Yudhishthira informed Arjuna and the other warriors of the plot and instructed them to ensure that the Kauravas did not succeed in their endeavour. Arjuna reassured his elder brother. "I can't kill my guru, but so long as I am there, he won't be able to capture you."

The battle this day was planned with the sole aim of capturing Yudhishthira alive. The first charge was forceful enough to create confusion amongst the Pandavas. Arjuna was drawn away from Yudhishthira. Shikhandi was led away by Bhurishrava and Abhimanyu was engaged in a battle by Jaidratha. Drona attacked the soldiers mercilessly and killed them in thousands. The Panchala prince Kumara intercepted Drona before he could get to Yudhishthira. But Drona was a great warrior. He easily broke the defence of Yudhishthira. First, he broke Yudhishthira's bow, then killed the Panchala prince Kumara and with the next few volleys injured Shikhandi and the Pandava twins.

Virata, Drupada and Satyaki made a valiant effort to defend the eldest Pandava, but the combined strength of the three warriors was no match for the furious guru, who swept them away like fallen leaves. Drona's men surrounded Yudhishthira. No one had any doubt that Yudhishthira would be captured. Suddenly, Arjuna appeared like a whirlwind, breaking Kaurava's defence. A fiery burst of arrows forced Drona to retreat. When the sun set, Pandavas had reasons to rejoice. Not only had the Kauravas suffered a heavy loss, but their attempt to capture the eldest Pandava was foiled as well.

The Twelfth Day
Yudhishthira Runs Away From The Battlefield

Since Drona had failed to capture Yudhishthira alive because of Arjuna, he spoke about his limitation again to Duryodhana and suggested a sound plan, "Son, it's impossible to capture Yudhishthira with Arjuna around; but if someone threw Arjuna a challenge, he wouldn't refuse. Then ensure that he is led far away."

Susharma, the Trigarta king who had past scores to settle with Arjuna, took the initiative to challenge Arjuna and led him far away from Yudhishthira. He had a huge army and five brothers — Satyartha, Satyavarma, Satyavrata, Satyeshu and Satyakarma — with him. Then he performed a yajna and took a Samshaptaka oath before the sacred fire to either kill Arjuna or to fall fighting against him.

When Susharma's death-squad challenged Arjuna, he entrusted the protection of Yudhishthira to Satyajita, Draupadi's brother, and raced towards the southern end of the battlefield to meet the challenge. Susharma's men ran helter-skelter in a confused melee as Arjuna's arrows began to indiscriminately kill men and beasts. King Susharma encouraged and rearranged his men once again. This time Arjuna used two deadly missiles — Tvashtra and Vayavya. The two missiles were capable of destroying and annihilating the entire division of an army. But Susharma's men were not halted. They withstood Arjuna's charge, even though they knew death was sure. With the help of these two missiles, Arjuna killed thousands of men, but the resistance was not yet over.

On the other front, Drona attacked Yudhishthira's guard. As he drew closer to the eldest Pandava, Satyajita launched an attack, killing Drona's charioteer and his horses. Drona retaliated full of fury, killing Satyajita's charioteer, horses, his brother and his horses along with charioteer in the very next instant. Before Satyajita could even react, the great guru beheaded him with his crescent shaped bow. Yudhishthira panicked and fled, leaving the Matsyas, Kekayas and Panchalas to face the great brahmin warrior. Before Dronacharya could chase and capture Yudhishthira, Dhrishtadyumna rushed to check Drona's advance.

Duryodhana and Karna rushed in to aid the guru in his effort to capture Yudhishthira. They charged with a large regiment of war elephants. They had nearly surrounded the eldest Pandava and might have even captured him, had Bheema not arrived at that very instant. His onslaught forced the war elephants to run over their own men, trampling hundreds of men under their feet.

Bhagadatta, a mighty warrior, was perhaps the only one, who could have checked the fury of Bheema. He was mounted on a gigantic elephant, Supratika, known for its war tactics. Supratika, the mammoth elephant, took Bheema unawares, when it curled the great Pandava in its trunk and flung him to the ground with a great force. Before Supratika could trample the mighty Pandava, he quickly rose to his feet and pounded the beast with his mace. The elephant ran away from the battlefield trumpeting in pain, with Bhagadatta still on its back.

When Arjuna heard the loud trumpets of Bhagadatta, he became worried about the safety of Yudhishthira. Arjuna asked Krishna to drive his chariot towards Yudhishthira. He broke away from Samshaptakas.

Arjuna stunned Bhagadatta with a shower of arrows, but the old warrior, oblivious of his injuries, charged Vaishnava, a deadly missile, at Arjuna. Krishna edged a little and took the impact of the missile on himself. In the next instant it turned into a garland of flowers. Since Vaishnava was a weapon bestowed by a deity, only he could have checked it. Without wasting much time Arjuna shot a great shaft killing Supratika, the elephant, and with the next one, he finished the story of Bhagadatta.

At sunset, Dronacharya was still far from his goal, despite the Kaurava army having suffered huge losses.

The Thirteenth Day
Abhimanyu is Killed

On this day Drona arrayed his troops in an impenetrable Chakravyooha. As he was surveying his army, Duryodhana derisively spoke about the great guru's inability to capture Yudhishthira alive. Drona, aware of his failure, replied in a determined tone, "Not even Gods can wrest victory where Arjuna and Krishna are together. With Arjuna around, Yudhishthira can never be taken captive. But today, all I can assure is, a Pandava hero will definitely fall."

The Samshaptakas once again drew out Arjuna to the southern end of the battlefield throwing a challenge at him. Yudhishthira, leading the battle, didn't have an answer to Chakravyooha. After thinking it over, he summoned Abhimanyu and asked him to breach the Chakravyooha, as only four men knew how to do that, and amongst the four men — Arjuna, Krishna, Pradyumna and Abhimanyu — only he was present there.

Abhimanyu asked Bheema to follow him, as he knew how to penetrate through the Chakravyooha. It was expected, Bheema would help him get out of the Chakravyooha once he entered and was closed in by the Kaurava army. Along with Bheema, the great warriors like Dhrishtadyumna and Satyaki too were to guard the rear of Abhimanyu.

Finding a weak link, Abhimanyu shot through the Kaurava men like a hurricane, leaving in his wake death and devastation. The Chakravyooha had been shattered. Karna and Shalya were forced to retire and Duryodhana's men were scattered. The swift and courageous warrior waging a lone battle tirelessly drew an instant applause from the Kaurava warriors. Guru Drona himself was enchanted with the valour and skill of the young warrior as he kept on repeatedly praising the brave son of his best disciple.

Duryodhana could hardly tolerate the rise of yet another Pandava hero. Moreover, the open praise of the young warrior by the great guru added salt to his injury. "Look, how the great guru is in awe of Arjuna's son. He doesn't even make an attempt to kill that boy. Kill him! He has already done enough damage," Duryodhana commanded his generals.

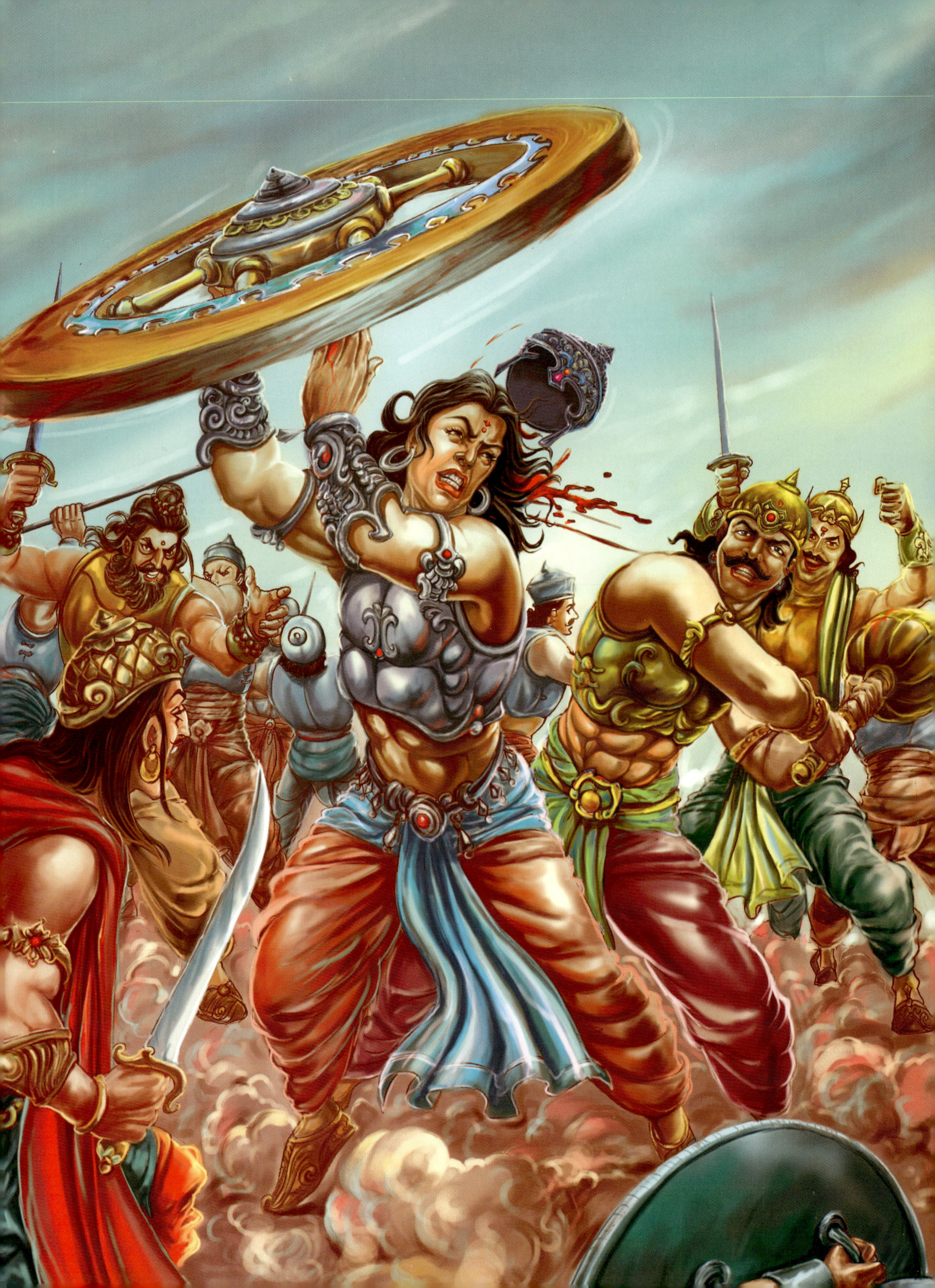

Jaidratha, the king of Sindhu, effectively blocked the breach made by Abhimanyu, as soon as he penetrated it, blocking the entry of the Pandava heroes.

The Pandavas — Yudhishthira, Bheema and the twins — and their generals could not succeed in breaking through Jaidratha. He had a boon from Lord Shiva to check the four Pandavas for one day.

Inside the array, Abhimanyu blazed through like the God of death. No one coming within his striking range was safe. Duryodhana sent his son Lakshamana with troops to check Abhimanyu. But Lakshamana was dead even before he could take his first aim at Abhimanyu. Duryodhana was wild with rage. "Kill the son of Arjuna this very moment. Observe no codes. Kill him or he will decimate us all alone. He has even killed my dear son."

Ethics and morality were shelved. Codes and rules were given up with the sole purpose to kill young Abhimanyu, no more than sixteen at that time. It was shameful that the great guru Drona also joined this evil game plan.

Six Kaurava warriors surrounded Abhimanyu, while Karna attacked him from the back. This was against the code of war.

The brave young Abhimanyu lost his armour, his quiver, his shield as well as his sword. But he kept fighting. He snatched a wheel out of a chariot and raising it, smashed about a dozen Kaurava men with it. After a while the wheel also gave up and cracked. Just then Dushasana's son attacked the unarmed Abhimanyu with his mace. Abhimanyu quickly snatched the mace from him, but finding him unarmed, threw away the mace, smiling derisively at his opponent. The Kaurava warriors rained every conceivable weapon upon him. Abhimanyu staggered and lay still.

Abhimanyu's death brought cheers to Kauravas but Yudhishthira was heart-broken. He bewailed loudly. He didn't know what answer he would give to Arjuna and Subhadra. Just then Vyasa reached there and told Yudhishthira not to grieve the death of a hero.

Arjuna, at the other end, had done away with the entire Samshaptakas of Susharma. The unethical assassination of his son broke his heart. He bewailed loudly as vengeance fuelled his anger.

"Tell me how he was killed," Arjuna asked in a harsh tone. "We had every intention of following Abhimanyu to the Chakravyooha and bringing him back safe, but Jaidratha blocked our way," Yudhishthira answered in defence as he cried.

"Jaidratha will die tomorrow. If I can't kill him by sunset, I will mount the pyre alive. This is the vow of a kshartiya," Arjuna uttered the vow and blew his conch with a threatening roar. The Kauravas in the camp heard the loud death-knell in utter fear.

The Land of The Dead

Duryodhana's spies told him about Arjuna's vow to kill Jaidratha before sunset next day, failing which, he had taken another vow to consign himself to the funeral pyre, alive.

Jaidratha, the king of the Sindhu, shook with fear and wanted to go home immediately. Duryodhana tried to instil confidence in him. "The greatest of our warriors like Drona, Karna, Shalya, Bhurishrava, Kripa and I will be there to protect you. No harm will come to you tomorrow," he said. But Jaidratha was still scared for his life. Jaidratha's fear subsided only when Drona promised to safeguard him from Arjuna.

While Kauravas were scared of Arjuna's vow, Krishna was worried how Arjuna would fulfill his vow to eliminate Jaidratha defended by topmost Kuru warriors, including Dronacharya. Moreover, Krishna had information about Drona's plan to array the troops in the highly complex half-lotus needle-mouth formation to protect him. Jaidratha was to be placed in the mouth, surrounded by the finest warriors.

The Fourteenth Day
Battle of Deceit and Treachery

Jaidratha was surrounded by the bravest warriors, who in turn were guarded by the elephant corps. Drona surveyed the troops and stationed himself directly in front of Jaidratha.

Duryodhana's brother, Durmorshana stood in the front position with his army consisting of war-chariots, war-elephants, horsemen, foot soldiers and archers. The war started and Arjuna smashed through the front lines routing Durmoshana's defence with lightning speed. Arjuna's chariot raced towards Drona. As he found himself facing the old warrior, he bowed his head in respect with folded palms. "Bless me victory, dear guru. I cannot kill Jaidratha without your blessing," Arjuna spoke to Drona.

"You must defeat me first before reaching Jaidratha," the old guru replied.

Arjuna instantly began to shower arrows on Drona's contingent, decimating his men, but the reinforcements poured in almost as quickly. Krishna asked Arjuna to move on without wasting his precious time in engaging himself with Drona. Krishna raced the chariot in the other direction, blasting through the front-line Kaurava men.

"Stop Arjuna," Duryodhana shouted to Drona, "How could you let him go? Had I known you were incapable of holding Arjuna, I would not have stopped Jaidratha from going back to his home."

Drona held his anger against Duryodhana and replied in a sharp tone, "I am well past my age. Let me concentrate on trapping Yudhishthira, while I leave it upon you to protect Jaidratha."

"Me? How can I? You know Arjuna. He is a great warrior who even Gods can't defeat. What chance do I have against him?" Duryodhana said in exasperation.

"Don't worry," Drona spoke reassuringly, "Here, I give you my enchanted armour. It will protect you against Arjuna's lethal arrows." Drona covered Duryodhana with the armour chanting the appropriate mantras.

When Arjuna came face to face with Duryodhana, a deadly battle took place and to Arjuna's surprise Duryodhana remained unharmed. The arrows fell off harmlessly to the ground after hitting Duryodhana. When Arjuna watched him closely, he discovered Drona's armour protecting Duryodhana.

Arjuna knew there was one way for his lethal shafts to penetrate Drona's armour. He chose a long, sharp and deadly arrow, hoping that this time it would penetrate the armour. Ashvathama saw the arrow flying at a great speed towards the king and destroyed it before it could strike. Arjuna's rage rose to ferocity in a moment and with quick volleys of sharply striking arrows, he broke Duryodhana's bows, killed his horses and destroyed his chariot.

Yudhishthira, battling on another front, grew worried about Arjuna as he didn't hear either the sharp, piercing sound of Devdutta or the twang of Gandiva. He asked Satyaki to go to the aid of Arjuna as he suspected him to be in a grave danger. Satyaki had been deputed by Arjuna to protect Yudhishthira. So he resisted the eldest Pandava's command. As Yudhishthira's worry for Arjuna magnified every moment making him miserable, he insisted and sternly commanded Satyaki to go in support of Arjuna.

Satyaki entrusted the task of guarding the eldest Pandava to Bheema and raced towards Arjuna. He successfully broke through Drona's guard and went past Karna without wasting his time in confrontation.

Drona found it easier to mount an offensive on Yudhishthira, breaking the front lines of his guard. The old brahmin warrior killed the king of Chedis and devastated Dhrishtadyumna's divisions.

Yudhishthira still feared for Arjuna and his fear was compounded when he lost sight of Satyaki's banner. He called Bheema to whom he expressed his worries. Bheema tried to reassure Yudhishthira but he was adamant on sending Bheema to Arjuna. Bheema faced heavy resistance from Drona, but the mighty warrior cared little and swashed through the defence killing thirty one of Duryodhana's brothers and thousands of men in a short and swift skirmish.

As the day passed, the battle was turning more savage and violent. The Kauravas were determined to save Jaidratha, while the Pandavas turned more savage and violent in their fight to finish. As the sun began to shift westwards, Bheema struck down ten more of Duryodhana's brothers.

The fourteenth day of the war claimed the maximum number of lives, with the Pandava warriors like Satyaki, Bheema, and Arjuna fighting with grim determination. Bheema on Yudhishthira's instruction, blazed through the Kaurava ranks and finding

Arjuna quite safe in Krishna's presence cheered loudly. When Yudhishthira heard Bheema's loud cheer, he was reassured about Arjuna.

Bheema was truly ferocious on this day. Anyone coming in his way fell dead as he rode through the vast enemy divisions like a bull charging through a herd of sheep.

As the Kaurava army retreated in a confused melee, Karna came forward to check the advance of Bheema. Sharp arrows greeted him, but he continued advancing like a thick-skinned rhinoceros. Soon Bheema found himself at a striking distance from Karna. Violent mace-blows rained over the steeds and chariots killing the horses and breaking Karna's chariot into pieces. Next, he broke Karna's bow and threw him on the ground. Duryodhana's brother Durjeya rushed to Karna's aid, who met an instant death as Bheema smashed his head with his mace. Durmukha, Duryodhana's yet another brother came next, only to meet with the same fate. Karna fled the battlefield now.

As Duryodhana's brothers kept pouring in, in the form of reinforcements, Bheema savagely struck them to their horrible end as quickly as they came. After decimating five more of Duryodhana's brothers, Bheema waited for more. Duryodhana's seven brothers were sent in next. They were Chitra, Upachitra, Chitraksha, Charuchitra, Chitrayndha, Chitravarma and Sharasan. Bheema killed them all one by one, waiting for still more of them to come. Kauravas were in complete awe of Bheema's strength. The next seven brothers who came after them met with a similar fate. The last of these seven brothers to be killed was Vikarna, who was loved by the Pandavas.

Karna came back to face Bheema once more with grim determination. Bheema had broken his bow eighteen times since morning and broke it once more, the nineteenth time. Undeterred, Karna continued raining arrows on Bheema, skilfully picking up the next bow. He even came close to killing Bheema, but held himself because of the promise made to Kunti — he wouldn't harm any of the Pandava brothers except Arjuna.

Satyaki found himself under attack by Bhurishrava, and after a long protracted battle, the Vrishni hero beheaded the old warrior under unfortunate circumstances leading to a controversy over the manner of his killing. The old warrior's right hand had been severed by Arjuna to save Satyaki from a sure death. Bhurishrava then sat in Praya (meditation) position to voluntarily relinquish his life. Satyaki beheaded the old, defenceless warrior with a single stroke of his sword, violating all norms of the war.

Arjuna defended his action claiming it his duty to defend Satyaki, his disciple. Satyaki too, found nothing wrong with his act as Bhurishrava had kicked him on his head, which was the worst possible insult.

Arjuna realised there was no time for arguments. Sun was in the western sky and Jaidratha was still alive. After hours of grim battling, Arjuna came close to the Sindhu king, Jaidratha. He, however, needed to get past Shalya and Kripa before he could inflict death upon the Sindhu king. Krishna noticed six warriors guarding the king and reckoned the enormity of the task in hand. The strategy had to be changed if Jaidratha was to be killed before sunset.

"I am going to create an illusion of darkness. Jaidratha, assuming the sun has set, will put away his weapons and so will his men guarding him. That's the time when you must strike. When you kill Jaidratha, make sure his head falls into his father's lap who is meditating in the forest. There's a curse on him that whoever drops Jaidratha's head on the ground, will meet the same fate as him," advised Krishna to Arjuna.

Soon darkness appeared due to Krishna's illusion. Kauravas cheered imagining the impossible feat of having vanquished Arjuna. Jaidratha put down his bow, amazed at his luck. Arjuna took his Gandiva and shot his finest arrow which no one saw in the dark. The arrow sliced Jaidratha's neck clean and carried the head to fall in Sindhu's old king's lap who was sitting in meditation in the forest since the time Jaidratha was a boy. When the king rose up from his meditation, the head fell down and in the next instant the king's head shattered into fragments.

Krishna withdrew the illusion. Crimson red coloured setting sun appeared on the horizon. Kauravas realised they had been hoodwinked. Hostilities, which ought to have been suspended with the setting of the sun, continued unabated. Jealousy, bitterness and acrimony magnified manifold in the darkness.

Kauravas, bitter and disappointed, were full of revenge. They carried the battle into darkness under lamps and torches.

The battle in the night made it more deadly and ferocious. It was only when Arjuna had mortally wounded Kripacharya and watched him fall that he realised the words of Vidura, "Disciples would raise arms against gurus and men would kill their friends and brothers."

Karna came close to killing Sahadeva, but held himself because of his having promised Kunti not to kill the four of the five Pandavas. Earlier in the day, he had spared Bheema's life too. Karna had created havoc in the battle. The Pandava men panicked at his very sight. Krishna was apprehensive of Arjuna's life so long as Karna possessed Indra's Vajra with him. "Karna is beating our men recklessly. Only you and Ghatotkacha can hold out against him. Send Bheema's son to deal with Karna before he sucks life out of our men," Krishna said to Arjuna.

The Death Dance of Ghatotkacha

When Ghatotkacha came, Krishna explained to him the need of the hour, his strength and qualities. He also told him that the hour for which he was born had come and now he was to deal with Karna.

"Tonight I will care for none. I will create an ugly dance of death," vowed Ghatotkacha and swooped upon the Kaurava army with his intensity magnified in the deadly hour of the night. With a blood curdling cry, he led his horde of fierce rakshasas against Karna. The severity of his attack terrified everyone in the battle.

The rakshasas, adept in the art of illusion, killed thousands of men. Karna shot arrows at illusory Ghatotkacha who rained shafts and arrows on Kauravas, killing them in thousands. He broke Karna's bow, killed the charioteer along with the horses and continued to decimate the Kauravas.

Kauravas pleaded with Karna to use Indra's Vajra against the rakshasa. They urged him to kill Ghatotkacha, otherwise, he was determined to butcher them all with his murderous rage.

Karna looked at the hopeless, distraught faces, frightened for their life and decided he could not have them slaughtered. He took out the Vajra and hurled it with grim determination upon Bheema's son. The missile went straight to its target, tearing Ghatotkacha's chest who let out a piercing shriek. Bheema's son made a quick decision in his dying moment, to bring about a gigantic destruction as a farewell to his Pandava family. He expanded his body to the size of a huge mountain scaling the sky above and fell to the ground as life ebbed out of him, crushing tens of thousands of warriors to death.

While the Pandavas mourned and wept bitterly over Ghatotkacha's death, Krishna displayed unseemly joy because Arjuna was safe now. Karna's Vajra was used once and could not now be used a second time. Yudhishthira loved Ghatotkacha even more than he loved Sahadeva, and bewailed his death.

The battle went on unabatedly. Drona rearranged his troops and led his men against Drupada. The brahmin warrior blazed through the Panchala troops. He first broke Virata's bow and then cut off his head.

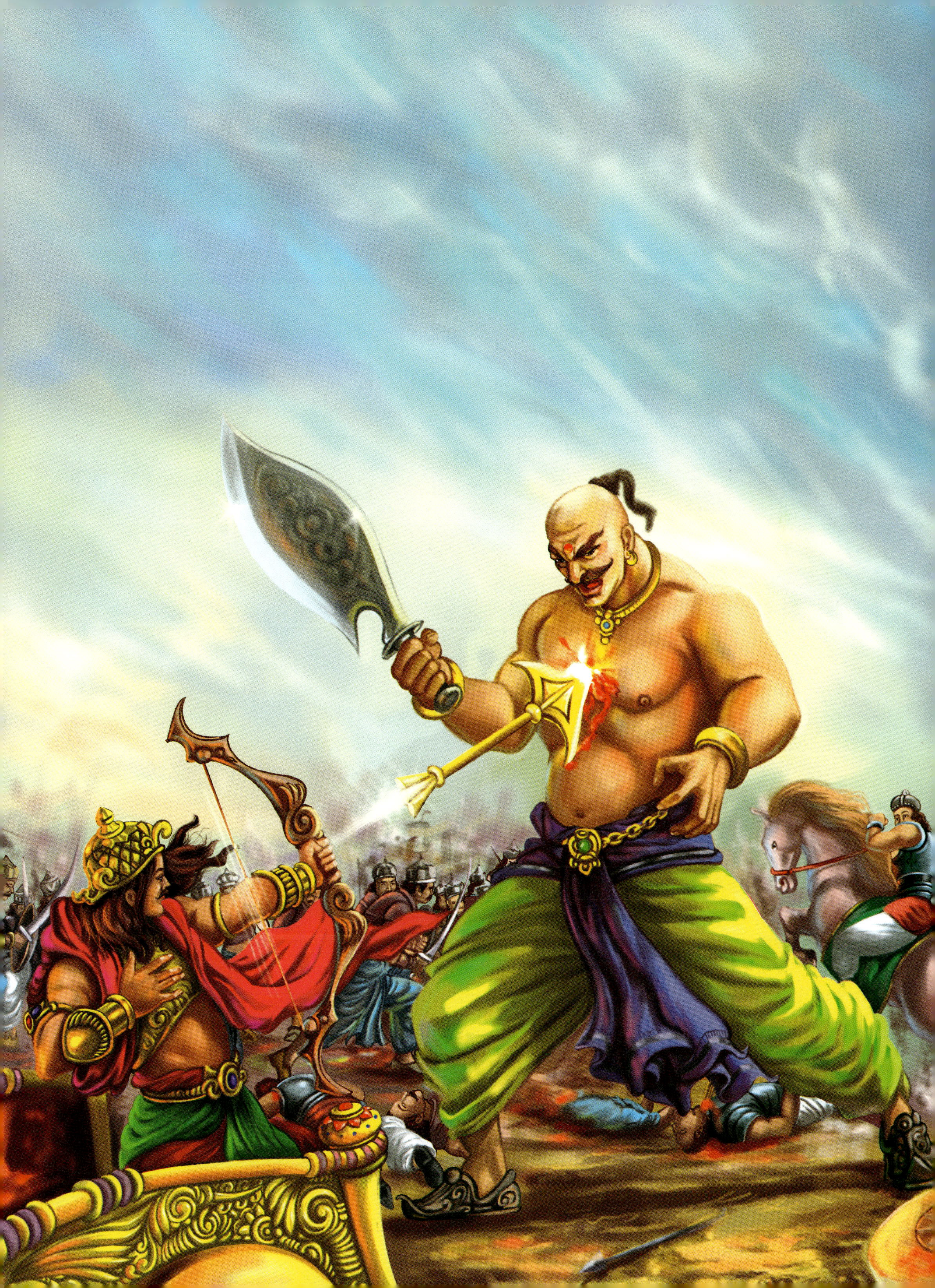

Dronacharya is Assassinated

When Dhrishtadyumna heard of his father's death at the hands of his old enemy, he vowed to kill Drona before the nightfall. Arjuna and Bheema joined Panchala against Drona and broke his ranks. Guru and disciple fought as if they were mortal enemies. The others stood amazed watching the combat in wonder. Thousands lost their lives but the two blood soaked warriors showed no sign of exhaustion. The Pandava troops shuddered at the sight of the massacre of their men. They complained bitterly about the way Drona was massacring them and only Arjuna was capable of killing him, but he wouldn't because he was his guru.

"It's impossible to kill him so long as he is armed," Krishna said to Arjuna. "We must disarm him somehow. If he is given the news that Ashvathama has died, he will lose all heart in the war and that's when he can be struck down," Krishna suggested.

Neither Yudhishthira nor Arjuna supported this strategy. But the majority of the generals favoured it. Bheema killed an elephant named Ashvathama and shouted, "Ashvathama is dead!"

Drona heard the cry to his great disappointment. He didn't believe the words. He thought his son couldn't have been killed so easily. He brushed the thought aside and launched a fresh attack on Dhrishtadyumna, killing his men in large number. The great brahmin warrior could not put himself whole-heartedly in the war. He worried for his son. The cry had worried him and now he was gripped with the sole thought of verifying the statement of Bheema. He decided to ask Yudhishthira, who never lied.

Krishna convinced Yudhishthira of the necessity of lies under certain circumstances. Drona could kill all of them if he continued fighting. If a lie saves life, it is no lie. Lies spoken to save a life, a marriage, a brahmin or a king are no lies. So when Drona asked Yudhishthira whether Ashvathama had died, Yudhishthira replied, "Ashvathama has been killed, not your son, but an elephant." Krishna arranged for a drum to be beaten as Yudhishthira spoke the latter part of the sentence, so that Drona could hear only "Ashvathama has been killed."

In any case, it was a lie spoken by Yudhishthira, the son of Dharmaraja, and as soon as the words crossed his lips, his chariot, which always remained above the ground, came to the ground.

Drona put away his arms in disappointment. His eyes looked vacant and with his son's name on his lips he spread Kusha grass on the ground and sat in meditation so as to enter in trance. Dhrishtadyumna grabbed the opportunity. He cut off his head and threw it amongst the Kauravas, who scattered away in panic.

When Ashvathama came to know of the manner of his father's death, he trembled with rage. In an instant he decided to wipe out the Pandavas, the Panchalas and all their allies, using Narayanastra, the deadliest weapon. Invoking the *astra*, he hurled it into the Pandava troops, totally annihilating a whole *akshavahini*. Before more damage could be done, Krishna instructed the Pandava army to lie down on the ground leaving their weapons. They followed Krishna's instructions, and the deadly weapon diffused and fell harmless. But Ashvathama had taken a heavy toll of the Pandava army, before the night fell.

The Fifteenth Day
Karna Leads

After Drona's death, the Kauravas unanimously elected Karna as the commander of the forces. In a single combat, Karna defeated and injured Yudhishthira, who retreated to his camp utterly frustrated and dejected.

Arjuna, battling Ashvathama's forces, noticed Yudhishthira's chariot missing. He asked Krishna to head for the camp. They were pleasantly relieved to find Yudhishthira there.

The eldest Pandava, bitter and humiliated after a humbling defeat at Karna's hands, thought Arjuna must have killed Karna. That was perhaps the reason for their presence in the camp, as Yudhishthira interpreted.

But when Yudhishthira came to know that Karna still lived, he turned furious and used insulting language against Arjuna and asked him to give the Gandiva to a more worthy warrior. This was enough provocation for Arjuna to raise his sword in an attempt to kill Yudhishthira. Krishna instantly intervened and the matter was amicably settled.

Arjuna, feeling remorseful at his deed, said that Karna would not live to see the next day's sunrise. Arjuna touched Yudhishthira's feet, "I will leave the battlefield only when I have killed Karna," he vowed, walking out of the tent.

Krishna and Arjuna were back in action amongst their men. Orders were issued to men to mount fresh attacks. Krishna noticed Arjuna was not in a right frame of mind and needed encouragement. He began motivating the archer to fight with Karna.

"You are the only one who can send Karna to Yama's court. Stop being emotional and just do your job with single-minded devotion. Fix your mind and even Gods won't be able to thwart you. Karna is Duryodhana's only hope. Kill him and he is finished. Remember, it was Karna who broke Abhimanyu's bow. He was amongst the six to attack and kill Abhimanyu when he was weaponless. He laughed at his death," said Krishna, instigating Arjuna.

"Karna will die before the sun sets today and Duryodhana will lose every hope of life and kingdom," Arjuna cried.

Bheema Drinks Dushasana's Blood

On the other front, Bheema was engaged with Dushasana with only one motive in his head, that of killing him. Dushasana's arrows pierced Bheema, but the mighty warrior was oblivious to everything. "Today I will drink your blood," roared Bheema, "and not even Gods can save you!" Next, he pounded the Kaurava with his mace and his head bled as it ruptured. Staggering, he fell out of his chariot and Bheema mounted over him. Bheema tore Dushasana's chest open and drank the fountain of blood gushing out, to the horror of everyone present there. Duryodhana and Karna watched helplessly. Ten of Duryodhana's brothers made a combined assault on Bheema, but all of them met with a swift death at Bheema's hand.

The Battle Between Arjuna and Karna

Karna's son Vrishasena was bravely facing the Pandavas, while he himself came forward to face Arjuna. At the sight of Vrishasena Arjuna was reminded of Abhimanyu's death at Kauravas' hand. "The time has come for you to see the death of your own son before your eyes. Six of you killed my son mercilessly when he was unarmed. I will kill your son first and then I will kill you." Arjuna shot ten deadly arrows at Vrishasena, who dropped dead immediately. Karna saw his dying son and rushed at Arjuna in rage.

The two mighty warriors rose towards each other in rage. The two were the best of warriors — tall, handsome and powerful, armed with God-given weapons.

Shalya, the charioteer of Karna and the maternal uncle of Pandavas, discouraged him, "You're going to fight against the best warrior on the planet. No one has ever defeated him." "Yes, I know," replied Karna, "and he has Krishna. Either I will kill him or he will kill me." Karna was clearly disappointed. On the other hand, Arjuna was gripped with the sole thought of killing Karna.

"Karna will not live today. I haven't forgotten that he disarmed Abhimanyu. Both Draupadi and Subhadra would be avenged today," Arjuna said to Krishna with determination in his voice.

As the two warriors clashed, the battlefield presented the ghastly sight of scattered and mutilated dead bodies of men and beasts. The surviving men trembled. The Gods, the demigods and the other heavenly beings came out of the heavens to watch the wonderful sight of the clash of the titans.

Ashvathama, unable to bear the deadly scene of destruction, ran to Duryodhana and requested him to make peace because otherwise everything was going to end in disaster. Duryodhana was drowned in sorrow and despair. All he could say was he did not want to be branded a coward. Moreover, Duryodhana was still hopeful that Karna will kill Arjuna.

Arjuna and Karna fought with killer's instinct. The deadly shafts of the two warriors clashed in mid air, while their missiles killed thousands of men and beasts of the two armies. Karna was furious and without giving a second thought, he hurled the Bhargava missile, killing thousands of Panchalas and Somakas.

Bheema was roused to fury. He reminded Arjuna of the misdeeds committed by Karna and asked him to show no mercy to him. Krishna was also annoyed. "Do you want me to strike his head off using my Sudarshan Chakra?" Krishna asked in irritation.

Arjuna shook away his inaction and said, "I'll use my Brahmastra now."

The missile charged with a deafening noise, illuminating the battlefield and filling the hearts of Kaurava men with fear. Karna knew how to save himself. The missile, nonetheless, annihilated a whole division of the Kaurava army when it fell.

The second half of the day had begun, but neither of the two had any considerable advantage over the other. Arjuna launched his next attack on Shalya, injuring him with ten deadly arrows and then with the next seven arrows he injured Karna. As he fell writhing in pain, the Kauravas panicked and their ranks broke.

Karna, unmindful of the pain, got ready to fight once again. A naga, Ashvasena, had a score to settle with Arjuna. His mother had died in the conflagration in Khandava, so he had long nourished his grievance against Arjuna. As Karna shot the arrow, he perched on it. The arrow might have killed Arjuna, had Krishna not acted promptly. When he saw the deadly naga on the arrow, he forced the horses on their knees and the chariot ducked low. The deadly arrow broke Arjuna's crown. His life was saved.

The naga came to his original form and appeared before Karna. He offered to help Karna in killing Arjuna, disclosing the reason for his grievance against Arjuna. But Karna refused to accept his offer, saying, "I would not require your help, even if I was confronting a hundred Arjunas!"

Ashvasena decided to go alone. As he leapt upon Arjuna, Krishna warned him, "Kill the naga immediately!" Arjuna released six deadly shafts, killing Ashvasena before he could strike Arjuna. And then he turned to meet Karna's attack.

Karna noticed the wheels of his chariot were sinking in the muddy ground. He was reminded of a curse he had on him. In his very young days, he had accidentally killed the cow of a brahmin, who had cursed him that he too would die helplessly as his chariot wheels would sink in the ground. At the same time Karna was also reminded of Parashurama's curse which was taking effect.

As he tried to use Bhargava, Parashurama's missile, he discovered to his consternation that he had forgotten the mantra. Parashurama had cursed him because he pretended to be a brahmin, so as to become his disciple.

When the great sage came to know of the truth, he cursed his disciple of not being able to use his weapons at an opportune moment. Karna leapt out of chariot and struggled to free the wheel. He pleaded with Arjuna to hold his attack as that was the code of war.

Krishna smiled sarcastically. "I wonder what makes you invoke rules when you forgot them completely at the time Draupadi was dragged to the court. You asked her to choose a Kaurava as her husband. Where were your codes when you killed Abhimanyu, who was unarmed?" Krishna asked. "Don't wait. Kill him!" he said, turning to Arjuna.

Arjuna instantly obeyed Krishna's advice. An arrow shot out of Gandiva, and neatly beheaded Karna. His head dropped to the ground. Arjuna and Krishna blew their conches to announce victory.

When Duryodhana came to know of Karna's death, he broke down, weeping bitterly. He launched an attack on Bheema with maniacal vengeance, but the sun had set and the day's battle was over.

The Sixteenth Day
Shakuni and His Son Are Killed

After the fall of Karna, Shalya was chosen as the commander-in-chief to lead the Kaurava army. The Kauravas launched a massive attack, breaking Yudhishthira's front lines.

Pandava men began falling like slender trees in a blizzard but Bheema arrived in time to check the tide. He shattered Shalya's bow, broke his armour and wounded him grievously. He also broke his uncle's sword and shield.

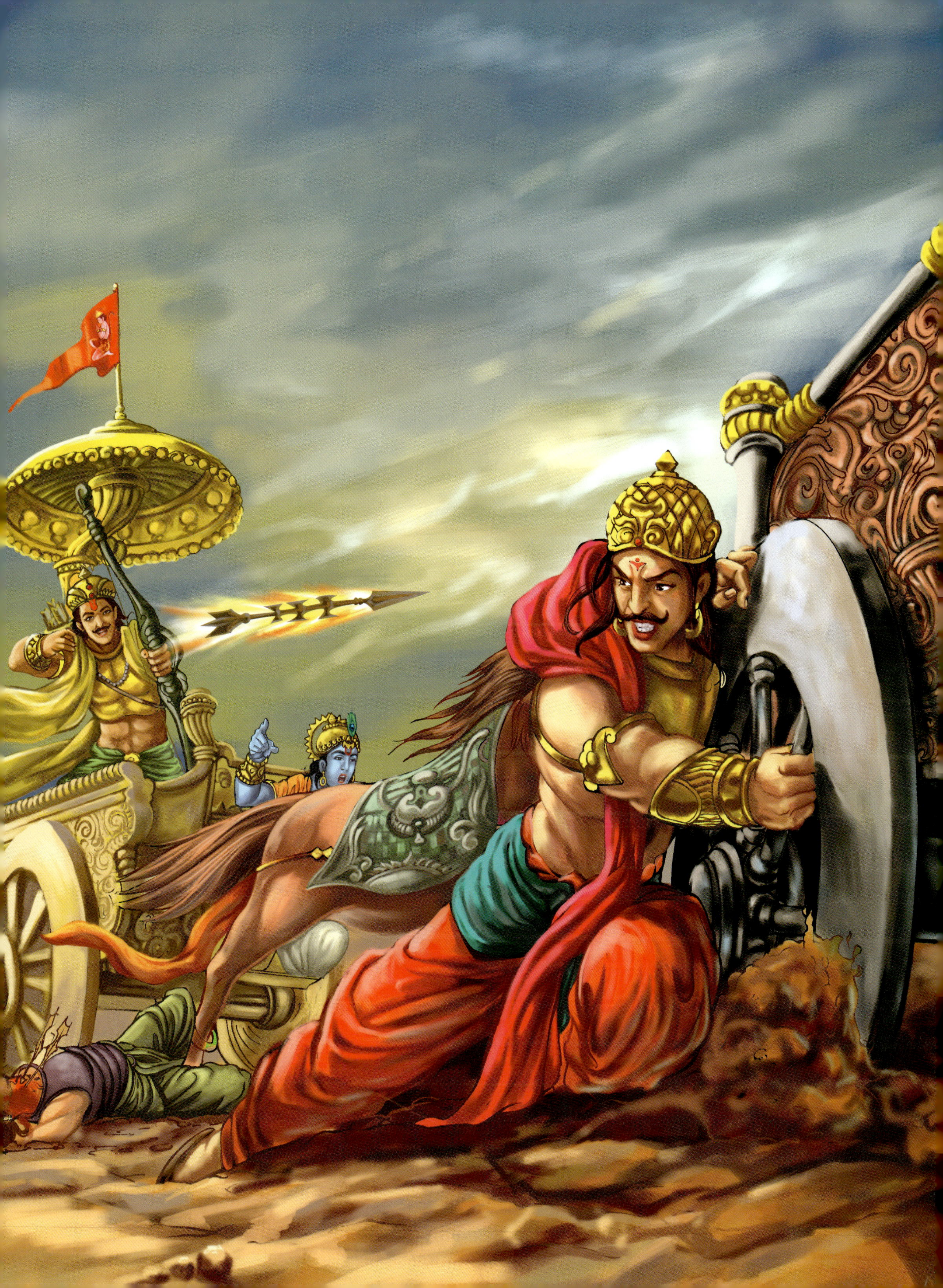

But Shalya fought his way through Yudhishthira's men and closed in upon him. Yudhishthira hurled his javelin at Shalya, who tried to duck but could not escape the powerful weapon, which plunged in his unprotected broad chest. Blood gushed out of his ruptured chest and he fell down dead.

Shalya's brothers attacked Yudhishthira, but he killed them one by one. Duryodhana and Kritavarma attacked Satyaki, but Duryodhana was under a constant attack by Pandava troops. His brave soldiers were being massacred. He asked his Mandraka warriors to retreat, but these brave warriors were also loyal. They refused to show their back to the enemy and died fighting. As they made a breach into the Pandava line, the troops encircled and wiped out the Mandraka division.

Duryodhana was alone, when Shakuni arrived with reinforcements to join Duryodhana. Shakuni was shattered when Sahadeva killed his son Uluka. Tears rolled down his cheeks. He remembered Vidura's words that war would bring untold grief. He went to battle Sahadeva but the Pandava broke his bow with a swift and accurate arrow and with the next one, Shakuni was beheaded.

The Seventeenth Day
Gandhari's Shield For Duryodhana

The sixteenth day of the war was over with Shakuni's death. On the seventeenth day Duryodhana was left alone. Of his eleven *akshavahinis*, only three men were alive. Duryodhana decided to go inside a lake to take some rest.

Using yogic powers, he solidified the lake and created an entrance through which he went inside. He sat inside to renew his strength and wait for the right moment to emerge.

Ashvathama, Kritavarma and Kripacharya were the only survivors of the Kaurava army. They were looking for Duryodhana when Sanjaya informed them that he was inside the lake to take some rest. They felt reassured that Duryodhana was still alive. The only other son of Dhritarashtra who was still alive was Yuyutsu, who had joined the Pandavas moments before the war began.

The three warriors went near the lake and shouted at Duryodhana to come out and fight the Pandavas. "The king of Kurus! You are so close to victory. Come out and fight the Pandavas. They have only a small division left. We are here to protect you," they cried.

"I know I have to fight, but today I must rest. I am tired and wounded. I will fight tomorrow," said Duryodhana.

Even before Duryodhana had entered the lake, Gandhari had reached Kurukshetra and was worried about her son. She asked her son to come unclothed after a bath in the river Saraswati, which was nearby. Gandhari's eyes were so powerful that Duryodhana's body could become as hard as steel if she looked at his body.

Somehow Krishna got a hint of the plan. When Duryodhana was going naked to his mother, Krishna interrupted him, "Won't you feel ashamed in going to your mother completely naked? You can do well to cover your loins." Duryodhana covered his loins with banana leaves and stood before Gandhari. Gandhari opened her blindfolded eyes to see Duryodhana. She cursed Duryodhana's fate as she discovered him partly covered. His body turned as hard as steel except for his hip which was covered.

When Duryodhana was hiding inside the lake and Ashvathama, Kritavarma and Kripacharya were conversing with him, some of the hunters in the forest overheard their conversation and came to know of the whereabouts of Duryodhana. They passed on the information to the Pandavas, who arrived at the lake.

Yudhishthira remarked sarcastically to Duryodhana hidden inside the lake, "Why do you hide? If you are a kshatriya and a Kaurava, get out and fight like a hero. Where's your self-respect, your pride, your honour?"

Duryodhana replied, "I am a Kaurava, a kshatriya and not afraid to die. I am here only to rest for a while. When I come out tomorrow, I will be ready to fight. Go back now."

As Duryodhana's voice wafted out of water, Yudhishthira lost his patience and challenged him to come out of the water and fight.

Duryodhana responded to the challenge. He challenged the Pandavas to come one by one in a single combat of mace fight. He came out of the lake with his mace. Bheema took up the challenge and the two warriors pounced on each other with deadly ferocity. The mace-duel went on for a considerable length of time without either of the warriors showing any sign of weakness.

Bheema Defeats Duryodhana by Foul Means

As the two mace warriors fought with each other, Balarama, their guru arrived. "I left forty days ago on a pilgrimage and I return today to find my disciples fighting," Balarama remarked.

Duryodhana and Bheema grappled viciously. Bheema gripped him, but he broke free and landed a massive blow on the mighty Pandava's chest. Both of them were drenched in sweat and blood but they continued to fight. Duryodhana hit Bheema on his head. Bheema reeled and before he could recover, a couple of more blows had already landed on his chest. He sprang up quickly and delivered a vicious blow at Duryodhana, bringing him down on his knees, but in a quick manoeuvre, the eldest Kaurava struck Bheema again on the head. Bheema fell down and rose up slowly, wiping blood and sweat off his forehead.

"Duryodhana is a far better mace warrior than Bheema. It's impossible to defeat him in a fair fight. Bheema has vowed to break Duryodhana's thighs. He will lose the fight, unless he resorts to treachery," Krishna confided truthfully to Arjuna.

Krishna hinted Bheema to hit at Duryodhana's thighs. As the Pandava warrior's eyes caught Krishna's, he patted at his thigh, showing Bheema where to strike. Moving cautiously, he waited for the right opportunity to strike. As he found an opportunity, he made full use of it and with the blows of his mace, broke Duryodhana's thigh bones. Duryodhana collapsed, unable to stand on his feet again.

Bheema roared wildly as Duryodhana cringed in pain. Then raising his foot, he placed it on Duryodhana's head. Everyone present there was shocked and aghast.

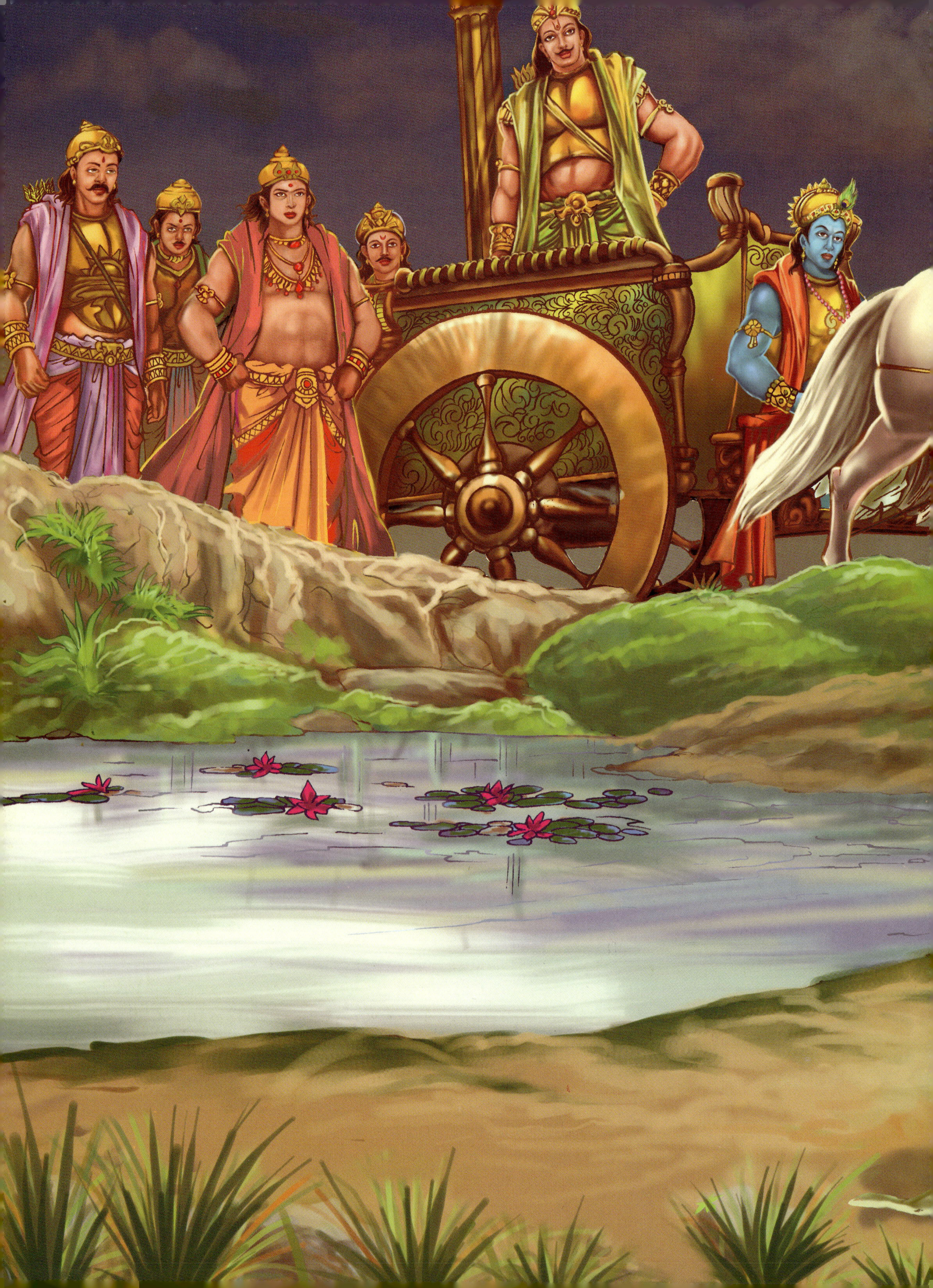

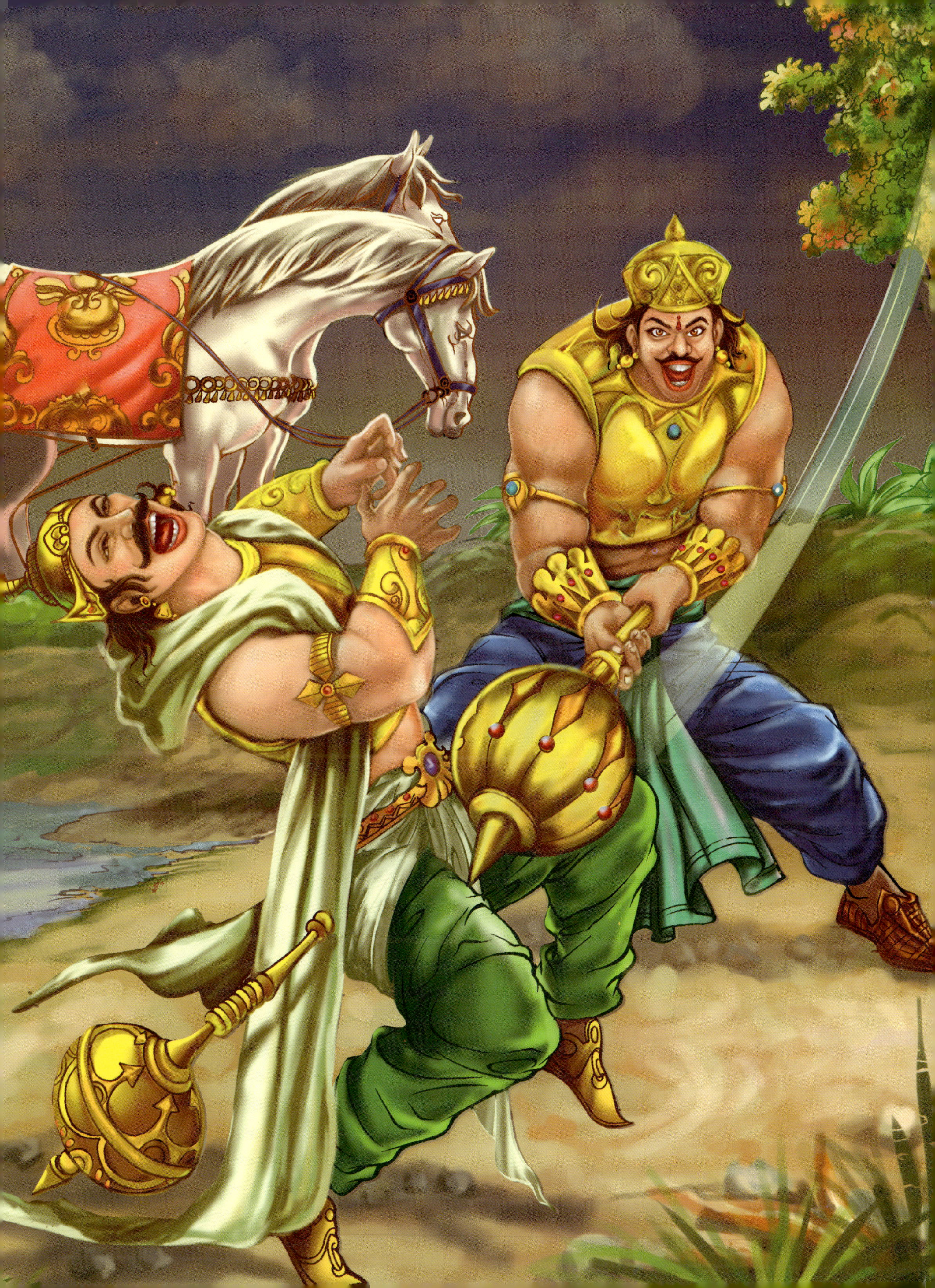

Balarama reacted violently and rushed to attack Bheema, saying, "Bheema has tarnished the image of true warriors. He struck Duryodhana below his waist and won using foul means."

As he was about to strike Bheema, Krishna held him and tried to reason with him, "Bheema had vowed to break Duryodhana's thigh in an open assembly. How could he have gone back on his words? Duryodhana insulted Draupadi in the open court. He killed Abhimanyu when he was unarmed. He had Draupadi abducted by Jaidratha. How can he expect the others to follow norms and rules when he himself does not follow them?" The words of Krishna pacified Balarama.

Duryodhana, writhing in pain, abused Krishna, "You accuse me of treachery, but look at yourself. You were behind Drona's death, spreading rumour about Ashvathama's death. You brought Shikhandi before Bhishma, knowing he would not fight a woman. You prompted Arjuna to kill Karna by foul means. You sent Ghatotkacha to ensure Karna used his Vajra against him. And now I saw you gesturing to Bheema to attack me below the navel. Can anyone stoop as low as you? I will die and attain heaven but you will live in grief and sorrow," Duryodhana cursed him.

Ashvathama was full of rage when he came to know Bheema had used foul means to defeat Duryodhana. He raced to be with Duryodhana, who lay immobilised suffering a painful and lingering death. Ashvathama, Kripa and Kritavarma wept in silence when they found Duryodhana lying helpless. Ashvathama could not hold himself at the pathetic sight of a crown prince in misery. "I vow to kill the Pandavas and Panchalas, O, honourable king and take revenge," he swore.

Duryodhana was immensely pleased to hear Ashvathama's words. He immediately anointed him as the next commander-in-chief of the Kaurava army as Kripacharya sprinkled water on Ashvathama's head. The three Kaurava warriors left seething in anger and with a determined vengeance.

Krishna advised the Pandavas to camp near the riverside that night as he suspected Ashvathama to adopt any means to seek vengeance.

That fateful night the Pandava men had already retreated to their camp, while Ashvathama was sleepless with anger and vengeance. He noticed an owl perched on a tree nearby. The owl crept into a crow's nest, and the next moment screeching sounds of the birds rented the stillness of night. Ashvathama found in this event, a lesson. He decided to creep into the Pandavas' camp and violently murder everyone sleeping there.

Kripacharya was aghast at the crooked plan and tried to reason with Ashvathama citing ethics and morality, but it was of no use. He countered arguing the immorality and violation of war codes in killing Dronacharya, Bhishma, Karna and Duryodhana. Finally Ashvathama, Kripacharya, and Kritavarma approached the Pandavas' camp in a determined move.

Ashvathama found a huge rakshasa guarding their camp and knew he needed to be avoided. Scouting around he found a small opening through which he crept softly, instructing Kripa and Kritavarma to slaughter every Pandava and Panchala who ran out of the gate. He found Dhrishtadyumna lying fast asleep in the very first tent itself, to his malicious satisfaction. He lifted him by hair and thrashed him to death.

Ashvathama systematically slaughtered the sleeping Panchalas with his sword. The Panchala princes, Draupadi's five sons, soldiers, guards, attendants were all killed ruthlessly and those who managed to escape to the gate were done to death by Kripacharya and Kritavarma.

Then the three of them, drenched in the blood of sleeping Panchalas, came to Duryodhana, who was barely alive. "You have been avenged, O king. All the Panchalas, including Dhrishtadyumna, Shikhandi and his brothers, and Draupadi's five sons lie dead. The Pandavas are now sonless. They have none left to rejoice their victory."

Duryodhana felt immensely satisfied to hear these words of Ashvathama. "You have done for me what Bhishma, Drona and Karna could not do. Now I will die in peace," he said. The eldest Kaurava prince finally breathed his last.

The Eighteenth Day
There Are No Winners in a War

The Pandavas were shocked and aghast at the tragedy of the previous night. There were only eight grief stricken Pandavas alive to mourn the cold-blooded massacre of their kin. They were five Pandava brothers, Draupadi, Uttara and Kunti.

Draupadi bewailed bitterly for the slaughter of her sons and declared she would mortify herself to death unless Drona's son paid for his crime. "I will begin living only when you get me the gem on his forehead he was born with," she said to Bheema, who immediately rushed out in search of Ashvathama. Krishna tried to stop him because Ashvathama still had the Brahmastra, capable of destroying the whole world.

Krishna and the Pandavas followed Bheema, who came to the banks of the Ganga, where they saw Ashvathama along with Vyasa and the other rishis.

Ashvathama trembled with fear as he saw the Pandavas and Krishna. He had the Brahmastra which he did not hesitate to use. He plucked a blade of grass and charged it with the mantra. The delicate tiny grass pulsated with energy of creation and moved. Arjuna immediately released the anti-missile. Vyasa then intervened and ordered them to withdraw their missiles because the collision would shatter the earth. Arjuna immediately obeyed, but Ashwathama did not know how to. Instead, he directed it to Uttara's womb, to kill Abhimanyu's unborn son and the last descendant of the Pandavas. He succeeded in killing the foetus.

Krishna was furious. He snatched the gem from Ashwathama's forehead, leaving a gaping wound. He cursed Ashwathama saying that he would live on, that he would be a leper, that his wounds would never heal and that it would be a very lonely existence. Krishna revived Uttara's stillborn child, when Uttara reminded him that he had promised her that she would have a son.

The Pandavas and Krishna, along with Narada, came to Draupadi and Bheema gave her the gem. She gave it to Yudhishthira. Thus the terrible war of Mahabharata came to an end with Ashvathama going into exile.

In Hastinapur, Dhritarashtra and Gandhari were grief stricken. Vidura tried to console them. Sage Vyasa also came there to console them and spoke of destiny which led to this war and caused great suffering. He advised them to accept Yudhishthira as their eldest son and the other Pandavas as their younger sons and crown the eldest prince as the king of Hastinapur.

When the Pandavas, along with Krishna, came to Hastinapur, Dhritarashtra embraced them. However, Dhritarashtra could not control his vengeance against Bheema, whom he held responsible for killing all his sons including Duryodhana. As he was about to hug Bheema, Krishna put an iron-statue in his place. Dhritarashtra had powerful arms. He hugged the statue with a powerful feeling of revenge. The statue instantly broke into pieces. Bheema stepped aside in shock.

Krishna rebuked Dhritarashtra for being blind in love for his son, which led to the war, and presently for trying to kill Bheema. The blind king realised his weakness and thanked Krishna for his timely intervention which saved Bheema's life.

Then the Pandavas went to Gandhari, who was in deep sorrow. She was about to curse Yudhishthira, but Vyasa intervened and she checked herself. She admitted to her reason being clouded by sorrow. She showered blessings on the Pandavas and blamed her son, Shakuni, Karna, and Dushasana for the tragedy.

Finally they went to the banks of river Ganga to perform the funeral rites of their near and dear ones. Gandhari fell unconscious when she saw the dead bodies of Karna, Drona and Dushasana. When she came back to her senses she lashed out at Krishna, "What were you doing when the kshatriyas slaughtered one another? You could have stopped this carnage, if you had wished to. I will curse you to witness your king and friends killing each other before your eyes, thirty six years from now. They will all perish but you will live to die in wilderness and your ladies will weep as the Bharata ladies are doing now!"

Krishna smiled and said, "I know that's going to happen."

When Karna's body was laid on pyre, Kunti wept bitterly and asked her sons to perform the last rites, as Karna was her son and their brother. The Pandavas were shocked at this revelation. Yudhishthira held himself guilty of fratricide even as he wept bitterly. "Had we known about it earlier, this war would not have taken place," Yudhishthira lamented.

Yudhishthira was so overwhelmed by grief that he decided to renounce the world and become an ascetic. His brothers and Draupadi tried their best to dissuade him against taking such an extreme step. They said such an example would make them a laughing stock. They said it was the kshatriya creed to win or die fighting. Finally they persuaded Yudhishthira to rule the kingdom for which so many kshatriyas died. Narada and Vyasa conveyed to Yudhishthira the truth of time and destiny being responsible for the war, rather than Yudhishthira himself.

After the end of the thirteen-day mourning period, the Pandavas went to Hastinapur. In a magnificent ceremony, Yudhishthira was crowned the king of the Kurus. His first command on attaining sovereignty was that Dhritrarashtra's word was law. When everything was going well and the reins of the government were in capable hands, Krishna told Yudhishthira that it was time he went to see Bhishma.

Bhishma Departs, Finally

Bhishma was still on the bed of arrows, waiting for the sun to move into the northern horizon. Yudhishthira, along with the other Pandavas and Krishna, went to see Bhishma. Krishna said the old general was the last repository of wisdom on the Vedas and the other scriptures and therefore, suggested Yudhishthira to enquire from him everything on morality, ethics and politics. So for the next many days Bhishma expounded on sovereignty, statecraft, truth and morality, the treatment of friends and foes, virtue and vice, justice and conduct. At last when the sun moved into the northern horizon, Bhishma decided to depart from the world. As his soul departed, fragrant flowers dropped out of sky. The Pandavas performed his last rites with the highest honour.

When Bhishma's mourning period was over, Sage Vyasa advised Yudhishthira to perform the great horse sacrifice and consolidate his kingdom. Arjuna followed the horse and established suzerainty of the king across the length and breadth of the country.

For fifteen years, everything went on well till Dhritarashtra and Gandhari decided to renounce the world and retire to the forest in Sanyas Ashrama. Kunti decided to accompany them. Yudhishthira requested the old couple to stay with them, but they were determined to retreat to the forest. Dhritarashtra and Gandhari left for the forest accompanied by Sanjaya and Kunti. Not long after their retreat to the forest, they died in a forest fire as they refused to run for their lives like animals in the forest. They sat facing east as the fire devoured them.

The Curse on Krishna Comes True

Thirty-six years after the Mahabharata war, Gandhari's curse on Krishna began to show effect. For thirty-six years, Krishna ruled over Dwaraka peacefully. The families of Yadavas and Vrishnis had grown very large.

One day, three powerful rishis — Vishwamitra, Kanva and Narada — arrived in Dwaraka. Some of the Yadava youths decided to play a nasty joke with the honourable rishis. The young men got drunk and dressed up a youth like a pregnant woman. They took him before the rishis, asking them to predict the sex of the child. The rishis were furious and cursed them. They said, an iron rod would be delivered to the man and that rod would be the cause of destruction of the Vrishnis and the Yadavas. Events took place as predicted.

The man gave birth to an iron staff, which the Yadavas ground to a powder and threw away in the sea. Waves washed the powder ashore which permeated into the reeds growing upon the seashore.

When Krishna, who had been away, learnt of the stupid joke; he banned brewing of alcohol. But the Yadavas and Vrishnis were cursed to meet a violent end. When Krishna left the city again, the youngsters held a picnic on the beach. They brewed alcohol on the beach and served it to all the warriors.

Tempers rose under the influence of alcohol. Long suppressed animosity between Satyaki and Kritavarma resurfaced. Thousands of men died fighting. Krishna arrived on the scene after Satyaki was killed. He was mad in anger and killed all the Yadavas. At the end of the day only Krishna and Daruka remained alive. Balarama was highly shocked and aggrieved.

Balarama went to meditate on the shores of the ocean and a white serpent emerged from his mouth and entered the ocean. No one saw any more of Balarama after this incident.

Krishna sent for Arjuna and asked him to take the Yadava ladies to Hastinapur. He himself departed to the forest. He was quite tired, therefore, he went to relax under a tree and soon dozed off. A hunter at a distance mistook him for a deer, perhaps because of his yellow robe giving a dazzling golden impression. He shot an arrow at him, which pierced the heel of his foot, the only vulnerable part of his body, and Krishna knew his end had come. Before dying an unmourned and lonely death, he blessed the hunter.

Arjuna arranged for the funeral of the Yadavas and left for Hastinapur with the Yadava ladies. On his way back, bandits attacked him. Arjuna was shocked to discover that the mighty Gandiva had lost its power and his inexhaustible quiver was empty of arrows. The bandits boldly took away some of the ladies, while Arjuna felt helpless and defeated.

Arjuna realised that Krishna was dead. He came to Hastinapur and told Yudhishthira of Krishna's death. Yudhishthira knew their time had come. He installed Parikshita, Arjuna's grandson, on the throne. Having anointed Abhimanyu's son as king, the Pandavas, along with Draupadi, left for their heavenly abode.

The Pandavas Leave For Their Heavenly Abode

They went north to the Himalayas, followed by a dog. The journey to the Himalayan heights was difficult. On the way Draupadi was the first to die. Bheema asked Yudhishthira as to why Draupadi died first of all. Yudhishthira replied that she was the first to go because she should have loved all of them equally, but she loved Arjuna the most.

The next amongst them to die was Sahadeva. The reason for his death in the second place, Yudhishthira said, was that he prided himself in his wisdom and learning. Nakula died after Sahadeva and the cause of his death was vanity. The next to die was Arjuna. Bheema wanted to know the weakness in his nature that led to his death. Yudhishthira said, it was his pride in archery. Soon after, it was Bheema's turn to die, but before dying he asked why was he dying. Yudhishthira told him, it was his gluttony. He was always greedy for food and ate too much. Yudhishthira was left alone, with only the dog to accompany him.

Suddenly Lord Indra appeared before him on a chariot and invited him to heaven in his bodily form. When the dog was refused a place in heaven, Yudhishthira too refused to go to heaven saying, he cannot desert the dog who has been with him since the beginning of his journey. He flatly declined to abandon the dog even if it meant losing the pleasures of heaven. The dog disappeared and in its place was Dharmaraja, the God of justice and Yudhishthira's father. He praised Yudhishthira for his love of justice.

On entering heaven, he found Duryodhana occupying a place of honour, but to his surprise, he found Draupadi and his brothers missing. Yudhishthira was enraged. He told the Gods in clear terms that he did not want a place in heaven, devoid of Draupadi and his brothers. The heaven which honoured a vicious man like Duryodhana was not for him. Saying so, the eldest Pandava strode out of heaven. Indra asked him to stop and summoned a guide to escort him to hell where Draupadi and the four Pandava brothers were to be found.

The sight of hell was terrible. The path to hell was strewn will dead bodies, disembodied flesh, dirt and blood. Yudhishthira found the offensive smell and ghastly sights in hell unbearable. So he decided to turn back and leave the place. Just then he beheld Draupadi and his brothers undergoing the trauma and pain of life in hell. They begged him not to leave them. Not just the Pandavas and Draupadi, but even Draupadi's five sons, Abhimanyu and Kunti were there in hell. Yudhishthira decided to stay with them. The Gods told him his place was in heaven. Hell was not for him, but Yudhishthira firmly refused to leave his brothers, sons, wife and mother to their fate.

All of a sudden, Dharmaraja appeared before him and as he appeared, the hellish scenario vanished and in its place appeared, light, fragrance and charming faces. Lord Dharmaraja said to the eldest Pandava, "My son, I am highly pleased with you. You came out successfully in every test that I presented to you. Your first test was when I followed you as dog and the last one now, when you refused the joys of heaven."

The illusion of hell vanished and Yudhishthira found himself in heaven. He saw his brothers, Draupadi, Kunti, Abhimanyu, and his sons enjoying a blissful life in heaven.

Yudhishthira asked Dharmaraja the reason why he had to undergo this illusory experience of pain and trauma. The God of morality said it was because he had lied once about the death of Ashvathama.

Parikshita, the son of Abhimanyu and Uttara, grew as a healthy, intelligent, and brave prince. He had succeeded King Yudhishthira, the Pandava king, to the throne of Hastinapur. For many years, Parikshita ruled with love, care, and compassion towards all. All over, in his kingdom, was peace and prosperity.